Learn XML

In a Weekend

ERIK WESTERMANN

Premier
Press

Premier

Press

The Premier Press logo and related trade dress are trademarks of Premier Press, Inc. and may not be used without written permission.

Publisher: Stacy L. Hiquet
Marketing Manager: Heather Hurley
Managing Editor: Sandy Doell
Acquisitions Editor: Todd Jensen
Project Editor/Copy Editor: Sean Medlock
Editorial Assistants: Margaret Bauer, Elizabeth Barrett
Technical Reviewer: Michelle Jones
Interior Layout: Marian Hartsough
Cover Designer: Mike Tanamachi
Indexer: Katherine Stimson
Proofreader: Lorraine Gunter

ISBN: 1-59200-010-X
Library of Congress Catalog Card Number: 2002106524
Printed in the United States of America

02 03 04 05 BH 10 9 8 7 6 5 4 3 2 1

Premier Press, a division of Course Technology
2645 Erie Avenue, Suite 41
Cincinnati, Ohio 45208

For the two greatest boys in the world,
my sons, Vikranth and Siddharth.

FOREWORD

The first time I met Erik was while running the popular CodeGuru Web site a few years ago, where he was responsible for writing the book reviews. While Erik's reviews had proven to be one of the most popular aspects of the site, we never had a system in place that would allow us to easily provide a means for the user to read archived reviews. Obviously, we could have simply organized the reviews much like we did the code articles, but we also wanted a means by which reviews could be searched using criteria such as rating, publisher, author, and title.

The solution Erik came up with was both elegant and functional. By combining the powers of ASP (Active Server Pages), XML, and XSL, in a weekend he wrote the foundations for the book review archive section that is still in use today at CodeGuru, as well as many other popular Web sites. His application design was so flexible that his work was later expanded to work with archived newsletters and many other document types.

Okay, so we know that Erik is great with XML, but will reading this book make you as productive as he is? I'll admit that when I was approached about writing this foreword, I was a bit wary that any reasonable amount of XML could be learned in a single weekend. I told Erik that I would need to read the entire book to make sure my name would be associated with something that I believe in. Well, two days later, not only was I surprised that the book does indeed deliver on its promises, but I actually learned several new bits of information about XML despite having used it for over two years now!

If you're new to XML and have no time to waste on theoretical discussions, this book is a goldmine of information. By the end of Saturday afternoon's lesson, many XML documents that you may have seen but never quite understood will begin to make sense. By the end of Saturday afternoon's lesson, you will understand basic XML constructs such as elements and attributes, you will have worked with XML namespaces and fully comprehend how to use them properly, and you'll understand how XML fits into practical applications. By Sunday evening, you will have done everything from working with document models and DTDs, to creating and interfacing your own XML documents with style sheets (both CSS and XSL), to programmatically accessing XML documents from your applications using the XML DOM.

The key is that Erik takes a pragmatic approach, helping you become productive quickly while taking the time to explain important details along the way. I found the discussions on character sets, character encoding, and schemas particularly interesting because they were so detailed, yet so easy to read and understand. That's unique in books like this. Erik enjoys teaching others, and his experience shines though on every page. The numerous sample XML documents throughout the book make it an interesting read, but Erik goes beyond that and includes code for Web pages and applications using programming languages like VBScript, JavaScript, and C#. Also, the samples are interesting even if you're not a programmer, because they provide you with another perspective on how developers work with XML.

Simply put, the clear explanations, real-world examples, and a focus on relevant technologies make this book an essential addition to your bookshelf if you're serious about XML.

Tom Archer
http://www.theCodeChannel.com
July 2002

ACKNOWLEDGMENTS

First and foremost, I'd like to thank Brad Jones for helping me get this project off the ground; Todd Jensen, acquisitions editor, for putting up with my "short" e-mails; Amy Pettinella, my project editor, for overseeing the project from (almost) the beginning; and Michelle Jones, technical editor, for her comments and suggestions.

I would also like to thank Altova, the producers of XML Spy, for the copy of XML Spy, and Jon Bachman at eXcelon for helping to get a copy of eXcelon Stylus Studio for the readers of this book.

I'd like to thank Tom Archer for his support throughout the project, and for helping me get my writing career started in the first place. I could not have done it without you. Thanks, Tom!

I'd also like to thank my sons, Vikranth and Siddharth, for understanding when I was busy, and for the time they gave up spending with me so that I could produce this book for you. I'd also like to thank my wife, Shanthi, for her ceaseless support in all of my endeavors.

ABOUT THE AUTHOR

ERIK WESTERMANN is an independent, accomplished developer with more than 10 years of experience in professional programming and design. Erik also enjoys writing and has written for a number of publications on the Internet and in print. Erik's professional affiliations include the IEEE Computer Society (http://computer.org), the Association for Computing Machinery (http://acm.org), and the Worldwide Institute of Software Architects (http://wwisa.org), where he is a practicing member. Erik has spoken at conferences including VSLive 2001 in Sydney, Australia. Erik's Web site is http://www.designs2solutions.com.

CONTENTS AT A GLANCE

CONTENTS

INTRODUCTION

Welcome to *Learn XML In a Weekend*. This book contains seven lessons and other resources that are focused on only one thing: getting you up to speed with XML, its related technologies, and its latest developments. The lessons span a weekend, beginning on Friday evening and ending on Sunday evening. Yes, you can learn XML in a weekend!

As you look at all of the other XML books that line the shelves, you might ask, "What's so special about this book?" This book is different from the rest of the pack because not only does it explain what XML is and how to use it, but it presents relevant, practical, and real-world uses of XML. While a lot of books focus on core XML (its syntax, DTDs, and so on), which is very useful information, they often assume that you have the expertise to integrate XML into your organization's operations.

This book focuses on relevant XML technologies like XPath, XSD, DTD, and CSS, and explains why other technologies, like XDR, may not be important in certain scenarios. This book also takes a practical approach to working with XML. After showing you the core syntax and other rules, I'll show you how to work with XML using two of the best XML editors on the market today: eXcelon's Stylus Studio and Altova's XML Spy. There's not much point in writing XML documents, schemas, and transformations by hand if XML editors can generate a lot of the XML for you!

I'll also discuss how to use XML in Internet Explorer, Microsoft Active Server Pages, and Microsoft's latest offerings: the .NET Framework and the Visual C# .NET programming language.

This book succinctly describes XML and its related technologies, focusing only on what's relevant in today's rapidly changing marketplace. I'll help you make choices that can mean the difference between a successful solution and one that fails because it uses irrelevant, incompatible, or outdated standards. Skim through the book now and take a look through Saturday afternoon's lesson, which describes how to create XML documents. That single lesson covers everything you need to know, from basic syntax to creating XML documents using different languages (important in today's global marketplace). By the end of that lesson alone, you'll already understand terms like entity reference, character sets, and namespaces.

How This Book Is Organized

This book is organized into seven lessons that span a weekend, beginning on Friday evening and ending on Sunday evening. By Monday morning, you'll be right up to speed with XML and its related technologies. If you're like me and cannot devote an entire weekend to reading a book because of other commitments, feel free to read this book whenever you like.

Here's an overview of each lesson:

Friday Evening focuses on introducing XML: what it is, why it's useful, and how people use it.

Saturday Morning is a slightly longer lesson that focuses on using XML in Internet Explorer with HTML and XSL, and using XML with Microsoft's Active Server Pages. This lesson gives you an overview of what you can do with XML. Don't worry if you're not a programmer or don't understand the programming language that's used in the lesson. The idea is to expose you to these technologies so that you'll gain a better understanding of how others use XML.

Saturday Afternoon is a slightly longer lesson, focusing on how to write XML documents by following the rules that XML imposes. This lesson covers basic document structure, working with attributes, comments, and CDATA sections. The lesson also covers character encoding, which allows international users to read your XML documents, and namespaces, a feature that makes your XML documents more useful by allowing you to share them with others.

Saturday Evening is one of the longest lessons in the book, focusing on document modeling using DTD and XSD. I suggest that you start reading this chapter as soon as you can after you complete Saturday afternoon's lesson so that you can complete it in one evening.

Sunday Morning focuses on using XML Spy and Stylus Studio to create and work with XML solutions. The lesson also covers XSL debugging using Stylus Studio, which can save you hours of frustration when your XSL code doesn't work as you expect it should. This lesson also describes Microsoft XML Core Services, how to determine what version is installed on your system, and how to get the latest updates.

Sunday Afternoon is a longer lesson, so I recommend you try to start it as soon as possible after completing the previous lesson. This lesson focuses on presenting data on the Web using presentation technologies like CSS and XSL. It examines how to repurpose an XML document using XSL that you create using Stylus Studio's graphical XSL editor.

Sunday Evening shows you how to use XML with Internet Explorer's Data Source Object (DSO), the XML Document Object Model (XML DOM), and Microsoft's .NET Framework. The DSO produces impressive results, like support for paging through long sets of data without any programming. The XML DOM is useful for creating and manipulating an XML document programmatically (via an application's code), and the Microsoft .NET Framework offers support for XML throughout.

Appendix A provides an HTML and XPath reference to help you become more productive. This appendix includes examples and screen shots.

Appendix B presents the W3C XML 1.0 Specification. This is a shorter specification than the one published by the W3C and uses examples throughout.

Appendix C is a list of Web resources.

The Glossary is a comprehensive listing of terms, along with their definitions. Most terms are used in the book, but there are some additional terms that you'll come across as you work with XML but do not appear in the book.

Conventions Used in This Book

This book uses a number of conventions that make it easier to read:

NOTE Notes provide additional information.

TIP Tips highlight information that appears in the surrounding text.

Code that appears within the body of a paragraph is shown in another font to make it stand out from the rest of the surrounding text.

Code listings appear in another font, sometimes including bold lines to highlight certain parts of the listing. The following is an example of a listing that contains bold text:

```
<?xml version="1.0" encoding="UTF-8"?>
<xs:schema xmlns:xs="http://www.w3.org/2001/XMLSchema">
  <xs:complexType name="license_t">
    <xs:simpleContent>
      <xs:extension base="xs:string">
        <xs:attribute name="licenseNumber" type="xs:string"/>
        <xs:attribute name="ownerName" type="xs:string"/>
```

REFERENCES

The following is a list of materials I used to prepare this book:

W3C, Extensible Markup Language (XML) 1.0 (Second Edition),
World Wide Web Consortium, 2000,
http://www.w3.org/TR/REC-xml

W3C, XML Path Language (XPath) Version 1.0,
World Wide Web Consortium, 1999,
http://www.w3.org/TR/xpath

W3C, XSL Transformations (XSLT) Version 1.0,
World Wide Web Consortium, 1999,
http://www.w3.org/TR/xslt

W3C, Cascading Style Sheets, level 1,
World Wide Web Consortium, 1996,
http://www.w3.org/TR/REC-CSS1

Nikola Ozu et al, Professional XML, Wrox Press, 2001

Khun Yee Fung, XSLT: Working with XML and HTML,
Addison Wesley, 2000

The Unicode Consortium, UNICODE STANDARD
VERSION 3.0, 2000

Introducing XML

- ➤ What Is XML?
- ➤ Biography of an XML Document
- ➤ Elements of XML Documents
- ➤ XML in the Real World
- ➤ XML Vocabularies

ood evening! Tonight you begin learning how people use XML in real-world scenarios. This evening introduces you to what XML is, how to create XML documents and play by XML's rules, the benefits of using XML, and how XML relates to HTML. The remainder of the evening discusses the typical life cycle of an XML document, describes how others make XML work for them, and covers the basics of the types of XML documents you'll probably encounter.

What Is XML?

XML stands for *extensible markup language*, a *syntax* that describes how to add structure to data. A *markup language* is a specification that adds new information to existing information while keeping the two sets of information separate. If it were as simple as that, I could describe XML to you in just a few pages.

However, XML is more complicated than that. It's a simple syntax that describes information, a set of technologies that allows you to format and filter information independently of how that information is represented, and the embodiment of an idea that reduces data to its purest form, devoid of formatting and other irrelevant aspects, to attain a very high level of usefulness and flexibility.

Oddly enough, XML is not a markup language. Instead, it defines a set of rules for *creating* markup languages. There are many types of markup languages, the most popular of which is HTML (Hypertext Markup Language), the publishing language of the Internet. HTML combines formatting information with a Web page's content so that you see the page in the way the designer intended for you to see it.

The two most important elements that make HTML work are the HTML itself and software that's capable of interpreting HTML. When you view a Web page, your browser retrieves the page, interprets the HTML, and displays the resulting document on your screen. The same two elements, XML itself and software that's capable of interpreting XML, are needed with XML.

Assume that you're working with a file that looks like this:

```
Learn XML In A Weekend, Erik Westermann, 159200010X
```

This file describes information about a book using three fields: the title, author, and ISBN (a number that uniquely identifies a book). While it's clear to you and me that `Learn XML In A Weekend` represents the title of a book, a computer would have a tough time figuring out that

➤ There are three fields in the file (separated by commas).

➤ Each field represents an individual piece of data.

XML enables you to add structure to the data. Here's the same file marked up with XML:

```
<books>
  <book>
    <title>Learn XML In A Weekend</title>
    <author>Erik Westermann</author>
    <isbn>159200010X</isbn>
  </book>
</books>
```

It's now apparent, both to us and to software that's capable of interpreting XML, that the file contains information about a collection of books (there's only one book in this collection) broken into three fields: title, author, and ISBN. For software to be able to interpret the XML, the sample follows certain rules:

➤ Text inside the angle brackets (< and >) represents a markup element.

➤ Text outside of the angle brackets is data.

➤ The beginning of a unit of data has a start tag prefix.

➤ The end of a unit of data is marked with an end tag. This is almost identical to a start tag, except that it begins with a slash (/).

For example, `<title>` is a start tag, `Learn XML In A Weekend` represents a unit of data, and `</title>` is an end tag. XML defines only the syntax—the rules—and leaves it to you to decide how you structure it and what data you store in it.

XML documents reside in files that you can create with an editor like Windows Notepad, making XML very accessible. Specialized editors are available to help you manage XML documents and ensure that you follow the rules of the XML specification. I'll cover two such editors later in this book.

NOTE

Windows Notepad is a simple text editor that comes with Windows. You can start Notepad by clicking Start, Run, and then typing **notepad**.

It is important to understand that XML is an enabling technology, which is analogous to any written or spoken language. A language doesn't communicate for us. We're able to communicate because we use language.

Just as you play a role in reading the words on this page (the words are meaningless, unless someone reads them), XML becomes useful only in the context of a system that's able to interpret it. Unlike written and spoken languages, you're not likely to directly read or write XML. People rarely read XML documents—in most cases, software creates an XML file and then other software uses it without anyone actually viewing the XML document itself. However, you still need to understand what XML is and how to use it to your advantage.

There are three important characteristics of XML that make it useful in a variety of systems and solutions:

➤ XML is extensible.

➤ XML separates data from presentation.

➤ XML is a widely accepted public standard.

XML Is Extensible

Think of XML like this: one syntax, many languages.

XML describes the basic syntax—the basic format—and rules that XML documents must follow. Unlike markup languages like HTML, which has a predefined set of tags (items with the angle brackets, as in the previous sample), XML doesn't put any limitations on which tags you can use or create. For example, there isn't any reason you couldn't rename the <book> tag to <manuscript> or <record>.

XML essentially allows you to create your own language, or vocabulary, that suits your application. The XML standard (described shortly) describes how to create tags and structure an XML document, creating a framework. As long as you stay within the framework, you're free to define tags that suit your data or application.

XML Separates Data from Presentation

Take a close look at the page layout of this book—it contains several types of headings and other formatting elements. The information on this page wouldn't change if you changed its format, though. If you remove the headings, italic characters, and other formatting, you'll be left with the essence of this book—the information that it contains, or its content.

XML allows you to store content with regard to how it will be presented—whether in print, on a computer screen, on a cellular phone's tiny display screen, or even read aloud by speech software. When you want to present an XML document, you'll often use another XML vocabulary (set of XML tags) to describe the presentation. Also, you'll use other software to perform the transformation from XML into the format you want to present the content in, as shown in Figure 1.1.

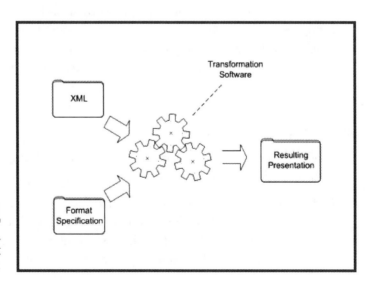

Figure 1.1

Presenting an XML document by first transforming it.

XML Is Widely a Accepted Public Standard

XML was developed by an organization called the World Wide Web Consortium (W3C), whose role is to promote interoperability between computer systems and applications by developing standards and technologies for the Internet. The W3C members include people from technology product vendors, content providers, corporate users, research labs, and governments. Their goal is to ensure that its recommendations (commonly referred to as *standards*) are vendor-neutral (not specific to a particular company or organization) and receive consideration from a broad range of users and developers.

The W3C's standards cannot be changed or dropped altogether without input from its members and from the general public (if they choose to participate in the process). This process is in contrast to proprietary standards that some vendors implement. For example, Microsoft could decide to stop developing a standard it has created, and subsequently stop incorporating it into its products. This is not likely to happen to standards that the W3C develops.

Is XML a Programming Language?

A *programming language* is a vocabulary and syntax for instructing a computer to perform specific tasks. XML doesn't qualify as a programming language because it doesn't instruct a computer to do anything, as such. It's usually stored in a simple text file and is processed by special software that's capable of interpreting XML. For example, if the processing software is designed to change the behavior of an application based on the contents of an XML file, the software will carry out the changes. XML acts as a syntax to add structure to data, and it relies on other software to make it useful.

Is XML Related to HTML?

HTML, the publishing language of the Internet, is related to XML through a language called SGML (Standard Generalized Markup Language).

SGML is a complex markup language that has its roots in GML, another markup language developed by a researcher working for IBM during the late 1960s. HTML is an SGML application, which means that HTML is a type of document that SGML directly supports. XML is a drastic simplification of SGML that removes its less frequently used features and imposes new constraints that make it easier to work with than SGML. However, like HTML, XML is a representation of SGML.

Why Not Use HTML?

Web developers are a very resourceful group of people. HTML has many shortcomings, and the Web developer community at large has worked to overcome them. The underlying problem with HTML is that it's a language that describes how to present information—it doesn't describe the information itself (with the exception of a few tags like <title> and <body>). Some people ask why the W3C doesn't extend HTML so it describes information. The problem with that approach is backward-compatibility with existing HTML pages and Web browsers. The syntax that describes how to format HTML and the software that processes HTML aren't as strict as the rules that XML imposes. Along with less strict rules comes an increase in the complexity of the software that interprets HTML, and adding new tags and capabilities to HTML would make the software even more complex.

The W3C has created a recommendation (a standard, in practical terms) called XHTML to address some of these complexities. XHTML is essentially a strict version of HTML—it combines the strength of HTML with the power of XML by imposing XML rules on HTML documents. For example, this is a fragment of a simple HTML document:

```
<TABLE width=50% ALIGN=center>
  <tr>
    <td>
      <ul>
        <li>List Item 1
        <li>List Item 2
      </ul>
    </tr>
</table>
<p>The above table contains a list
<HR>
<p>Contact the author for details
```

Notice that the <TABLE> element includes two attributes, width and align, and the end tag, </table>, is in lowercase as opposed to the uppercase start tag. The list items (the ones that start with the <li> tag) don't have an end tag, as is the case with the <p> tags that appear after the table. The <hr> tag doesn't require an end tag, since the tag stands on its own. This listing represents completely legal HTML. Browsers will display the page as the designer intends it to be shown.

If you rewrite the fragment using XHTML, it would look something like this:

```
<table width="50%" align="center">
  <tr>
    <td>
      <ul>
        <li>List Item 1</li>
        <li>List Item 2</li>
      </ul>
    </tr>
</table>
<p>The above table contains a list</p>
<hr/>
<p>Contact the author for details</p>
```

The difference between the two fragments is subtle:

➤ All tags and attributes must be in lowercase.

➤ Attribute values must appear in quotes (refer to the <table> tag's width and align attributes).

➤ All tags must have both a start and end tag.

➤ Empty tags, like the HTML <hr> tag, must appear as empty XML elements using the syntax shown in the previous listing (<hr/>—note the slash character just before the last angle bracket).

XHTML allows Web developers to combine HTML with XML either in the same file or in separate files. The final result on HTML, however, is that its rules are too relaxed and the software that processes it is too complex to survive a major revision. The restrictions that XHTML imposes alleviate these problems to allow for further development.

Biography of an XML Document

Throughout the chapter I've hinted at the stages an XML document passes through, beginning at its creation and ending at its presentation. Figure 1.2 summarizes how to create an XML document. It shows a person using Windows Notepad to create an XML document and store it in a file.

Figure 1.3 shows what happens when a user requests a page from a Web site that uses XML documents to manage its content.

The process starts with the user making a request for a page from a Web site (step 1). The Web server (the computer that runs the Web site) retrieves the document the user wants. However, the document is in XML, and the user

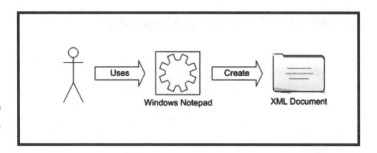

Figure 1.2

Creating an XML
document.

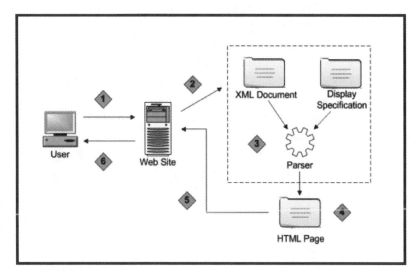

Figure 1.3

Later stages
of an XML
document's life.

expects the document to be a Web page that's marked up using HTML. In step 3, the Web server transforms the XML document into HTML by combining it with another document that describes how to perform the transformation. The software that performs the actual transformation is called a *parser*. An XML parser interprets the tags in an XML document and can perform other functions, like transforming XML into other formats. In step 4, the parser produces the resulting HTML document, which gets passed on to the Web site in step 5. The final step in the process occurs when the Web site delivers the HTML file to the user's computer. The user's browser interprets the HTML file and displays it onscreen (not shown in the figure).

This scenario is just one of many ways to use XML documents. The next section describes how people use XML documents in real-world applications.

Elements of XML Documents

The best way to learn what makes up an XML document is to work from a simple example. The following listing is a complete XML document that lists the names of two people:

```
<?xml version="1.0" encoding="UTF-8"?>
<!DOCTYPE people [
  <!ELEMENT people (person+)>
  <!ELEMENT person (name)>
  <!ELEMENT name (first, last)>
  <!ELEMENT first (#PCDATA)>
  <!ELEMENT last (#PCDATA)>
]>
<people>
  <person>
    <name>
      <first>Essam</first>
      <last>Ahmed</last>
    </name>
  </person>
  <person>
    <name>
```

```
      <first>Tom</first>
      <last>Archer</last>
    </name>
  </person>
</people>
```

XML lets you name the parts of the document anything you want. It doesn't matter how you're going to use the document, and the final appearance of the document doesn't matter either. All that matters is that you follow the basic rules for creating tags, as described earlier. This sample document contains some markup at the very beginning that obviously doesn't follow the basic rules—I'll explain what those parts are in a moment. Figure 1.4 highlights the various elements of the sample document.

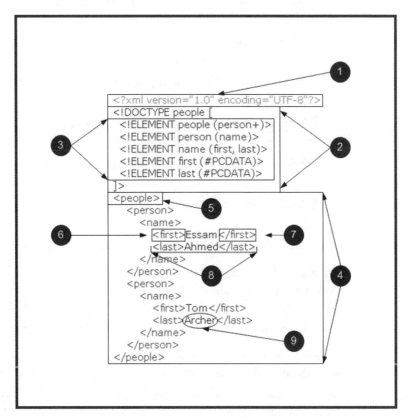

Figure 1.4

Elements of an XML document.

The sample document, like all XML documents, has content interspersed with markup symbols. Take a closer look at the parts that make up this document. The numbers refer to the numbers in black circles in Figure 1.4:

1 XML declaration: Describes general characteristics of the document, such as that it's an XML document, which version of the XML specification it complies with (1.0 is the only known version at the time of this writing), and which character encoding it uses. (I'll describe character encoding in Saturday morning's lesson, "Separating Content from Style.")

2 Document Type Declaration (DTD): This describes the structure of the document in terms of which elements it may contain, along with any restrictions it may have. (I'll describe the DTD in detail on Saturday morning.)

3 Internal DTD subset: A DTD can contain references to other DTDs. However, the one in this example uses internal declarations that are local to the XML document.

4 XML information set: This represents the XML document's content—the information the document conveys.

5 Root element: This encloses all the information. An XML document can have only one root element.

6 Start tag: XML elements have a start and end tag—the start tag provides the name of the XML element.

7 End tag: The name of the end tag must exactly match the name of the start tag.

8 XML element: The start and end tags are collectively referred to as an XML element.

9 Data: XML elements can contain data between the start and end tags.

An XML document represents information using a hierarchy. That is, it begins with a root element, which contains sub-elements, which in turn can contain other sub-elements, text, or both. One way of depicting such a hierarchy is an upside-down tree structure, as shown in Figure 1.5.

Although XML is designed so that people can read it, it isn't intended to create a finished document. In other words, you can't open up just any XML-tagged document in a browser and expect it to be formatted nicely. XML is meant to hold content so that when the document is combined with other resources, such as a style sheet, it becomes a finished product.

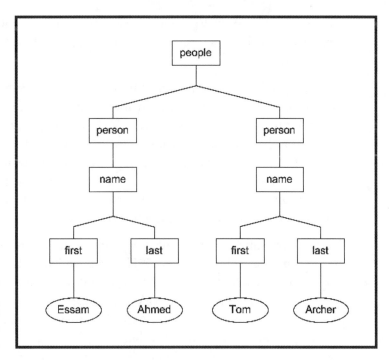

Figure 1.5

Tree view of an
XML document.

XML in the Real World

XML enjoys broad support from major software vendors, programming languages, and platforms (operating systems). Since XML is platform- and vendor-neutral, it's easy to integrate in a variety of ways. XML plays three primary roles:

➤ Application integration

➤ Knowledge management

➤ System-level integration

Using XML for Application Integration

A classic example of integrating applications is adding package-tracking functionality to a company's Web site that fulfills customers' orders. For example, assume that you run an online store and want to let your customers track the status of their orders without leaving your site. You could implement a page that displays the order, along with a link that allows the customer to check the order's status and get package-tracking information after the order ships.

Your company uses several couriers to deliver orders to customers, and you want to present this tracking information regardless of the courier. XML is perfect for this scenario. It allows your Web site to request package-tracking information from another site on the customer's behalf, and the results are delivered in a predictable format that's easy to integrate into your site. As long as the software on your Web site knows the format (structure) of the XML document(s) on the other couriers' Web sites, your site will be able to integrate the results into the customer's order status page.

That's a very simple example of integrating applications. A more complex example involves Microsoft's .NET Platform, which makes extensive use of XML to achieve a high degree of interoperability between distributed applications. Using the .NET Framework, a developer could create an application that requests information and interacts with other applications on the Internet using standardized XML vocabularies (XML tags), without the users even being aware that it's happening. The developer could integrate Internet-based applications that provide paid services or free information, or that simply perform processing on behalf of the user. The possibilities are limitless.

This level of integration is possible because XML is platform-neutral. As long as two applications "speak" XML, using a predetermined vocabulary, they can interact with each other regardless of where they physically reside or how they're implemented.

Using XML for Knowledge Management

Most personal Web sites are made up of HTML pages that contain static (unchanging) content. Using HTML pages to provide content to your site's visitors works well, as long as the number of pages you need to manage remains relatively small. If you want to update your existing pages, you have to edit them directly. If you want to change the appearance of some or all pages on your Web site, you have to edit them directly as well. As your site grows, changing sitewide characteristics such as the site's overall appearance, navigation aids, and interactive capabilities becomes a significant problem because you have to change a large number of pages.

Managing a Web site's content is easy with a class of applications called Content Management Systems (CMS). CMS allows Web site owners, content providers such as journalists, and other (usually) nontechnical users to add new information to a Web site without any knowledge of the site's underlying structure or operation. Web sites that display ads in certain positions on each page, or that track how their visitors use them, are particularly difficult to manage because they often incorporate additional programming to manage those functions.

XML has made great strides toward integrating CMS solutions. XML-based CMS stores a Web site's content in XML files and delivers the content to users in a variety of formats, including HTML. In fact, there are some free, XML-based CMS's available on the Internet. FullXML is a free, XML-based CMS that uses Microsoft technologies like Windows, Microsoft Internet Information Server (Web server), and the Microsoft XML parser (software that interprets XML). Visit http://www.fullxml.com for more information.

XML is also being used as a portable database system. I use portable in terms of easily moving a data store (a repository of data) that's stored on one system to another system. Popular database systems are based on proprietary formats that their vendors have invented. For example, if you use a database system from one vendor, it's very difficult to integrate it with a database system from another vendor. Besides the obvious competitive reasons, there are incompatibilities in the system's file formats and methods of communication.

XML addresses these problems by allowing you to retain the structure that a database system provides while making it easy to access and move the entire set of data from one system to another. For example, you can move a data set from a Unix-based system to a Windows-based system without using any special software, which is practically impossible with proprietary database systems. The advantage of XML is that the data store (repository) becomes open (easily accessible without having to use any special software) and vendor-neutral. Those are two very important characteristics in the face of fast-paced economic changes that could lead to vendors going out of business or dropping entire product lines.

Another aspect of knowledge management is content reuse. With the increasing demand for quality content, providers are looking for interesting ways to reuse and integrate content that they've spent a lot of money to acquire. XML makes it easy to aggregate content from a number of XML documents into a new document and present it in various formats.

Using XML for System-level Integration

The software you use every day relies on the fundamental functions of other software (such as a Web server) and operating systems (such as Windows). Sometimes developers need to move data and system-level entities (objects, if you're interested) from one computer to another, or from one application to another on the same computer. For decades, this has been a difficult problem to address.

XML helps by providing a format that's easy to marshal (transport). Documents are stored as simple text files, which easily translate into strings that are relatively easy to marshal between computers and processes. For example, the Microsoft .NET Framework uses XML to marshal data on a single system or across systems interconnected by a network, like the Internet. If I've lost you, don't worry. All you need to understand is that XML can help you quickly achieve interoperability at very low levels within a system.

XML Vocabularies

As you've learned, XML allows you to create your own vocabulary that suits your application or data. A vocabulary is simply a set of tags with specific meanings that developers and applications understand. For example, the "books" XML document at the beginning of this chapter uses an XML vocabulary that defines the meanings of the <books>, <book>, <title>, <author>, and <isbn> tags. Specifically, when an application reads the "books" XML document, it understands that the <books> tag refers to a set of books, while a single book is represented by the <book> tag.

Since XML is so flexible, new XML vocabularies are being developed at an incredible pace. Some vocabularies have become so popular and useful that the community at large, and even the W3C, have adopted them as industry standards. Once a vocabulary becomes standardized, it's easier for developers and vendors to support the vocabulary and integrate it into applications and other systems.

XML vocabularies are broadly divided into two groups, horizontal and vertical, as shown in Figure 1.6.

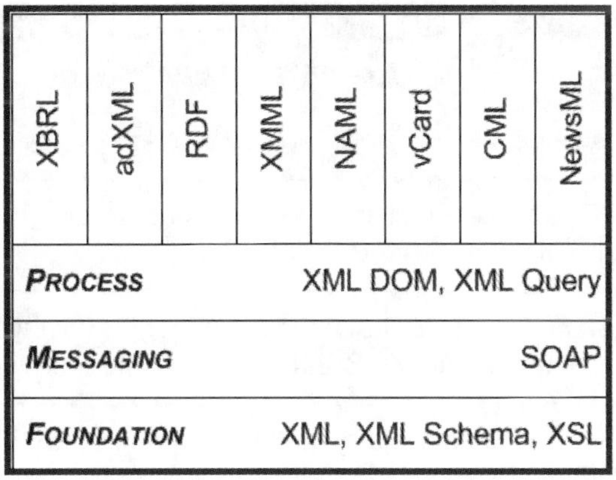

Figure 1.6

Groups of XML vocabularies.

Horizontal XML vocabularies represent core definitions and elements upon which all industry-specific XML vocabularies rely. For example, SOAP is a vocabulary that's useful for all types of XML applications that need to communicate with each other over a network like the Internet. Vertical XML vocabularies are industry-specific.

Table 1.1 lists some industries and the names of some of their XML vocabularies, either in use or under development.

The following sections describe some popular vocabularies to give you an idea of how much development has already taken place. Keep in mind that these are all XML vocabularies. That is, they represent XML documents that developers and software applications have agreed to use to facilitate communication and interoperability.

XSL

XSL, the Extensible Stylesheet Language, is an XML vocabulary that describes how to present a document. In other words, you write XSL using XML. When you combine XSL with XML using a parser, as shown in Figure 1.3, the parser produces a new file that's based on the formatting commands that you specify using XSL. You can present the resulting document on a screen, in print, or in other media. XSL enables XML content to remain separate from its presentation. If you don't fully understand how this works, it's described in more detail on Sunday afternoon. For now, it's important to understand the underlying concept of using XSL to describe the presentation of an XML document.

TABLE 1.1 INDUSTRY-SPECIFIC XML VOCABULARIES

Industry	Examples of XML Vocabularies
Accounting	XFRML (Extensible Financial Reporting Markup Language), SMBXML (Small and Medium Sized Business XML)
Entertainment	SMDL (Standard Music Description Language), ChessGML (Chess Game Markup Language), BGML (Board Game Markup Language)
Customer relations	CIML (Customer Information Markup Language), NAML (Name/Address Markup Language), vCard
Education	TML (Tutorial Markup Language), SCORM (Shareable Courseware Object Reference Model Initiative), LMML (Learning Material Markup Language)
Software	OSD (Open Software Description), PML (Pattern Markup Language), BRML (Business Rules Markup Language)
Manufacturing	SML (Steel Markup Language)
Computer	XML (Extensible Logfile Format), SML (Smart Card Markup Language), TDML (Timing Diagram Markup Language)
Energy	PetroXML, ProductionML, GeophysicsML
Multimedia	SVG (Scalable Vector Graphics), MML (Music Markup Language), X3D (Extensible 3D)

For example, consider the "books" XML document at the beginning of this chapter. Suppose that you want to format the document as a table, as shown in Figure 1.7.

Figure 1.7

Presenting an XML document in a browser using HTML.

Title	Author	ISBN
Learn XML In A Weekend	Essam Ahmed	1931841942

Using XML Spy, a tool that I discuss on Sunday morning and Sunday afternoon, you can easily generate the necessary XSL with drag-and-drop editing. Here's a fragment of the XSL that the parser uses to perform the transformation (note that this is only a small part of the complete document):

```
<?xml version="1.0" encoding="UTF-8"?>
<xsl:stylesheet version="1.0"
xmlns:xsl="http://www.w3.org/1999/XSL/Transform">
  <xsl:template match="/">
    <html>
      <head/>
      <body>
        <xsl:for-each select="books">
          <xsl:for-each select="book">
            <xsl:if test="position()=1">
              <xsl:text disable-output-escaping="yes">
                &lt;table border="1"&gt;</xsl:text>
            </xsl:if>
            <xsl:if test="position()=1">
              <thead>
                <tr>
                  <td>Title</td>
                  <td>Author</td>
                  <td>ISBN</td>
                </tr>
              </thead>
            </xsl:if>
```

For the moment, you don't need to understand what the XSL means. The point is that this is an XML document that happens to use the XSL vocabulary. The document follows all of XML's rules with regard to start and end tags (and several other rules that I'll describe in the next lesson). If you combine the complete XSL document with the "books" XML document, you'll end up with the table back in Figure 1.4. If you want to display the "books" XML document in another format, such as a bulleted listing, just change the XSL document and transform the XML document again. The XML document remains the same, regardless of which format you choose to display it in.

CDF

CDF, the Channel Definition Format, is an XML vocabulary invented by Microsoft to automatically notify Web users that new content is available. That way, users can find out about new content without having to actually visit the site.

CDF pushes information out to users who are interested in receiving updates. Web publishers use CDF to describe the information they want to publish, and how frequently they want to update interested users in any changes. When a Web publisher changes its site, interested users' systems are automatically updated. In fact, CDF is integrated into Microsoft Windows through the Active Desktop, so a user can have Web site updates appear as part of his or her Windows desktop.

CDF also allows users to customize how they want to be notified when a Web site is updated. Users can choose from several notification methods, including e-mail, screen saver, desktop component, and channel. The first two formats are self-explanatory. A desktop component is a special window that remains open on your screen but resides on the desktop itself (where the wallpaper is). It always has the latest information in it, and when you click on a link, it starts Internet Explorer and opens the Web site. Figure 1.8 shows a desktop component that the W3C publishes.

A *channel* is like an item in Internet Explorer's Favorites menu—you simply select the channel, and IE opens up a page that has information about the Web site's updates. The twist with the channel format is that you may be able to browse through some or all of the content when you're not connected to the Internet. (The Web publisher determines if you can view the content offline.) The channel format is a benefit to mobile users, or users who prefer to use a portable device to catch up on the latest from their favorite Web sites.

Figure 1.8

A desktop component displaying updates from the W3C Web site.

The only browser that's capable of working with CDF is IE. Microsoft submitted the CDF format to the W3C in 1997 for consideration and possible development as a widely accepted standard, but the W3C hasn't pursued the format since then.

MathML

Presenting mathematical expressions and equations in Web documents is usually difficult, because most systems support only basic symbols for operators like addition, subtraction, multiplication, and division.

MathML, the Math Markup Language, meets the needs of a broad set of users, including scientists, teachers, the publishing industry, and vendors of software tools that allow you to create and manipulate mathematical expressions. It's a W3C recommendation, which means it's a broadly accepted industry standard. For example, Figure 1.9 shows a complex mathematical expression with characters that most browsers, including IE, cannot display using standard HTML.

NOTE The samples for this book include a page called `testMathML.html` in the `chapter01` folder. You need to download and install a browser that's capable of interpreting MathML documents, like the freely available Amaya browser at `http://www.w3.org/Amaya/`. Select the Distributions option and pick the download file for your operating system. The sample is located in the \XMLInAWeekend\chapter01 folder. Please see the Preface for information on where to obtain the samples.

Figure 1.9

A mathematical equation based on a MathML document.

$$A = \int_0^1 \frac{\ln(x+1)\sqrt{x^2+2x+2}}{x+1}dx$$

MathML can get rather complicated. For example, the following listing represents the MathML for the expression in Figure 1.9:

```
<?xml version="1.0" encoding="UTF-8"?>
<!DOCTYPE math PUBLIC "-//W3C//DTD MathML 2.0//EN"
"http://www.w3.org/TR/MathML2/dtd/mathml2.dtd">
<math
    xmlns="http://www.w3.org/1998/Math/MathML"
    xmlns:xlink="http://www.w3.org/1999/xlink">
  <mrow>
    <mi>A</mi>
    <mo>=</mo>
    <mrow displaystyle='true'>
      <msubsup>
        <mo>&int;</mo>
        <mn>0</mn>
        <mn>1</mn>
      </msubsup>
      <mfrac>
        <mrow>
          <mo moveablelimits='true'>ln</mo>
          <mrow>
            <mo stretchy='false'>(</mo>
            <mi>x</mi>
            <mo>+</mo>
            <mn>1</mn>
            <mo stretchy='false'>)</mo>
          </mrow>
          <msqrt>
            <mrow>
              <msubsup>
                <mi>x</mi>
                <mrow></mrow>
                <mn>2</mn>
              </msubsup>
              <mo>+</mo>
              <mn>2</mn>
              <mi>x</mi>
              <mo>+</mo>
```

```
            <mn>2</mn>
          </mrow>
        </msqrt>
      </mrow>
      <mrow>
        <mi>x</mi>
        <mo>+</mo>
        <mn>1</mn>
      </mrow>
    </mfrac>
    <mi>d</mi>
    <mi>x</mi>
  </mrow>
  </mrow>
</math>
```

There are three types of MathML elements: presentation elements, content elements, and interface elements. *Presentation elements* describe mathematic notational structures, such as rows (mrow), identifiers (mi), and numbers (mn). Content elements represent mathematical concepts like addition and constructs like matrixes.

There is only one interface element: the math element. It allows MathML to coexist with HTML, providing MathML-capable software with a general overview of the MathML document. It also allows special style sheets (formatting instructions) to be associated with MathML documents.

DocBook

DocBook is an XML vocabulary designed to help publishers and authors create books. Although DocBook works particularly well for books on computer software and hardware, it's useful for other types of books too. It's not a W3C standard, but a group called Organization for the Advancement of Structured Information Standards (OASIS) promotes its use and develops it, along with other important industry specifications.

The following listing demonstrates some of the content from this chapter, marked up using DocBook:

```
<chapter id="Chapter 1">
  <title> What is XML?</title>
```

```
<warning>
 <para>I have changed the content a little</para>
</warning>

<para>XML provides a means to add <emphasis>structure</emphasis>
to the data, making the structure more apparent. Here's the same
file marked up with XML:<para>
<programlisting><![CDATA[
<books>
  <book>
    <title>Learn XML In A Weekend</title>
    <author>Erik Westermann</author>
    <isbn>159200010X</isbn>
  </book>
</books>]]>
</programlisting>
</chapter>
```

The preceding listing is based on the DocBook specification, which is a
DTD (briefly described in the "Elements of XML Documents" section ear-
lier in the chapter). The following listing is a very small fragment of the
DTD that describes DocBook:

```
<![%book.element;[
<!ELEMENT book %ho; ((%div.title.content;)?, bookinfo?,
    (dedication | toc | lot
   | glossary | bibliography | preface
   | %chapter.class; | reference | part
   | %article.class;
   | %appendix.class;
   | %index.class;
   | colophon)*)
   %ubiq.inclusion;>
<!--end of book.element-->]]>
<!ENTITY % book.attlist "INCLUDE">
<![%book.attlist;[
<!ATTLIST book    fpi    CDATA    #IMPLIED
    %label.attrib;
    %status.attrib;
    %common.attrib;
```

```
    %book.role.attrib;
    %local.book.attrib;
>
<!--end of book.attlist-->]]>
<![%chapter.element;[
<!ELEMENT chapter %ho; (beginpage?,
                        chapterinfo?,
                        (%bookcomponent.title.content;),
                        (%nav.class;)*,
                        tocchap?,
                        (%bookcomponent.content;),
                        (%nav.class;)*)
    %ubiq.inclusion;>
<!--end of chapter.element-->]]>

<!ENTITY % chapter.attlist "INCLUDE">
<![%chapter.attlist;[
<!ATTLIST chapter
    %label.attrib;
    %status.attrib;
    %common.attrib;
    %chapter.role.attrib;
    %local.chapter.attrib;
>
<!--end of chapter.attlist-->]]>
```

SVG

SVG, Scalable Vector Graphics, is an XML vocabulary for describing two-dimensional graphics. Most graphics on the Internet are referred to as bitmaps. A bitmap is a file that contains information about a graphical image, including the location and color of each individual element. Bitmaps store a lot of information, so the files can get very large. That's why it takes longer for pages with lots of graphics to download into your browser.

SVG makes it possible to describe images using XML instead of a bitmap. It describes an image in terms of its lines and curves instead of its individual picture elements, making it much more descriptive and compact than bitmaps. For example, Figure 1.10 shows a simple graphic that takes about

Figure 1.10

A simple SVG-
based image.

54,000 bytes to store in a bitmap file (specifically, a JPG file). Expressing the
same file using SVG requires about 3,000 bytes—that's 18 times less space.

The following is a partial listing of the SVG used to generate the image in
Figure 1.10:

```
<?xml version="1.0" standalone="no"?>
<!DOCTYPE svg PUBLIC "-//W3C//DTD SVG 1.0//EN"
  "http://www.w3.org/TR/2001/REC-SVG-20010904/DTD/svg10.dtd">
<svg width="200" height="300">
  <path
    d="M122.966 199.448 C124.37 199.448 125.509... "
    style="fill:rgb(192,192,192);stroke:rgb(0,0,0);stroke-width:1"/>
  <text x="81px" y="91px" transform="translate(9 8)...">Learn</text>
  <text x="80px" y="111px" transform="translate(11 7)...">XML in
a</text>
  <text x="77px" y="122px" transform="translate(0 1)...">Weekend</text>
</svg>
```

The following listing is a fragment of the DTD that describes the SVG
vocabulary. It doesn't include attribute and entity declarations:

```
<!-- ================================================================
      PARTIAL DECLARATIONS CORRESPONDING TO: Document Structure
     ================================================================ -->
<!ENTITY % svgExt "" >
<!ELEMENT svg (desc|title|metadata|defs|
  path|text|rect|circle|ellipse|line|polyline|polygon|
```

```
  use|image|svg|g|view|switch|a|altGlyphDef|
  script|style|symbol|marker|clipPath|mask|
  linearGradient|radialGradient|pattern|filter|cursor|font|
  animate|set|animateMotion|animateColor|animateTransform|
  color-profile|font-face
  %ceExt;%svgExt;)* >
<!ELEMENT g (desc|title|metadata|defs|
  path|text|rect|circle|ellipse|line|polyline|polygon|
  use|image|svg|g|view|switch|a|altGlyphDef|
  script|style|symbol|marker|clipPath|mask|
  linearGradient|radialGradient|pattern|filter|cursor|font|
  animate|set|animateMotion|animateColor|animateTransform|
  color-profile|font-face
  %ceExt;%gExt;)* >
<!ELEMENT defs (desc|title|metadata|defs|
  path|text|rect|circle|ellipse|line|polyline|polygon|
  use|image|svg|g|view|switch|a|altGlyphDef|
  script|style|symbol|marker|clipPath|mask|
  linearGradient|radialGradient|pattern|filter|cursor|font|
  animate|set|animateMotion|animateColor|animateTransform|
  color-profile|font-face
  %ceExt;%defsExt;)* >
<!ELEMENT desc (#PCDATA %descExt;)* >
<!ELEMENT title (#PCDATA %titleExt;)* >
<!ELEMENT symbol (desc|title|metadata|defs|
  path|text|rect|circle|ellipse|line|polyline|polygon|
  use|image|svg|g|view|switch|a|altGlyphDef|
  script|style|symbol|marker|clipPath|mask|
  linearGradient|radialGradient|pattern|filter|cursor|font|
  animate|set|animateMotion|animateColor|animateTransform|
  color-profile|font-face
  %ceExt;%symbolExt;)* >
<!ELEMENT use (%descTitleMetadata;,
  (animate|set|animateMotion|animateColor|animateTransform
  %geExt;%useExt;)*) >
<!ELEMENT image (%descTitleMetadata;,
  (animate|set|animateMotion|animateColor|animateTransform
  %geExt;%imageExt;)*) >
```

```
<!ELEMENT switch (%descTitleMetadata;,
  (path|text|rect|circle|ellipse|line|polyline|polygon|
  use|image|svg|g|switch|a|foreignObject|
  animate|set|animateMotion|animateColor|animateTransform
  %ceExt;%switchExt;)*) >
<!-- ==============================================================
      PARTIAL DECLARATIONS CORRESPONDING TO: Basic Shapes
     ============================================================== -->


<!ELEMENT rect (%descTitleMetadata;,
  (animate|set|animateMotion|animateColor|animateTransform
  %geExt;%rectExt;)*) >
<!ELEMENT circle (%descTitleMetadata;,
  (animate|set|animateMotion|animateColor|animateTransform
  %geExt;%circleExt;)*) >
<!ELEMENT ellipse (%descTitleMetadata;,
  (animate|set|animateMotion|animateColor|animateTransform
  %geExt;%ellipseExt;)*) >
<!ELEMENT line (%descTitleMetadata;,
  (animate|set|animateMotion|animateColor|animateTransform
  %geExt;%lineExt;)*) >
<!ELEMENT polyline (%descTitleMetadata;,
  (animate|set|animateMotion|animateColor|animateTransform
  %geExt;%polylineExt;)*) >
<!ELEMENT polygon (%descTitleMetadata;,
  (animate|set|animateMotion|animateColor|animateTransform
  %geExt;%polygonExt;)*) >
  points %Points; #REQUIRED >
```

WML

WML is the Wireless Markup Language, a derivative of XHTML and a style sheet language called Cascading Stylesheet Mobile Profile. (Recall that a style sheet allows you to indicate how you want to display a document.) WML is designed to work with WAP (Wireless Application Protocol) to bring Internet content to mobile wireless devices such as cellular phones and Personal Digital Assistants (PDAs), which have very little memory and processing capabilities.

The following listing is a small fragment of the WML Document Type Definition:

```
<!--
Wireless Markup Language (WML) Document Type Definition.

Copyright Wireless Application Protocol
Forum Ltd., 1998,1999. All rights reserved.

WML is an XML language.  Typical usage:
   <?xml version="1.0"?>
   <!DOCTYPE wml PUBLIC "-//WAPFORUM//DTD WML 1.1//EN"
          "http://www.wapforum.org/DTD/wml_1.1.xml">
   <wml>
   ...
   </wml>

Terms and conditions of use are
available from the Wireless
Application Protocol Forum Ltd. web site at
http://www.wapforum.org/docs/copyright.htm.
-->
<!--============ Decks and Cards =============-->

<!ELEMENT wml ( head?, template?, card+ )>
<!ATTLIST wml
  xml:lang         NMTOKEN         #IMPLIED
  %coreattrs;
  >

<!-- card intrinsic events -->
<!ENTITY % cardev
 "onenterforward  %HREF;         #IMPLIED
  onenterbackward %HREF;         #IMPLIED
  ontimer         %HREF;          #IMPLIED"
  >

<!-- card field types -->
<!ENTITY % fields
 "%flow; | input | select | fieldset">
```

```
<!ELEMENT card (onevent*, timer?, (do | p)*)>
<!ATTLIST card
  title          %vdata;        #IMPLIED
  newcontext     %boolean;      "false"
  ordered        %boolean;      "true"
  xml:lang       NMTOKEN        #IMPLIED
  %cardev;
  %coreattrs;
  >


<!-============= Event Bindings =============->


<!ELEMENT do (%task;)>
<!ATTLIST do
  type           CDATA          #REQUIRED
  label          %vdata;        #IMPLIED
  name           NMTOKEN        #IMPLIED
  optional       %boolean;      "false"
  xml:lang       NMTOKEN        #IMPLIED
  %coreattrs;
  >


<!ELEMENT onevent (%task;)>
<!ATTLIST onevent
  type           CDATA          #REQUIRED
  %coreattrs;
  >
```

The following listing shows a simple WML document:

```
<?xml version="1.0"?>
<!DOCTYPE wml PUBLIC "-//WAPFORUM//DTD WML 1.1//EN"
"http://www.wapforum.org/DTD/wml_1.1.xml">
  <wml>
    <card id="sample" title="WMLSample">
        <p>Hello World!</p>
    </card>
  </wml>
```

Its resulting output on a cellular phone display is shown in Figure 1.11.

Figure 1.11

A cellular phone displaying a WML document.

SOAP

SOAP, the Simple Object Access Protocol, is an XML vocabulary that enables computers to exchange structured information based on a request-response model. It's used for computer-to-computer communications, beginning with a computer making a request and ending when it receives a response. End users might not even know that the systems they use are SOAP-based. However, end users derive the benefits of SOAP message exchange, as described in the "Using XML for Application Integration" section earlier in this chapter.

SOAP enables applications and services that have been developed by separate, and often unrelated, businesses to exchange information or provide services to each other. The following listing is a SOAP request that requests a system to call the GetEvent method, passing in the parameters month=1 and day=1:

```
<SOAP-ENV:Envelope
   xmlns:SOAP-ENV="http://schemas.xmlsoap.org/soap/envelope/"
   SOAP-ENV:encodingStyle="http://schemas.xmlsoap.org/soap/encoding/"
>
   <SOAP-ENV:Body>
     <e:GetEvent
xmlns:e="http://www.designs2solutions.com/Namespaces/LXIAW">
       <e:when>
         <e:Date>
           <day>1</day>
           <month>1</month>
         </e:Date>
       </e:when>
     </e:GetListings>
   </SOAP-ENV:Body>
</SOAP-ENV:Envelope>
```

When the server receives the request, it calls the method and returns a SOAP response to the requesting system. The following listing is the SOAP response:

```
<SOAP-ENV:Envelope
  xmlns:SOAP-ENV="http://schemas.xmlsoap.org/soap/envelope/"
  SOAP-ENV:encodingStyle="http://schemas.xmlsoap.org/soap/encoding/"
>
  <SOAP-ENV:Body>
    <e:GetEventResponse
     xmlns:c="http://www.designs2solutions.com/Namespaces/LXIAW">
      <![CDATA[
        <TABLE>
          <TR>
            <TD>01-01</TD>
            <TD>New Years Day</TD>
          </TR>
        </TABLE>
      ]]>
    </e:GetEventResponse>
  </SOAP-ENV:Body>
</SOAP-ENV:Envelope>
```

RDF

RDF, the Resource Description Framework, is a general-purpose language to identify something that has a URI (Uniform Resource Identifier). You can assign a URI to just about anything that's meaningful to you, including a Web site or a book. It's a means of expressing information about Web resources so that applications can exchange it without any loss of information.

For example, when you go to the library or visit an online bookstore, you can look up information about books by author, subject, title, publisher, and other properties. This information describes a book, but it's not the book itself. Similarly, RDF describes things in terms of three key pieces of information: resource, property, and statement. (A *statement* is a combination of a resource and a property.)

For example, I am the creator of my Web site, designs2solutions.com. In RDF, the resource is my Web site, the property is the creator, and the value of the property is my name. The statement is "Erik Westermann is the creator of http://www.designs2solutions.com". The following RDF document describes this statement:

```
<?xml version="1.0" encoding="utf-8">
<RDF:RDF
  xmlns:RDF ="http://www.w3.org/RDF/RDF"
  xmlns:ew ="http://www.designs2solutions.com/Namespaces/LXIAW" >
    <RDF:Description href="http://www.designs2solutions.com">
      <ew:creator>Erik Westermann</ew:creator>
    </RDF:Description>
</RDF:RDF>
```

RSS

RSS, the RDF Site Summary, is an RDF-compliant vocabulary that allows Web authors to easily syndicate content they create. For example, let's say you regularly write articles about geology and want to make those articles available to a broad audience. You can create an RSS document that describes the articles and submit it to an RSS-compliant service to publicize those articles. Unlike advertising, which simply makes potential customers aware of something, syndication republishes content and redistributes it to reach a larger audience.

RSS is based on the idea of a *channel*, which is very similar to a channel in CDF but has a different purpose. An RSS channel contains information about the content you want to syndicate—specifically, it has title, link, description, and language elements. RSS also supports an image element that contains the logo of the content producer. The RSS items element contains a reference to the content you actually want to syndicate—the articles themselves.

For example, the following listing is an RSS 1.0-compliant channel:

```
<rdf:RDF xmlns:rdf="http://www.w3.org/1999/02/22-rdf-syntax-ns#"
xmlns="http://purl.org/rss/1.0/">
  <channel>
    <title>Learn XML In A Weekend</title>
    <link>http://designs2solutions.com/LXIAW</link>
    <description>Support and information about the popular book,
      Learn XML In A Weekend</description>
```

```
<language>en-us</language>
<copyright>Site content Copyright Essam Ahmed</copyright>
<webMaster>Erik Westermann</webMaster>
<item>
  <title>Updated Samples</title>
  <link>designs2solutions.com/LXIAW/samples</link>
  <description>Download updated samples which encompass
    the latest updates to the W3C XML specification
  </description>
</item>
</channel>
</rdf:RDF>
```

This listing describes a channel that I publish called Learn XML in a Weekend. The item element contains one article about new samples that are available for the book. I can submit this file to an RSS content aggregation service to ensure that everyone who has a copy of the book gets the latest updates.

VoiceXML

VoiceXML is a vocabulary for defining voice dialogs, such as an interactive phone-based banking system for accessing your account, registering for services, or checking the balance of your credit card account. Telephones, both traditional and wireless, are more pervasive than personal computers, and VoiceXML makes it easier to bring Web content and other types of text-based content to them.

VoiceXML is different from WML because it doesn't attempt to deliver content to devices with small displays using a visual approach. Instead, it uses interactive voice systems that read content to you aloud over the phone. It relies on infrastructure like the Internet, Interactive Voice Response (IVR) devices, and VoiceXML gateways to deliver its content. This makes it easier to adapt existing content or create new content for voice-based systems.

The following listing demonstrates what a VoiceXML document looks like:

```
<?xml version="1.0"?>
  <vxml version="1.0">
    <menu>
      <prompt>Would you like to access your<enumerate/></prompt>
```

```
        <choice next="http://...news.vxml">  News updates</choice>
        <choice next="http://...stocks.vxml"> stock market
updates</choice>
        <choice next="http://...sports.vxml"> sports scores </choice>
        <nomatch>I didn't understand your selection.</nomatch>
        <noinput>Please say your request in plain English</noinput>
    </menu>
</vxml>
```

This system reads choices to you and then asks for your selection, which you make by speaking it aloud.

What's Next?

We've come a long way in a short time! Time for a long break to let all this new information soak in. We'll start off tomorrow morning with a sample application that demonstrates the benefits of using XML to publish book reviews on the Internet instead of using plain HTML pages.

Separating Content from Style

➤ **The Problem**

37

Good morning! Last night you got an overview of XML, in terms of what it is and the benefits it provides. You also saw the typical life cycle of an XML document, got an idea about how XML is used in the real world, and were introduced to some important XML vocabularies. While the theoretical background is helpful, sometimes it's better to take a pragmatic approach and jump right into working with XML.

This lesson presents a simple book review site, called the Computing Book Review Service, that provides book reviews to help people decide which books to buy. This book review site comes in three different implementations, although the end result of each implementation is identical. The implementations use a variety of technologies and techniques, including HTML, XML, XSL, JavaScript, the XML DOM, and Microsoft's Active Server Pages. Don't worry if you're not familiar with some or all of these technologies. I'll cover them in more detail on Sunday Evening. I go into some detail here when appropriate, so feel free to skim through sections that are too involved for you right now.

The Problem

Let's say you have a Web site and want to publish reviews of books that you've read to help people make buying decisions. While it seems straightforward to create a single page that lists books along with their reviews, you can see how this page would become very long very quickly with just a few book reviews. A better approach would list all available book reviews on one page and present each book review on its own page, making it easier to find an individual book review. Figure 2.1 shows the first page of a book review section.

This page presents some basic information about the book review. Each book review header includes the date that the book was reviewed, the reviewer's name, and the title and author of the book. The reviewer's name is hyperlinked to a page listing all of the reviews the reviewer has written.

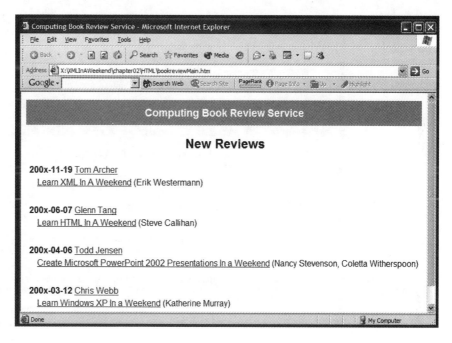

Figure 2.1

Main book review page.

Since this is a sample application, I haven't included the capability to list books by reviewer. However, if you're familiar with technologies like HTML, JavaScript, and XML, it's relatively straightforward to add that capability yourself. The book title also appears as a link, but this one leads to a page containing the book review, as shown in Figure 2.2.

The book review page repeats some information that was shown on the main page, including the title of the book, the date it was reviewed, and the name of the reviewer. At the top of the page is the name of the publisher and year that the book was published. The main section of the page contains the book review, followed by a table with the book's ISBN, number of pages, and the book title and the name of the publisher again.

As mentioned, this lesson presents three different ways of storing, retrieving, and presenting the book reviews. Each method has benefits and tradeoffs that affect both the readers who access the Web site and the person who maintains the site. I'll explain these tradeoffs as I discuss each implementation.

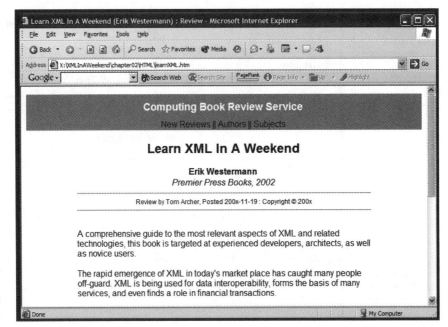

Figure 2.2

Displaying an individual book review.

HTML: Quick and Easy

The first implementation is based entirely on HTML pages. HTML is quick and easy to learn, and it's simple to produce good-looking pages when you combine HTML with CSS. The HTML pages for this implementation are located in the \XMLInAWeekend\chapter02\HTML folder. Double-click on the bookReviewMain.htm file for the listing of book reviews. To see how the page is put together, right-click anywhere on the list of reviews and select View Source from the menu that pops up. Close the source view by selecting File, Close from the menu of the application that contains the page's code.

Figure 2.3 is a *sequence diagram* that describes some of the processing that occurs when you request an HTML page. A sequence diagram focuses on events that occur over time. Time flows from the top of the diagram to the bottom. In other words, things that appear towards the bottom of the diagram occur after those that appear towards the top of the diagram. The boxes with the vertical lines sticking out from them represent things that are interesting in the context of what the diagram describes. For example, there are two boxes in Figure 2.3, Browser and Operating System, since these are items that are important to what the diagram describes. Arrows with text are referred to as messages. Arrows that point to the right are outgoing messages. Arrows that point to the left are incoming messages, which are usually shown using a dashed line because incoming messages are generated only after an outgoing message has been sent. The dashed lines show that the incoming message is present, but the diagram just highlights that fact. Arrows that loop back to the line they originate from, such as the arrow for the Format Page message in Figure 2.3, indicate a message that something sends to itself, usually in response to an incoming message. The stick figure on the left side of the diagram is called an actor, representing the people who use this system.

This sequence diagram shows that when a user loads an HTML page, Internet Explorer (*Browser* in the diagram) works with the operating system (Windows) to request the file and wait for the operating system to provide it. Once the file is loaded, IE formats the page by sending itself a message to render the page based on the HTML tags. Finally, IE returns the page to the user by displaying it on the screen. That's how it works behind the scenes. This discussion will now focus on how the rest of the HTML solution functions.

If you're not familiar with HTML, you'll find a quick reference in Appendix A. This page is essentially a collection of links wrapped up within a couple

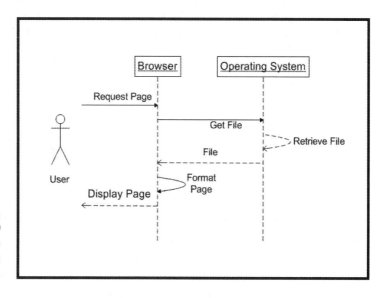

Figure 2.3

Sequence diagram: viewing an HTML page.

of tables that control the page's layout. The following listing demonstrates how each review header is laid out and how the links work:

```
<table>
  <tr>
    <td>
      <div class="reviewDate">200x-11-19</div>
      <a href="underConstruction.htm">Tom Archer</a></td>
  </tr>
  <tr>
    <td class="rl">
      <A href="learnXML.htm">Learn XML In A Weekend</A> (Erik
        Westermann)
    </td>
  </tr>
</table>
```

The table's first row contains the reviewer's name and the date that the book was reviewed. I wanted the date to appear in bold, so it's in an HTML `div` tag that makes it easy to change the enclosed text's style using CSS. I could have used the HTML `B` tag to make the text bold just as easily, but that limits your ability to easily change the formatting in the future. If I wanted to have the date appear in italics and underlined, for example, I would have to change all `B` tags to `I` and `U` tags throughout the document. Using CSS and a `DIV` tag makes changing the formatting throughout the document a snap because the CSS needs to change in just one place in the document!

The `A` hyperlink tag that contains the reviewer's name uses the `href` attribute to point to the `underConstruction.htm` page, which explains that the section is not yet complete. You could create a page to list all reviews that a reviewer has written, making it easy for readers to find reviews written by Tom Archer. The next link points to the book review itself. The name of the book review page in this example is `learnXML.htm`, and the link presents the book's title followed by the name of the author.

So far, so good. You can easily discern that there's a one-to-one relationship between review headers and book reviews, as shown in the preceding listing. When you want to add another book review to the list, just add some more HTML elements like the ones shown in the previous listing. The sample code (see the Preface for direction on how to obtain the sample code) includes comments with pointers to help you add your own review header.

Each book review has its own HTML file. In the previous example, you saw that the book review for this book is in the `learnXML.htm` file. Most of the HTML elements in the file are there to control layout and provide navigational links. I'll explain how this works now, so that you'll have a better understanding of the benefits that the two other implementations provide.

One prominent characteristic of each book review is the large navigational region at the top, just after the page's heading. The navigational controls allow a reader to return to the listing of books, list books by author, and list books by subject. The last two features aren't available in any of these three implementations, but they're in place to give you an idea of the complexities of creating a seemingly simple set of Web pages.

The following listing demonstrates how to create the navigational controls:

```
<table style="COLOR: white;  BACKGROUND-COLOR: #ff9900;"
  cellpadding="10%" width="100%">
  <tr>
    <td style="FONT-WEIGHT: bold;font-size:120%" align="center">
      Computing Book Review Service
    </td>
  </tr>
  <tr>
    <td style="padding:0;color:black" align="center">
      <a class="menu" href="bookReviewMain.htm">New Reviews</a> ||
      <a class="menu" href="underConstruction.htm">Authors</a> ||
      <a class="menu" href="underConstruction.htm">Subjects</a>
    </td>
  </tr>
</table>
```

As with most other visual elements, the controls reside in a table and are implemented using the sequence of three A tags in the bottom half of the listing. Each A tag uses a CSS class attribute to make it easier to format its contents. One aspect of formatting each link is that its background color changes from orange to silver when you hover the mouse pointer over it, and reverts back to the original color when you move the mouse away. Another aspect of the links is the page that each refers to through the `href` attribute. If you want to change where one of the links points to, you have to change the link in each book review document. This can make maintenance and upgrades very time-consuming.

Another characteristic of individual book reviews is that they contain a lot of repeated elements. For example, the book's title appears in three different places throughout the book review, as does the name of the author. The following listing shows fragments of the learnXML.htm file that contain the book's title. The comment lines describe each case where the book's title appears:

```
<html>
  <head>

    <!--
      TITLE of the document - the title appears in bar that runs
        across the very top  of the browser's window
    -->

    <title>Learn XML In A Weekend (Erik Westermann) : Review</title>

    <!--
      The large, centered title that appears immediately after
        the navigational controls
    -->
    <h2 align="center">Learn XML In A Weekend</h2>

      <!--
        Part of the table that summarizes information about
        the book at the bottom of the review
      -->

      <tr>
        <td>
          Title . . . . .
        </td>
        <td>Learn XML In A Weekend
        </td>
      </tr>
      <tr>
```

When you write a new HTML file for a book review, you have to remember how many times to repeat elements like the title of the book and the author's name, and where to place them throughout the document. This can become tedious and confusing, whether you add new reviews only occasionally (you may forget that you need to repeat certain elements) or add reviews often (making all of the repetition tedious).

The benefits of using an approach based on HTML include

➤ It's easy to add a new book to the listing of available book reviews.

➤ You can create book review pages relatively easily.

➤ The pages work with up-to-date versions of the major browsers.

The drawbacks appear throughout this discussion:

➤ There's a one-to-one relationship between the number of book reviews and files that you must maintain.

➤ You need to change many pages' content as a result of a single change, such as a change to the navigational controls.

➤ Repetition of certain elements, like the book's title, within pages and across pages makes it easy to make a mistake, leading to possibly confusing book reviews.

To gain more from the benefits of using the purely HTML-based approach, and to reduce or eliminate some of the drawbacks, use XML.

XML Mixed with HTML and XSL: Flexible and Cool

"Cool" is really the best word to describe this implementation, because it's based completely on XML mixed with XSL, HTML, and JavaScript code. You can find the files for this implementation in the `\XMLInAWeekend\ chapter02\XML` folder.

The twist to this implementation is that the listing of book reviews isn't in an HTML page. The page that contains the listing is called `bookReviews.xml`. Double-click on it to open the file in Internet Explorer (see Figure 2.4).

The first thing you should notice is that the page appears to be identical in every way to the preceding HTML-based solution. The only difference is that you're reading an XML document instead of an HTML document. You'll recall from the previous lesson that XML is made up of markup tags that follow certain syntactical rules. Unlike HTML, it doesn't convey any information about how to present information. You can apply formatting to

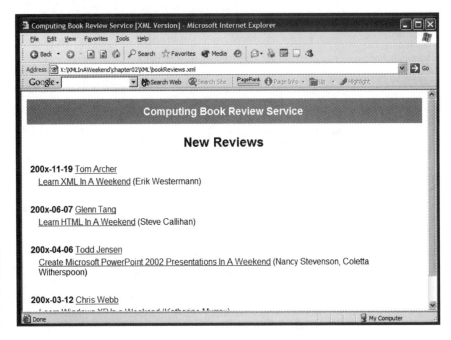

Figure 2.4

Viewing a listing of
available reviews
using an XML
document.

an XML document using a Cascading Style Sheet (CSS) or Extensible Stylesheet Language (XSL) document. This implementation uses XSL to format the listing of book reviews.

Figure 2.5 is a sequence diagram that describes how this solution works when the user requests a particular book review. First, the browser requests an HTML page from the operating system. This page contains instructions that tell the browser to load an XML file and an XSL file (which I'll discuss soon). (The return messages are implicit and have been left out of the diagram to make it easier to read.) When the browser has both the XML and XSL files, it requests the XML Parser to parse the XSL and XML files, combines them, and displays the resulting page on the user's screen.

I'll describe how XSL is used in this solution in a moment, but first you need to understand the structure of the XML document. All information about book reviews resides in a single file, `bookReviews.xml`. This file uses a relatively simple structure, as shown in the following listing:

```
<books>
  <book>
```

```
<xsl:template match="/">
  <html>
    <head>
      <title>Computing Book Review Service [XML Version]</title>
    </head>
    <body>
      <table>
        <tr>
          <td style="FONT-WEIGHT: bold;font-size:120%" align="center">
          Computing Book Review Service
          </td>
        </tr>
      </table>
      <h2 align="center">New Reviews</h2>
      <xsl:for-each select="books">
        <xsl:for-each select="book">
          <xsl:value-of select="review/reviewDate"/>
          <xsl:element name="a">
            <xsl:attribute
name="href">underconstruction.htm</xsl:attribute>
            <xsl:value-of select="review/reviewer"/>
          </xsl:element>
          <xsl:element name="a">
            <xsl:attribute name="href">displayReview.htm?
              <xsl:value-of select="title"/>
            </xsl:attribute>
            <xsl:value-of select="title"/>
          </xsl:element>
          (<xsl:for-each select="author">
            <xsl:value-of select="."/>
            <xsl:if test="position()!=(count(../author))">, </xsl:if>
          </xsl:for-each>)
        </xsl:for-each>
      </xsl:for-each>
    </body>
  </html>
</xsl:template>
```

This listing begins with a special XSL element called a template, which contains a pattern indicated by the `select` attribute that limits the template to processing only parts of an XML document. In this example, however, the template works on the whole XML document because the `select` attribute contains a slash character (/), which represents the XML document's root element. The directives within the template produce the listing of book reviews by using a combination of HTML tags and content from the XML document. Immediately following the template is some HTML code that defines the document's title, which appears in Internet Explorer's title bar as well as in the orange box at the top of the document.

The XSL gets interesting at the line that reads `<xsl:for-each select="books">`, because that's where the listing of reviewed books is generated. The directives within the `<xsl:for-each...>` element create the links to the reviewer's name and the book review document. This section also includes directives for generating the listing of authors (if there's more than one author), and it's capable of inserting commas between multiple authors' names.

If you closely review the XSL, you'll notice that it also contains a number of HTML tags. In fact, the XSL document actually creates an HTML document that Internet Explorer displays but never saves to disk. (The HTML document exists only in memory, and just long enough for Internet Explorer to draw it on the screen.)

When a user clicks on the title of a book, the browser loads another page called `displayReview.htm`, regardless of which book the user selects. The `displayReview.htm` file contains an HTML document with some JavaScript code that transforms the raw book review information into the formatted document you see in Internet Explorer.

Click on one of the books' titles on the main listing of book reviews and note the address that shows up in the browser's address bar. Here's most of what shows up in my browser's address bar when I click on the link for *Learn XML In A Weekend*:

```
displayReview.htm?Learn%20XML%20In%20A%20Weekend
```

The address has the name of the HTML page (`displayReview.htm`), followed by a question mark, followed by a strange-looking string of characters. This is actually the title of the book, with the character sequence %20 in place of the space between each word.

`displayReview.htm` contains some basic HTML that controls the layout of the page, as shown in the following listing:

```
<html>
  <head>
    <style type="text/css">
      BODY { FONT-FAMILY: Sans-Serif; }
      A.menu {text-decoration:none}
      A.menu:hover {background:silver}
      TD.reviewer {font-size:75%}
    </style>
    <!-- JavaScript code removed from here -->
  </head>
  <body onload="Init()">
    <div id="bookReviewText">(default)</div>
  </body>
</html>
```

This listing is very basic as far as HTML documents go, since it only contains `html`, `head`, `style`, `body`, and `div` elements. If you were to open this page with Internet Explorer, it wouldn't be interesting because it would display the word "(default)" and generate an error. So where does the book review come from? The page contains some JavaScript code that executes and formats the book review text when the page loads, according to some XSL instructions that reside in another file.

Let's ignore the details of JavaScript code for now and consider the XSL that formats a single book review. When the user clicks on a book review, the `displayReview.htm` file isolates that review from the rest of the reviews in the `bookReviews.xml` file. Recall that XML is designed to add structure to data, not format it, so `displayReview.htm` can reuse the information in `bookReviews.xml` to display a single book review. The JavaScript code in `displayReview.htm` is responsible for isolating the single book review in memory and then combining it with the XSL that formats it for display on the screen. The XSL is rather involved, roughly 130 lines, because it generates a lot of HTML to control the layout of the final document. Rather than rewrite the HTML tags starting again from the beginning, I reused one of the HTML-based solution's book review files and put it into the XSL document, along with a number of modifications, to produce the end result.

The more interesting parts of the XSL start with the basic information about the book that appears just below the navigational controls at the top of the page: the overview of the book. This overview information is made up of four parts: the book's title, the names of the authors, the name of the publisher, and the year the book was published. Here's the XSL that generates the overview:

```
<xsl:element name="h2">
  <xsl:attribute name="align">center</xsl:attribute>
  <xsl:value-of select="../title"/>
</xsl:element>
<center>
  <b>
    <xsl:for-each select="../author">
      <xsl:value-of select="."/>
      <xsl:if test="position()!=(count(../author))">, </xsl:if>
    </xsl:for-each>
  </b>
  <br/>
  <i>
    <xsl:value-of select="../publisher"/>,
    <xsl:value-of select="../publicationYear"/>
  </i>
</center>
```

It looks rather involved at first, but it's actually straightforward. Ignore the rest of the listing and focus on the xsl:value-of and xsl:for-each elements. Specifically, consider the item that appears in quotes after the select= part of each xsl:value-of and xsl:for-each element. The select= part contains references to elements in the bookReviews.xml document. For example, the reference to ../title in the first xsl:value-of element represents the value of the title element as shown in the bookReviews.xml document. A few lines farther down, the XSL produces a listing of authors using an xsl:for-each element. Even farther down in the listing, the XSL formats the name of the publisher and the year the book was published using xsl:value-of elements.

Essentially, the preceding listing produces HTML code in memory that looks like this:

```
<h2 align="center">Learn XML In A Weekend</h2>
```

```
<center>
  <b>Erik Westermann</b><br>
  <i>Premier Press Books, 2002</i>
</center>
```

The book review text itself also resides in the bookReviews.xml document in an element called reviewText, which is a child of the review element, which in turn is a child of a book element. (If this discussion is going too fast for you, don't worry. I'm covering a lot of ground early in the book so that you'll be in a better position to understand later lessons. You don't have to understand all of the details now.)

What's interesting about the book review text is that only a single XSL directive produces it:

```
<xsl:value-of select="../review/reviewText" disable-output-
escaping="yes"/>
```

This directive is one of those xsl:value-of elements you just saw. This time, the element refers to ../review/reviewText in the select= part, which corresponds to the reviewText element in the bookReviews.xml document. There's a new directive at the end of the xsl:value-of element: disable-output-escaping. This single directive allows you to store the book review text in HTML in the bookReviews.xml document.

The XSL that follows the book review looks really involved, but it boils down to only a few lines:

```
<xsl:value-of select="../title"/>
<xsl:for-each select="../author">
  <xsl:value-of select="."/>
  <xsl:if test="position()!=(count(../author))">, </xsl:if>
</xsl:for-each>
<xsl:value-of select="../publisher"/>
<xsl:value-of select="../isbn"/>
<xsl:value-of select="../details"/>
```

This XSL generates the table immediately following the book review. The first line renders the book's title, followed by a section that renders the names of the authors, adding a comma between each author's name. The final three lines render the name of the publisher, the book's ISBN, and the details element, which usually lists the number of pages.

What's interesting about all of this XSL is that it works with the same XML document that you used to view the listing of book reviews, and it handles the details of repeating elements like the author's name and book's title, making the whole solution easier to maintain. If you're really curious about how I wrote all of this XSL, I invite you to read through the `singleBookReview.xsl` file. If you have questions about the content of the file, please refer to Sunday afternoon's lesson, "Presenting Data on the Web," and Appendix A. Also, you can visit this book's supporting Web site at http://www.designs2solutions.com for additional resources.

The next section discusses the details of how the JavaScript code combines the `bookReviews.xml` XML document with the XSL that's being discussed here. Not familiar with JavaScript? That's not a problem. For now, all you need to understand is that the code in the preceding listing executes inside Internet Explorer and causes it to display a book review from the `bookReviews.xml` file within the essentially empty HTML document.

Try this experiment: Click on one of the book reviews on the main page to display an individual review, and then right-click anywhere within the document and select View Source from the menu that pops up. The document you're looking at represents the document's *source* (the directives that Internet Explorer uses to format the page). Look through the source document and try to locate the book review text. You won't be able to find it, because it's not there. The preceding code causes Internet Explorer to create a sort of virtual document that exists only in the computer's memory. This document exists just long enough in memory for Internet Explorer to render it on the screen.

The following section gives you an idea of how the JavaScript code works. If you're not interested in the details of how the code works, skip the next section and go directly to the section called "ASP: Flexible and Far-Reaching."

How the JavaScript Code Works

This section goes into some details that you can skip if you're not familiar with terms like JavaScript, ActiveX, or COM. You need only a basic understanding of these terms to understand this section.

When you click on a book's title, you load a document called `displayReview.htm` into Internet Explorer, using a specially formatted address. Here's part of the address that appears in Internet Explorer when you click on the title of a book on the main book review document, bookReviews.xml:

```
displayReview.htm?Learn%20XML%20In%20A%20Weekend
```

This address contains the name of the page, followed by a question mark, followed by the title of the book that the user has clicked on (with %20 replacing each space). The displayReview.htm file contains JavaScript code that extracts the name of the book that appears after the question mark, uses it to isolate the book review from the rest of the reviews in the bookReviews.xml document, and then combines the single book review with the XSL document discussed in the preceding section.

Here's what the JavaScript code looks like (the lines that begin with // are comments that describe the actions a section of code carries out):

```
function Init() {
  var xpq=unescape(window.location.search);
  if(xpq.length>1)
    bookName=xpq.substring(1,xpq.length)
  else
    bookName="Learn XML In A Weekend";

  // Load and parse the bookReviews.xml document
  xmldoc = new ActiveXObject("Microsoft.XMLDOM");
  xmldoc.async = false;
  xmldoc.load("bookReviews.xml");

  // Load and parse the XSL document that's capable of
  // formatting a single book review
  xsldoc = new ActiveXObject("Microsoft.XMLDOM");
  xsldoc.async = false;
  xsldoc.load("singleBookReview.xsl");

  // Extract the book's title from the
  // address bar in Internet Explorer
  var xpathExpr;
  xpathExpr="/books/book/title[. = '";
  xpathExpr+=bookName;
  xpathExpr+="']";
```

```
// Isolate the book from all others in the XML document
var singleBook = xmldoc.selectSingleNode(xpathExpr);
// Transform the single book review using the XSL document
bookReviewText.innerHTML=singleBook.transformNode(xsldoc);
// Set the title of the document. The title appears
// in the bar that runs across the top if Internet Explorer
document.title=bookName + " : Review";
}
```

This code does some really interesting things. It starts by reading the value that appears after the question mark in the address in Internet Explorer's address bar. The code does this by accessing the value in the `window.location.search` variable exposed by Internet Explorer, which contains the string which appears after the question mark. Since the string has %20 characters instead of spaces, the JavaScript code uses an Internet Explorer function called `unescape` to convert the %20 character sequences back into spaces.

Immediately following the first comment, the next three lines load the `bookReview.xml` document into memory using the XML Document Object Model (XML DOM). The XML DOM makes it easier for programmers to write programs that read, manipulate, navigate, update, and transform an XML document. It's easy for programmers to use and understand because it's based on a cohesive, conceptual representation of XML documents, using terms like "document," "node," "node list," and "processing instruction," which are the same terms XML document designers use.

Although the XML DOM is available to all applications on a Windows system, it's typically used through Internet Explorer, using a programming language like JavaScript or VBScript. The XML DOM exposes its functionality to programming languages using an interface (a common factor between two disparate parts of a system that allows both parts to interact with one another) that's accessible through COM (a set of Microsoft technologies that allows programmers to interact with parts of a system using a set of predefined rules). The JavaScript code invokes the XML DOM using this statement:

```
xmldoc = new ActiveXObject("Microsoft.XMLDOM");
```

The code within the page invokes one XML DOM for the `bookReviews.xml` document and one for the XSL document. It isolates the book review the user has selected by building an XPath expression that's passed on to the `selectSingleNode` method, which returns a node containing only the elements for a particular review. For example, when the user clicks on the book review for *Learn XML In a Weekend,* the JavaScript code isolates that book review from all others in the `bookReviews.xml` document by generating the following XPath expression:

```
/books/book/title[ . = 'Learn XML In A Weekend']
```

This XPath expression is passed on to a method called `selectSingleNode`, which evaluates the expression and attempts to locate the part of the `bookReviews.xml` document that has the string "Learn XML In A Weekend" in the `title` element. The `selectSingleNode` method returns a node object that contains the requested book review. The next thing the JavaScript code does is combine the single book review with XSL to render it on the screen. The following line combines the XML with the XSL:

```
bookReviewText.innerHTML = singleBook.transformNode(xsldoc);
```

The code on the right side of the equals sign performs the actual transformation and returns a string that contains the result of the transformation. The expression on the left side assigns the results of the transformation to a part of the HTML document, which Internet Explorer renders on the screen. The final action the JavaScript code takes is to set the title of the document, which is shown in the bar across the top of Internet Explorer.

The JavaScript code is executed when the page loads, so the user doesn't have to do anything. The HTML document's `body` tag contains a directive to execute the code when the document has been loaded, as shown in the following line:

```
<body onload'="Init()">
```

The code that you saw in this section resides in a function called `Init`. The `body` tag's `onload` attribute causes the `Init` function to execute when the page is loaded into Internet Explorer.

The benefits of using this approach include the following:

➤ It's easy to add a new book to the listing of available book reviews.

➤ All the book reviews and information about the books reside in a single file.

➤ It's easy to change the appearance of all pages in the solution because two pages control most of the layout.

➤ XSL handles the details of where to put certain values throughout a document, reducing the possibility of errors and omissions.

The drawbacks of this approach include the following:

➤ The solution is supported only by browsers that can work directly with XML, XSL, and JavaScript. Not all browsers provide the same level of support for all three technologies.

➤ Using the XML DOM in this way makes this solution usable only in modern versions of Internet Explorer. A lot of systems still have very early or outdated versions of Internet Explorer, so they won't be able to access the site's pages.

➤ All processing takes place directly within the browser. It may take longer for slower computers to work with the XML and XSL, causing delays for end users.

➤ When a user reviews the listing of available books or a single book review, the entire XML document is sent to Internet Explorer. This is okay for a small solution like the one in this lesson, but it can cause a problem as the number of book reviews increases because the XML document must be sent to the user's system each time the user navigates to one of the pages.

The final implementation extends these benefits and addresses these drawbacks so that the producer of the Web site and its users derive the most use and functionality from the site.

ASP: Flexible and Far-Reaching

The two solutions that you've just learned about have some great benefits, but also some important drawbacks. You derive the benefits of both solutions when you initially create each solution and when you add a book review. You see the drawbacks of the HTML solution when the number of reviews grows past a certain number, and you see the drawbacks of the XML solution when you don't want to be concerned with which browser is used to access the site. Each solution is at one end of an extreme. The HTML-based solution is easily accessible by users on any browsers, and it's very simple but difficult to maintain, whereas the XML solution requires an up-to-date copy of Internet Explorer, and it's more complex but very easy to maintain.

This last incarnation of the book reviews site uses Microsoft's Active Server Pages (ASP) technology in a way that frees users from having to use a particular browser, makes the site easy to maintain, and uses all of the XML and XSL that you've seen so far.

ASP is part of Microsoft's Web server, called Internet Information Server (IIS), and it allows programmers to create Web sites that dynamically generate Web pages for users on a per-request basis. To get an idea of how an end user interacts with dynamically generated pages, visit an online book seller and request details about a few books. When you make a request for a book, the book seller's Web server accesses a database, looks up the details of the book, and generates a Web page based on that information. This process is repeated each time you request information on a different book. The book seller uses dynamically generated Web pages based on content from a database because it's easy to maintain. Adding a new book for sale is a (relatively) simple matter of adding information to a database. The Web server handles the details of how to format the information at the point when a user requests information about the new book. From an end user's perspective, dynamically generated Web pages offer a certain level of interactivity. Instead of reviewing unchanging pages, each page is generated at the time you request it and (hopefully) contains information that you're interested in.

Microsoft's Web server, IIS, provides integrated support for dynamically generating Web pages using a mixture of HTML, which is sent directly to end users, and code written in a language like JavaScript, which IIS executes before the results are sent to the end user. The result is that pages are generated when the user requests them, and they're easy to maintain because they're made up of familiar HTML and JavaScript code.

As I mentioned earlier, support for the XML DOM in Windows-based systems is provided by a component that's available to all applications through COM. You realize the benefit of this broad support when you want to programmatically use the XML DOM from within ASP, instead from within Internet Explorer, because the code that does most of the work is almost exactly the same in both scenarios. Figure 2.6 is a sequence diagram that describes how this solution works.

Figure 2.6 introduces a new entity, the Web server. Take a close look at this diagram and compare it with Figure 2.5. You should notice that, apart from an extra message, the diagram captures the same set of actions as those shown

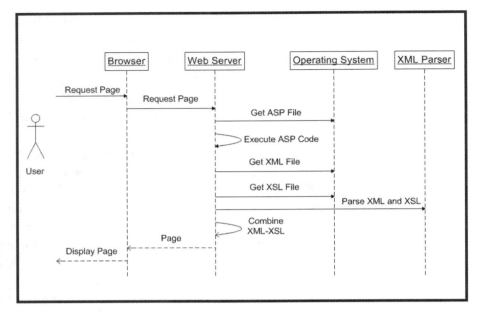

Figure 2.6

Viewing book
reviews using
ASP and XML.

in Figure 2.5, except that the Web server is now doing all of the work instead of the browser. The Web server in this case is Microsoft's IIS, and it generates actions based on code in an ASP. The solution renders all pages in plain HTML, while still allowing you to maintain the site in XML and take advantage of XSL to format the pages. It's an interesting solution because it allows you to realize these benefits simply by shifting all of the work from the browser to the Web server, thereby extending the reach of this solution to all users' browsers.

Before you continue, you need to understand that all processing occurs on the Web server. It begins after the user requests a page, but it's completed *before* the page is sent back to the user's browser. This is an important concept that's easy to overlook.

Unlike the previous two solutions, you cannot simply open a file and work with the solution. You need to use Microsoft's Internet Information Server to read, interpret, and process the pages. The system requirements for this solution (as outlined in the Preface) are Windows 2000 Professional or Server or Windows XP Professional, along with Internet Information Server (any version after 3.0). It's essential that you have version 3.0 or later of Microsoft XML Core Services, Microsoft's name for its XML parser. The sample code includes an XML parser sniffer, an HTML page with some JScript code that determines which version of the XML parser is installed on your system. The sniffer is located in the `\XMLInAWeekend\sniffer` folder. Locate the file using Windows Explorer (click the My Computer icon on your system's desktop) and double-click on the file to open it (you must have Internet Explorer 5.0 or later to use the page). Open the page on the system that has IIS installed on it to ensure that you have at least version 3.0 of Microsoft XML Core Services installed. If you don't, please visit the address provided on the page's recommendations and install the current version.

Use the following directions to configure your system to host the ASP-based solution:

1. Extract this book's sample code onto the system's hard drive.
2. Start Windows Explorer by double-clicking on the My Computer icon on your system's desktop.
3. Locate the `\XMLInAWeekend\chapter02` folder.
4. Right-click on the ASP folder that appears on the right side of the window.
5. Select Properties from the menu that pops up beside the pointer.
6. Select the Web Sharing tab from the dialog box that pops up.
7. Click on the Share This Folder option.
8. Click on the OK button in the dialog box that pops up.
9. Click on OK to close the folder properties dialog box and show Windows Explorer again.

Once you've completed these steps, start Internet Explorer and type the following address into the address bar:

```
http://localhost/ASP
```

You should see a Web page that lists available book reviews. This Web page will be identical to the pages you saw in the HTML and XML solutions. Depending on the configuration of your Web server, there's a small chance that your browser may not be able to find the first page of the application. If that happens, the browser will display this message: "The page cannot be found." You can correct the problem by changing the address that you type into the browser's address bar, as shown:

```
http://localhost/ASP/default.asp
```

If you get a message that the page cannot be found using the preceding address, chances are that your Web server either isn't running or isn't configured properly. For more information on how to troubleshoot this problem, please consult Microsoft's online documentation or visit its support Web site. If your version of Windows didn't come with a Web server, such as Windows XP Home Edition or Windows 98, you can still try out the samples at my Web site, http://www.designs2solutions.com/LXIAW.

When you first visit the book reviews site, whether on your own system or my Web site, the first page you'll see is the page that lists available book reviews. This page is dynamically generated by some code that resides in the default.asp file. The following listing shows the contents of this file:

```
<%@ Language=JavaScript %>
<html>
  <head>
  <%
    xmldoc = Server.CreateObject("Microsoft.XMLDOM");
    xmldoc.async = false;
    xmldoc.load(Server.MapPath("bookReviews.xml"));
    xsldoc = Server.CreateObject("Microsoft.XMLDOM");
    xsldoc.async = false;
    xsldoc.load(Server.MapPath("bookReviewMainASP.xslt"));
  %>
  <title>Computing Book Review Service [ASP Version]</title>
    <style type="text/css">
      BODY { FONT-FAMILY: Sans-Serif; }
      A.menu {text-decoration:none}
      A.menu:hover {background:silver}
      TD.reviewer {font-size:75%}
    </style>

  </head>
  <body>
  <%
    Response.Write(xmldoc.transformNode(xsldoc));
  %>
  </body>
</html>
```

Basically, this is an HTML page with some additional directives throughout. The first directive appears in the very first line of the page. Essentially, it says that the Web server should treat the page as an Active Server Page that uses the JavaScript programming language to dynamically generate the page's contents. Another directive, just after the HTML head tag in the form of the character sequence <%, informs the Web server that what follows is JavaScript code it should execute, and not HTML code. As a result, the Web server processes the code before sending its results to the end user's browser.

The JavaScript code in this listing has a very simple job. It loads the bookReviews.xml document and the XSL document, and combines them to produce a listing of available book reviews. The XML-based solution didn't require this code because that page was an XML file that referred to an XSL file. In this case, however, the Web server needs to load the XML file, load the XSL file, and combine the two to produce a page that's delivered to the end user's browser. In the previous example, this occurred within the user's browser so that an HTML page was never produced. In this case, the Web server produces a plain HTML page that almost all browsers can render accurately on the screen.

The ASP that renders the page containing a single book review is a little more complex than the page that lists available book reviews, since it needs to segregate the book review that the user is interested in before formatting it. The good news is that the code is almost exactly the same as the code that appears in the displayReview.htm file you saw earlier in this lesson, as shown in the following listing:

```
<%@ Language=JavaScript%>
<html>
  <head>
  <%
    var xpq=Request.QueryString("bookTitle");
    bookName=xpq;
    xmldoc = Server.CreateObject("Microsoft.XMLDOM");
    xmldoc.async = false;
    xmldoc.load(Server.MapPath("bookReviews.xml"));
    xsldoc = Server.CreateObject("Microsoft.XMLDOM");
    xsldoc.async = false;
    xsldoc.load(Server.MapPath("singleBookReview.xsl"));
```

```
var xpathExpr;
xpathExpr="/books/book/title[. = '";
xpathExpr+=bookName;
xpathExpr+="']";
xmldoc.setProperty("SelectionLanguage", "XPath");
var singleBook;
singleBook = xmldoc.selectSingleNode(xpathExpr);
%>

<title><%=xpq%> : Review</title>
<style type="text/css">
    BODY { FONT-FAMILY: Sans-Serif; }
    A.menu {text-decoration:none}
    A.menu:hover {background:silver}
    TD.reviewer {font-size:75%}
</style>

</head>
<body>
  <%
  Response.Write(singleBook.transformNode(xsldoc));
  %>
</body>
</html>
```

The differences between the code in displayReview.htm and the code in the previous listing relate to how the XML DOM is invoked and how the XPath expression is created. Like the previous page, the Web server generates plain HTML that most browsers can easily and accurately render on the screen. This is very much unlike the XML-based solution, which requires users to have the current version of Internet Explorer installed on their system in order to use the book reviews sample.

The benefits of using this approach include the following:

➤ It's accessible to almost all browsers in existence today because the output is in regular HTML.

➤ Users don't need to have systems capable of processing XML and XSL documents, because all processing occurs on the Web server.

➤ The system is still easy to maintain, because the structure of the XML and XSL files hasn't changed from the previous solution.

The drawback to this approach is that it must run on a Microsoft operating system, like Windows 2000 or Windows XP, that has all of the latest releases of software like Microsoft XML Core Services.

What's Next?

This lesson introduced several new concepts to you in a relatively short time. Don't worry if you didn't understand some of it. The important thing is that you have an idea of how people use XML in practical ways to solve real problems.

The next lesson is just a little longer than this lesson, and it covers how to write XML documents by introducing the rules that all XML documents must follow. Since both this lesson and the next are relatively short, that leaves you with some extra time that you'll need for this evening's lesson, which is slightly longer than both of this morning's and afternoon's lessons combined.

Marking Up Isn't Just for Graffiti Artists

➤ Elements of XML

➤ Expressing More by Using Attributes

➤ Adding Data to Your XML Documents

➤ Adding Comments

➤ Using Processing Instructions

➤ Declaring an XML Document

➤ Composing a Well-Formed XML Document

➤ Languages and Character Sets

➤ The Fundamentals of Namespaces

O n Friday evening, you looked at the basic rules for creating an XML document. This afternoon's lesson goes into more detail by describing how to create *well-formed* documents, the elements that make up an XML document, and advanced topics like namespaces and data modeling.

Elements of XML

Figure 3.1 shows an HTML anchor element. I chose this element because it's easy to understand and should be familiar to those who've worked with HTML. The sidebar describes the anchor element's role.

Figure 3.1 highlights some of the features of the anchor element, which are described in Table 3.1.

The parts in Table 3.1 are collectively known as an *element*; specifically, an HTML element. XML structures its elements in exactly the same way.

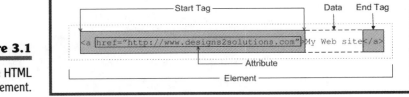

Figure 3.1

A sample HTML element.

THE HTML ANCHOR ELEMENT EXPLAINED

The HTML anchor element is also known as a link. When you browse the Internet, you find your way through a site by clicking on either text links or image links. A text link usually appears as blue underlined text. (Note: Not all Web sites style their links in this way because it's very ordinary. Some sites style their links so that they blend in with the surrounding text, or stand out a great deal. Most Web site designers give readers a visual clue that's consistent within a site to indicate links.) When you move your mouse over a link, the pointer changes into a hand to indicate that you can click to follow the link. This is shown in Figure 3.2.

Figure 3.2

Clicking on a link.

The anchor tag has two essential parts: the text that serves as the link (*Reviews* in the figure) and the name of the document that the link leads to. When you click on the text, the browser loads the document.

TABLE 3.1 THE PARTS OF AN HTML ANCHOR ELEMENT

Part	Description
Start tag	The start tag offsets an HTML element from the surrounding text, signaling the beginning of an HTML element. The tag begins with a less-than symbol (<) and is immediately followed by the name of the tag (a in this example).
Attribute	An attribute is data that has a very close relationship with the tag in which it appears. The attribute in this example is called href. Its role is to tell the browser the address of the document to load when the user clicks on the text link.
Data	An anchor's data indicates to the user that the text is a link ("My Web site" in this example). The text usually appears in some other color to distinguish it as a link (see the sidebar "The HTML Anchor Element Explained" for details).
End tag	The end tag indicates where an HTML element ends and where the rest of the surrounding text begins. In this example, the end tag is </a>.

Structure of XML Elements

Figure 3.3 shows a basic XML element.

The element is made up of a start tag, some data, and an end tag. The start tag in the figure has an attribute (type). However, attributes may or may not be optional. (You'll learn how to figure out which attributes are optional in this evening's lesson, "Document Modeling.") The key is that all elements must have a start tag *and* an end tag.

There's only one case where you don't have to explicitly provide an end tag for an element: when the element is empty. For example, suppose you're creating an XML document that contains some paragraphs. You use the <para> tag to indicate the beginning of a paragraph and the </para> tag to indicate the end of a paragraph, as shown in the following listing:

```
<para>Elements are made up of a start tag, some data, and an end
tag.</para>
<para></para>
<para>There is only one case where you don't have to...</para>
```

The paragraph in the middle of the document is empty because there isn't any text between the start and end <para> tags. This is called an *empty element*. These elements occur in XML documents so often that they have their own shorthand notation:

```
<para />
```

An empty element looks just like a start tag, except that instead of having just a greater-than symbol at the end of the tag, there's a single space and a slash character (/). It's not strictly necessary to have a space before the />

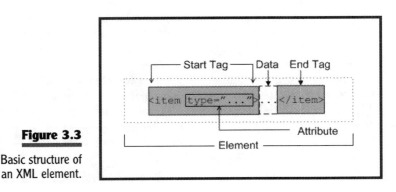

Figure 3.3

Basic structure of an XML element.

character sequence, but it can avoid problems later on when you're trying to figure out why an XML parser claims an XML document has an error, when in fact it looks fine to you. The effect of the shorthand notation is identical to that of the longer notation that uses both the start and ending tags. The difference is that the shorthand notation is easier to type.

XML elements do not necessarily have to contain data. They can contain any of the following three types of information:

➤ Data (arbitrary text)

➤ Other elements

➤ A mixture of data and other elements

These types of elements are so pervasive in the world of XML that each one has a special name, referred to as a *content model*. This is simply a description of what an element contains. Table 3.2 summarizes the three XML content models.

TABLE 3.2 XML CONTENT MODELS	
Content Model	**Elements Contain...**
Text-only	Only data—no other elements
Element-only	Only other elements—no data
Mixed content	Text-only and element-only type elements

Naming Elements

Every element must have a name that's at least one character long. You use an element's name to form its start and end tags. For example, the previous example used <para> and </para> tags to represent a single paragraph in a document. The name of each paragraph element in the document is para; as a result, its start and end tags use the element's name.

Element names have one or more characters in them, but the first character is a little different from all of the other characters. The first character of an element's name can be either a letter or an underscore character (_). If you decide to use a letter, it can be in upper- or lowercase. This implies that you cannot create elements that don't have a name (such as <>), nor can you create an element that's named using a single space (such as < >). This rule also implies that the name of the element begins immediately following the less-than symbol (<). An element named < book> is *not* a valid element name because it begins with a space.

Characters following the first character can be any letters, numbers, underscores (_), hyphens (-), and periods(.); letters can be in upper- or lowercase. Element names *cannot* include the following characters: punctuation marks, such as commas, apostrophes, ampersands (&), and asterisks (*), and space or tab characters (collectively known as *whitespace* characters). Figure 3.4 summarizes these rules.

Later on you'll come across elements that have a colon (:) in their names. The colon is a legal character for naming your elements, as long as it comes *after* the first character. It serves a special purpose in XML for namespaces, which I'll describe later. This introduces you to the first rule about all XML documents: All elements must follow strict naming rules.

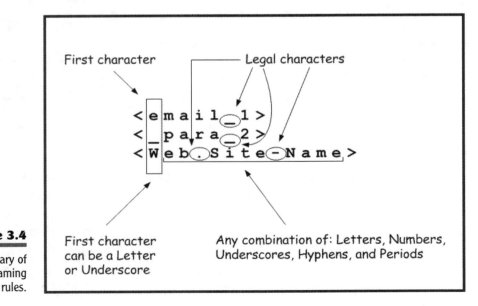

Figure 3.4

Summary of element naming rules.

Structuring Elements

An XML element by itself isn't all that interesting because it describes only one thing, or a part of something. Elements are more interesting in the context of an XML document since they provide structure to the data. Figure 3.5 shows the conceptual structure of an XML document.

The figure shows that the document contains elements with all three types of content models. At the very top of the figure is an element-only element, which represents the *root element*. The root element is different from other elements in an XML document because all XML documents must have one. A root element encloses all of the other elements in the XML document. Think of it as a description of the document's subject. For example, here's what to do if the XML document describes books:

1. Name the root element books.

2. Begin the XML document with a <books> tag.

3. End the XML document with the </books> tag.

This introduces you to the second rule about all XML documents: They must have a root element.

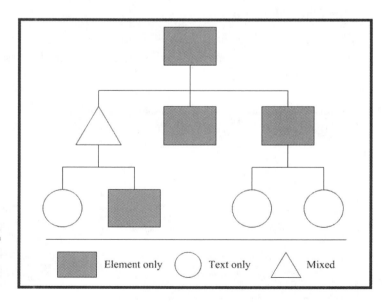

Figure 3.5

The conceptual structure of an XML document.

The rest of the figure represents the document's structure within the root element. Here's an XML document that follows this structure:

```
<rootElement>
  <mixedElement>Item One
    <textOnlyElement>Item Two</textOnlyElement>
    <emptyElement />
  </mixedElement>
  <emptyElement />
  <enclosingElement>
    <textOnlyElement>Item Three</textOnlyElement>
    <textOnlyElement>Item Four</textOnlyElement>
  </enclosingElement>
</rootElement>
```

The root element, `rootElement`, exemplifies the element-only content model because it contains all of the document's other elements. The `mixedElement` is a mixed-content element because it contains both text ("Item One") *and* other elements (`textOnlyElement` and `emptyElement`). When the content for the `mixedElement` ends, so does the `mixedElement` element, with a closing tag. The `enclosingElement` uses the element-only content model because it contains two other elements. Both of the elements that `enclosingElement` contains use the text-only content model because they contain only text ("Item Three" and "Item Four").

This listing also demonstrates that you nest elements to structure your XML documents. Nesting, shown in Figure 3.6, works by enclosing elements within other elements.

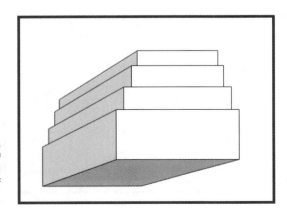

Figure 3.6

Conceptual
representation of
nesting elements.

It is important to nest elements correctly. They cannot overlap. Here's an example of *incorrectly* nested elements:

```
<bus><route>85E</bus></route>
```

The bus and route elements overlap because their closing tags are in the reverse order of their starting tags. This brings us to the third rule for all XML documents: Elements may nest, but they may not overlap.

Expressing More by Using Attributes

Elements sometimes have attributes whose role is to annotate the element they're associated with. You saw an example of an attribute in Figure 3.1, where the HTML anchor element has an attribute that provides the address of the document to load when the user clicks on the text part of the link.

XML also supports attributes, as shown in the following listing:

```
<books>
  <book isbn="159200010X" author="Essam Ahmed">
    Learn XML In A Weekend
  </book>
</books>
```

This contains the same information about books that the sample in Friday evenings lesson does, except that it uses attributes instead of separate elements to describe the book. So which is more appropriate to use, elements or attributes?

Unlike elements, which convey the structure of a document, attributes are essentially unstructured annotations since they convey information in the form of a *name-value* pair. This is a simple structure that associates an arbitrary *name*, like isbn in the previous listing, with a *value*, like "159200010X" in the previous listing. XML elements, in contrast, convey a much richer structure that's easy to process with XML-based software. Attributes are useful when you expect people to directly read your XML documents, whereas elements are useful in the context of applications that use XML. While XML is easy for you and me to read, it's not a great way to convey information directly between people. XML is more useful when systems process it to transform information into a more usable format. As a result, many XML document authors prefer to use elements in most situations.

Another factor in deciding whether to use attributes is how you plan to present your XML documents. Later on, I'll describe how you can display your XML documents using CSS (Cascading Stylesheets) and XSL (Extensible Stylesheet Language). CSS requires less processing power than XSL, and it's easier to use. However, CSS cannot access information in an element's attributes. XSL has access to all of an XML document's structure, including its attributes, but it's a little more difficult to use than CSS. I'll describe both techniques later in the book.

Like XML elements, attributes also have to follow a set of rules to ensure that XML parsers can work with them:

➤ Attributes must always appear in the starting tag of an element.

➤ Attributes cannot contain other attributes or elements.

➤ An attribute can appear only once within a given element.

➤ Attributes follow the same naming rules as elements.

➤ Attribute values must appear in quotes.

➤ An equals symbol must appear between an attribute's name and its value.

Figure 3.7 summarizes these rules.

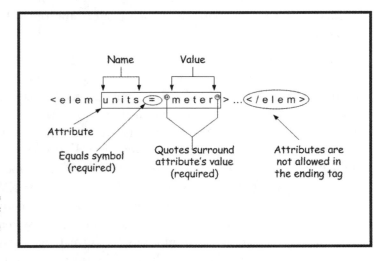

Figure 3.7

Summary of attribute usage rules.

Here are some examples of using attributes correctly:

```
<box color="brown" type="cardboard">
   <location>81C</location>
</box>
<price type="wholesale" amount="29.99" />
<season hemisphere="north" >
   <name>Summer</name>
   <startMonth month="06">June</startMonth>
   <endMonth month="09">September</endMonth>
   <averageTemperature units="Celsius" scale="degrees">28</averageTem-
perature>
</season>
```

The box element in the previous listing demonstrates how attributes add useful information, since the attributes describe the box's color and type. The price element is similar, except that it's an empty element and doesn't contain any information. In contrast, the attributes in the season element (and the elements it contains) make the information easier for applications to process. The attributes annotate the startMonth, endMonth, and averageTemperature elements, providing information that an application could determine on its own or find elsewhere (the attributes don't actually convey any new information).

While there aren't any restrictions on what you can name your attributes (provided that you follow the naming rules), XML reserves some names for its own use. You must avoid the reserved attribute names that are shown in Table 3.3.

Adding Data to Your XML Documents

As you've seen, the XML standard is strict about how you format your document's elements and attributes. The XML standard also describes what kinds of data (or content) you can have within your document.

A lot of XML's rules are based on *character sequences*. For example, an element's start tag begins with the less-than symbol (<) and ends in the greater-than symbol (>). An element's end tag begins with </ and ends with >. In contrast, an empty element begins with < and ends with />. Using charac-

TABLE 3.3 RESERVED XML ATTRIBUTE NAMES AND THEIR ROLES

Attribute	Description
xml:lang	Defines the language an element's data uses. See "Understanding the xml:lang Attribute" later in this lesson for more information.
xml:space	Declares whether an XML-aware application should preserve whitespace characters in an element. This attribute can have two values: default and preserve. The default setting indicates that the XML-aware application can treat whitespace characters using its own rules. The preserve setting indicates that you want the XML-aware application to consider whitespace characters to be part of the data and not change them in any way.
xml:link	Indicates that the element this attribute resides in is a link element.
xml:attribute	Used in conjunction with xml:link to rename attributes to avoid attribute naming conflicts.

ter sequences makes XML easier to understand, but it puts some restrictions on the data you can use in your XML documents since it could be misinterpreted as an XML tag.

Elements and attributes cannot contain the following characters:

➤ Less-than symbol (<)

➤ Ampersand (&)

➤]]

Although this list is short, it can put some restrictions on the type of information your XML documents can have. For example, the following elements contain *illegal* data:

```
<expression> a < b </expression>     <!-- Less-than symbol is illegal! -->
<story>Jack & Jill</story>           <!-- Ampersand symbol is illegal -->
<example>var1[var2[var3]]</example>  <!-- Character sequence ]] is
                                         illegal -->
<image> <img src="image.jpg"> </image> <!-- Contains a less-than
                                            symbol -->
```

```
<code description="check if a < b"> <!-- Contains a less-than symbol -->
  <script language="jscript">
    function testValue(a,b) {
      if (a < b)                    <!-- Contains a less-than symbol -->
        return a;
      else
        return b;
    }
  </script>
</code>
```

These three symbols cannot appear within your data because of how an XML parser processes your documents. For example, the less-than symbol (<) indicates that an element tag is starting, and the ampersand character indicates that the characters that follow represent an entity reference (described in the next section).

Before you start to get too concerned about what you can store in your XML documents, you should know that there are some easy ways of getting around these restrictions without having to resort to simply not including some of your data in an XML document. The workarounds include using entity references and using character data sections, both of which are described in the following sections.

Using Entity References

Entity references allow you to use special characters within XML documents that would otherwise make your XML data invalid. For example, consider the following JavaScript code (don't worry if you're not familiar with JavaScript):

```
for ( i = 0; i < 10; i++)
```

The less-than symbol is an illegal character. If you add this code to an XML element called code, it looks like this:

```
<code>for ( i = 0; i < 10; i++)</code>
```

When an XML parser comes along, it interprets the element like this:

```
<code>for ( i = 0; i
```

The XML processor reads the name of the element and its value up to the first less-than symbol, which appears just after the second letter *i*. At that point, it stops processing because there's a space immediately following the less-than symbol. The XML parser interprets the less-than symbol as indicating the beginning of an element (a start tag), and element names cannot start with a space. As a result, the XML parser stops processing the document. The way to address this problem is to use an entity reference in place of the less-than symbol:

```
<code>for ( i = 0; i &lt; 10; i++)</code>
```

This replaces the less-than symbol (<) with its entity reference, <. Table 3.4 describes the predefined entity references you can use in your XML documents.

Table 3.4 includes entity references that are outside the scope of invalid XML data. You can use these entity references wherever you would use the character directly. For example, the following is the same listing I showed you earlier that contained illegal data. This time, I use entity references to make the data legal in XML (the entity references appear in bold):

```
<expression> a &lt; b </expression>
<story>Jack &amp; Jill</story>
<example>var1&#91;var2&#91;var3&#93;&#93;</example>
<image> &lt;img src="image.jpg"&gt; </image>
<code description="check if a &lt; b">
   &lt;script language=&quot;jscript&quot;&gt;
     function testValue(a,b) {
       if (a &lt; b)
         return a;
       else
         return b;
   }
   &lt;/script&gt;
</code>
```

If you look closely at the entity references, you'll see some that have numeric values following the ampersand character. For example, [represents the opening square bracket ([), and [represents the closing square bracket (]). Table 3.4 showed the predefined XML entity references. This implies that there are non-predefined entity references available as well.

TABLE 3.4 PREDEFINED XML ENTITY REFERENCES

Character	Name	Entity Reference
<	Less-than	<
>	Greater-than	>
&	Ampersand	&
"	Quote	"
'	Apostrophe	'

You can replace any characters in your XML documents with entity references by using the entity reference character (&), followed by a pound symbol (#), followed by the numeric representation of the character. So where can you find numeric representations of characters? Use Table 3.5 to get you started. If you need more characters, search on the Internet for the term "ASCII character chart" or visit my Web site at http://www.designs2solutions.com/LXIAW.

TABLE 3.5 SELECTED CHARACTER CODES

Character	Name	Entity Reference
™	Trademark	™
©	Copyright	©
®	Register	®
±	Plus or minus	±
¼	One-quarter	¼
½	One-half	½
¾	Three-quarters	¾

Using Character Data Sections

The fact that you can use entity references in your XML documents implies that an XML parser reviews the data in your XML document. However, this is not the case. An XML parser has no way of knowing when your data ends and a tag begins, other than by checking each character for a less-than symbol. Entity references free you from the XML parser, since you can use any character you like to represent your XML data.

The problem with using entity references is that it makes your document a little more difficult to produce. You have to replace illegal data with legal entity references, as shown in the previous example. If you forget to replace illegal characters with entity references before you mark up a document using XML, it will be difficult to replace less-than symbols, greater-than symbols, and ampersands, because those symbols are pervasive throughout the XML markup itself.

If you have large sections within your XML document that use illegal characters, an alternative is to use a character data or CDATA section. This "fences off" an area within your XML document. When an XML parser encounters a CDATA section, it ignores the contents and simply continues to process the rest of the document, leaving you free to put whatever you like within the CDATA section.

TIP

XML parsers ignore the data in CDATA sections. Any non-CDATA sections within an XML document are referred to as *parsed character data* sections.

Here's what a CDATA section looks like (the CDATA tags appear in bold):

```
<code><![CDATA[for ( i = 0; i < 10; i++)]]></code>
```

This is how you can create a CDATA section:

1. CDATA sections must appear within an XML element.
2. Start the CDATA section using the following character sequence: `<![CDATA[`.
3. Add data to the CDATA section.
4. End the CDATA section using the following character sequence: `]]>`.

The following listing uses CDATA sections, where possible, to allow for longer sections of character data:

```
<expression><![CDATA[ a < b ]]></expression>
<story><![CDATA[Jack & Jill]]></story>
<example> var1&#91;var2&#91;var3&#93;&#93;</example>
<image><![CDATA[ <img src="image.jpg"> ]]></image>
<code description="check if a &lt; b">
<![CDATA[
  <script language="jscript">
    function testValue(a,b) {
      if (a < b)
        return a;
      else
        return b;
    }
  </script>
]]>
</code>
```

There are two places in the previous listing where I was unable to use a CDATA section. The first place is in the example element. I couldn't use a CDATA section because it includes two closing square bracket characters (]]), which indicates the ending of a CDATA section. The other place I couldn't use a CDATA section is in the code element's description attribute. Attributes are very simple structures, so you have to use entity references. You cannot use CDATA sections within attribute data.

Adding Comments

XML documents can get complicated, so XML document designers sometimes add comments so you can annotate your documents for the benefit of other users. XML parsers ignore comments. The following listing embeds comments throughout the XML document:

```
<!--The program evaluates the following expression: -->
<expression><![CDATA[ a < b ]]></expression>
<!-- ...and generates an image as the result: -->
```

```
<image><![CDATA[ <img src="image.jpg"> ]]></image>
<!-- This is the end of the document -->
```

A comment begins with the character sequence <!-- and ends with the character sequence -->. Comments can contain almost any characters, including the less-than (<) and ampersand (&) characters. The only character sequence you *cannot* include in a comment is the double hyphen (--), since that indicates the end of a comment.

You can put comments almost anywhere in an XML document *except* within an element's markup or in a CDATA section. For example, the following is an illegally placed comment:

```
<example <!-- Example One *ERROR* --> level="novice">
```

Comments within CDATA sections aren't recognized as comments because, by definition, XML-aware applications ignore CDATA sections. This means that comments within CDATA sections are essentially invisible to XML-aware applications.

You can put comments within a document type definition (DTD), provided that the comments are not within other markup that's in the DTD. You'll learn more about DTDs in Saturday evening's lesson, in the section called "Understanding and Using DTDs."

Using Processing Instructions

A Processing Instruction (PI) is a special directive that you can add to an XML document that contributes to the information in the document, but also conveys information to the application that processes the document. There isn't any requirement to include PIs in your documents, and XML-aware applications are allowed to ignore them if they wish. A PI has two parts, a target keyword and data, as shown in Figure 3.8.

The PI begins with a beginning delimiter, "<?", and ends with an ending delimiter, "?>". The target keyword immediately follows the beginning delimiter, and, as with XML elements, whitespace between the beginning delimiter and the target keyword is illegal. The target keyword is application-specific—it's up to you to decide what word you want to use, since it's meaningful only to you and the application that processes the target keyword. The

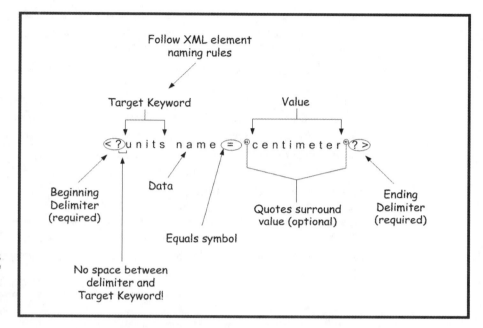

Figure 3.8

The structure of an
XML Processing
Instruction.

data in a PI can take two forms. Figure 3.8 shows one form, a name-value
pair. The other form is simply another word that's not followed by an equals
symbol or value. You can include as much or as little data as you like. If the
PI doesn't have any data, the application can treat the target keyword as data
instead. Here are some valid PIs:

```
<?hello?>
<?subTotal every=5 units="pages"?>
<?printer type=color?>
```

Declaring an XML Document

All XML documents begin with an XML declaration. It uses a special tag to
inform XML-aware applications, like an XML parser, that the document it's
reviewing is indeed an XML document. Here's what the XML declaration
looks like:

```
<?xml version="1.0"?>
```

This declaration states that the document contains XML that's compliant with version 1.0 of the XML specification (which is the only known version at the time of this writing). There are some other elements of the XML declaration that specify the character set (language) that the document uses, and if the document refers to other XML documents. Table 3.6 describes the elements of an XML declaration.

You'll learn how to use character encoding later in this lesson.

TABLE 3.6 ELEMENTS OF AN XML DECLARATION

Element	Description	Usage
`<?xml`	Starts the XML declaration.	Required
`version`	Describes which version of XML the document uses. Version 1.0 is the only known version at the time of this writing.	Required
`encoding`	Describes what character set the document uses. A character set contains the characters for a given language. The most common character set is UTF-8, and that's the default if you don't use this attribute in your declaration.	Optional
`standalone`	Specifies if the XML document refers to other XML documents. The value for this attribute can be "yes" or "no," and it's "yes" if you do not provide this attribute.	Optional
`?>`	Closes the XML declaration.	Required

Composing a Well-Formed XML Document

Now that you know how to play by the rules, you also know that all XML documents must be *well-formed*. A well-formed XML document follows all of the rules you've already learned about in this lesson. Your XML needs to be well-formed because otherwise XML parsers and XML-aware applications can't work with it.

You're now ready to create your first well-formed XML document! Your initiation into the world of XML is to create a traditional "Hello World" XML document. Figure 3.9 shows what the document looks like in Internet Explorer.

You'll use Windows Notepad to create the document. The easiest way to start Notepad is to click on your system's Start menu, click Run, type **notepad**, and then press the Enter key.

The first thing you need to do is type the XML declaration on the very first line:

```
<?xml version="1.0" encoding="UTF-8"?>
```

The declaration states that the document conforms to XML version 1.0 and uses UTF-8, the most common character encoding. (It's sometimes referred to as US ASCII in tech-speak.) The declaration must be the very first line of the XML file. There shouldn't be any lines or whitespace before the declaration.

The next item in the document is the comment that describes the document. Type the following on the line after the XML declaration:

```
<!-- This is a sample Hello World document that demonstrates how to
write a well-formed XML document-->
```

Figure 3.9

Displaying an XML document in Internet Explorer.

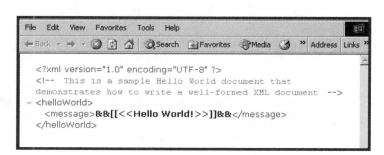

You can put the comment onto more than one line. Press the Enter key to end a line and start a new one. Just make sure to close the comment using the --> character sequence.

Next, start the *root element* by typing the following tag on the line immediately following the comment. Pay attention to the uppercase W:

```
<helloWorld>
```

The next line has the `message` element tag on it. Start a new line and press the Tab key to insert some space before the tag:

```
    <message>
```

XML allows you to freely format your documents. XML parsers and XML-aware applications ignore the additional spaces that appear around XML elements. This is not the case, however, with the contents of XML elements themselves. I'll describe the effect of whitespace in the discussion on XSL tomorrow afternoon. For now, enter the message as shown (press the Tab key twice on a new line before typing the message):

```
        &amp;&amp;&#91;&#91;&lt;&lt;Hello  World!&gt;&gt;&#93;&#93;&amp;&amp;
```

The message contains many characters that XML does not like, so it replaces them with entity references. An alternative is to use a CDATA section, but you can't do that in this case because the message has two closing square brackets (]]).

The last thing you need to do is close the document's elements. Type a Tab character before the closing `message` element:

```
    </message>
</helloWorld>
```

(Pay special attention to the uppercase W in the last closing element.) Figure 3.10 gives you an idea of what the document should look like at this point.

Save the document by selecting File, Save, choosing a directory to save the file in, and assigning the name helloWorld.xml to the file. You can view the file by starting Internet Explorer and typing the location and name of the file in the Address bar. (You don't have to be connected to the Internet.) For example, if you saved the file in your c:\temp folder, type the following address into the Address bar: **c:\temp\helloWorld.xml**.

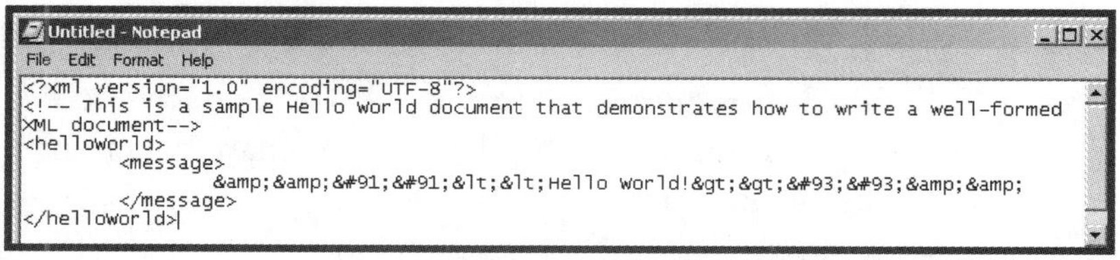

Figure 3.10

Editing the sample XML document using Windows Notepad.

Languages and Character Sets

The Internet is a worldwide network that contains documents, Web pages, and even e-mail messages that are written in languages other than English. People communicate using the written word, sounds, images, and a range of other media. Computers store all of it in the form of numbers, so if you want to store a document on a computer or send an e-mail message to someone, it needs to be transformed into a numeric representation first.

For example, assume you're sending an e-mail message to a friend that reads, "Hi, how are you?" When you send the message, your computer encodes the message using the English character set (assuming you're using a PC that has the English version of Windows installed on it). Here's what the message looks like when it is encoded:

```
72 105 44 32 104 111 119 32
97 114 101 32 121 111 117 63
```

So what does this mean? The numbers represent each character in the message. For example, 72 represents the "H" in "Hi," and 44 represents the comma after the "i." (If you look closely, you'll see the number 32 in several places. It represents the space character.)

If you live in Germany, chances are that you'll send your message in German, which has some letters that have umlauts, like ä, ö, and ü. These letters, and many others in use around the world, don't exist in English text, but there must be a way of representing them using numbers. Encoding systems address this issue by assigning numbers to letters, as in the previous example. When worldwide networks became more common, these encoding systems didn't work well because often a number represented the space character in English but represented another character in another language. In other words, the two languages' encoding systems overlapped with one another.

Understanding Unicode Character Encoding

Earlier, I introduced you to some ASCII character codes. Figure 3.11 shows 96 characters from the ASCII character chart, which includes most common English characters.

The ASCII character set is not sufficient for representing characters from other languages because it can hold references to only 255 characters. (Each cell in Figure 3.11 represents a reference to a character. For example, the number 32 references the space character, and the number 65 references the capital letter A.)

The Unicode character set is modeled on ASCII, but it goes well beyond ASCII's capabilities to encode upper- and lowercase letters A to Z, numbers 0-9, and other special and control characters. Unicode is a global character set, capable of encoding more than one million characters. That's more than enough to encompass characters from every current and historical language, as shown in Table 3.7.

The Unicode character set is far from completely used up. There's space available for new languages, and for developers to define symbols that are unique to their applications. Unicode characters are drawn on the screen or printed using a process called *text rendering*, where Unicode character values combine with a font to produce the final character or symbol, as shown in Figure 3.12.

If you want to use the complete Unicode character set in an XML document, set the XML declaration's encoding attribute to UTF-16:

```
<?xml version="1.0" encoding="UTF-16"?>
```

Figure 3.11

Common ASCII characters.

SP 32	! 33	" 34	# 35	$ 36	% 37	& 38	' 39	(40	) 41	* 42	+ 43	, 44	- 45	. 46	/ 47
0 48	1 49	2 50	3 51	4 52	5 53	6 54	7 55	8 56	9 57	: 58	; 59	< 60	= 61	> 62	? 63
@ 64	A 65	B 66	C 67	D 68	E 69	F 70	G 71	H 72	I 73	J 74	K 75	L 76	M 77	N 78	O 79
P 80	Q 81	R 82	S 83	T 84	U 85	V 86	W 87	X 88	Y 89	Z 90	[91	\ 92	] 93	^ 94	_ 95
` 96	a 97	b 98	c 99	d 100	e 101	f 102	g 103	h 104	i 105	j 106	k 107	l 108	m 109	n 110	o 111
p 112	q 113	r 114	s 115	t 116	u 117	v 118	w 119	x 120	y 121	z 122	{ 123		124	} 125	~ 126	DEL 127

TABLE 3.7 NAMES OF LANGUAGES AND SYMBOLS THE UNICODE CHARACTER SET ENCOMPASSES

Character Grouping	Language or Symbols
European	Latin, Greek, Cyrillic, Armenian, Georgian, Runic
Middle Eastern	Ogham, Hebrew, Arabic, Syriac, Thaana
South and Southeast Asia	Devanagari, Bengali, Gurmukhi, Gujarati, Oriya, Tamil, Telugu, Kannada, Malayalam, Sinhala, Thai, Lao, Tibetan, Myanmar, Khmer
East Asia	Han, Hiragana, Katakana, Hangul, Bopomofo, Yi
Philippine	Tagalog, Hanunóo, Buhid, Taganwa
Other Languages	Ethiopic, Cherokee, Canadian Aboriginal Syllabics, Mongolian
Symbols	Currency Symbols, Mathematical Operators, Technical Symbols, Geometrical Symbols, Braille

Canadian Aboriginal Syllabics unifies symbols from various native-Canadian into a single symbolic set.
Khmer is also known as Cambodian.
Han is a unified set of characters used in written Chinese, Japanese, and Korean.
Hiragana is a set of symbols used to write Japanese words phonetically.
Katakana is a set of symbols used to write non-Japanese words phonetically in Japanese.
Bopomofo, also known as Zhuyin-Zimu and Zhuyin-Fuhao, is used in teaching Chinese.
Yi, also known as Cuan or Wei, is a Sino-Tibetan language.

The drawback to using UTF-16 character encoding is that you lose compatibility with the ASCII character set, which is still in broad use today. A subset of the UTF-16 is UTF-8, which is ASCII-compatible and is still capable of encoding more than 24,000 characters and symbols (encompassing more than 100 languages). UTF-8 is said to be ASCII-compatible because the first 255 characters match the ASCII character codes and characters. This means you can use UTF-8 encoding in place of ASCII without having to be concerned about compatibility with older applications that may refer directly to ASCII characters using their encoded values.

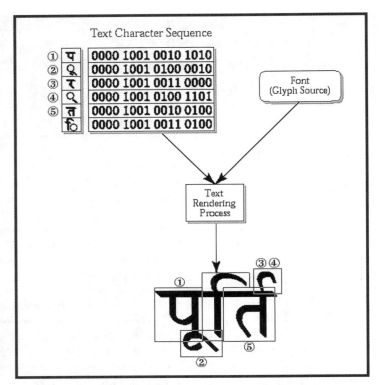

Figure 3.12

Rendering
(drawing) a
Unicode character.

The following listing provides just some of the languages whose characters
and symbols you can use through the UTF-8 character set:

➤ Latin

➤ French

➤ Spanish

➤ Italian

➤ Irish

➤ Russian

➤ Hindi

➤ Vietnamese

➤ Korean

➤ Thai

Since UTF-8 covers so many languages, it's probably sufficient for most of your non-English XML files. For example, Figure 3.13 shows an XML document that displays the message "hello" in Russian, Arabic, and Spanish using the UTF-8 character set.

If you want to use the Unicode character set (UTF-8 or UTF-16), you have to use an editor that can save files using Unicode character encoding. But not all editors support Unicode! For example, Windows Notepad on Windows 2000 and later supports saving files as Unicode, but Notepad on Windows 95, Windows 98, and Windows Me does not. Commercial editors such as XML Spy, which I discuss later, support Unicode. If you're not sure that your editor can save your XML documents in Unicode, simply save the document and try to open it using Internet Explorer. If the document is not saved using Unicode encoding, IE will report an error about invalid characters in the document.

The sample code that accompanies this book demonstrates two versions of the XML document shown in Figure 3.13: The file `hello-noUnicode.xml` was saved without Unicode encoding, and `hello-withUnicode.xml` was saved using Unicode character encoding. Note that regardless of the setting you use for the encoding attribute in the XML declaration, you must save XML documents that use UTF-8 or UTF-16 character encoding as Unicode files. Otherwise, Internet Explorer will not be able to interpret the characters.

There are some cases where using the Unicode character set isn't practical. For example, if you're converting existing documents that are written in a native character set into XML, it may be difficult to convert from the native character set into Unicode. In these cases, you can leave the document in its original character set and simply declare the XML document as being in a particular character set. Table 3.8 lists some common character sets and the languages they represent.

Figure 3.13

An XML document using three different languages.

```
<?xml version="1.0" encoding="UTF-8" ?>
- <hello>
    <message language="russian">привет</message>
    <message language="arabic">هناف للترحيب</message>
    <message language="spanish">¡hola!</message>
  </hello>
```

TABLE 3.8 COMMON CHARACTER SETS	
Encoding	**Language**
ISO-10646	Hindi
ISO-2022-JP	Japanese
BIG5	Traditional Chinese
GB2312	Simplified Chinese
ISO-8859-6	Arabic
ISO-8859-7	Greek
KOI8-R	Russian
ISO-8859-10	Nordic Languages
ISO-8859-3	Esperanto
ISO-8859-2	Hungarian, Polish, Czech, Croatian
ISO-8859-5	Macedonian, Ukrainian

For example, if you want to indicate that a document uses the Japanese character set, the XML declaration would look like this:

```
<?xml version="1.0" encoding="ISO-2022-JP"?>
```

Understanding the xml:lang Attribute

The discussion so far has focused on character encoding. While character encoding is great for using different languages in your XML files, you sometimes need to know which elements contain which languages. For example, Figure 3.13 shows an XML document that uses three different languages to display the word "hello." If the message elements did not have the language attribute, a computer would probably not be able to definitively determine the message's language. The problem with using an attribute like language is that it's not part of the XML standard. As a result, you could create XML elements that have a lang attribute, and someone else could decide to use something like lingo.

XML provides an attribute called xml-lang to indicate which language an element uses. The attribute does not have any effect on how an XML document gets processed, but applications can use the attribute for their own purposes. Figure 3.14 shows how to use the xml-lang attribute.

The xml-lang attribute uses standardized language codes based on the ISO-639 standard. ISO-639 defines two- and three-letter language codes and has since been supplanted by a newer standard. However, ISO-639 remains in broad use. Table 3.9 lists some ISO-639 two- and three-letter language codes. For a more complete listing, visit the supporting Web site for this book, or my personal Web site at http://www.designs2solutions.com/LXIAW.

Some languages have variations depending on what country the language is spoken in. For example, there's a difference between the English spoken in Canada, the United States, and the United Kingdom. You can supplement the language code you use in the xml-lang attribute by indicating which dialect of the language you're using. For example, the following listing indicates which dialects the words in the listing use:

```xml
<?xml version="1.0" encoding="UTF-8"?>
<words>
  <through>
    <word xml-lang="en-us">thru</word>
    <word xml-lang="en-ca">through</word>
  </through>
  <colors>
    <word xml-lang="en-us">color</word>
    <word xml-lang="en-gb">colour</word>
  </colors>
  <check>
    <word xml-lang="en-us">check</word>
    <word xml-lang="en-ca">cheque</word>
  </check>
</words>
```

```
<?xml version="1.0" encoding="UTF-8"?>
<hello>
    <message xml-lang="ru" language="russian">привет</message>
    <message xml-lang="ar" language="arabic">هتاف للترحيب</message>
    <message xml-lang="es" language="spanish"> ¡hola!</message>
</hello>
```

Figure 3.14

Using the
xml-lang attribute.

Language	Two-Letter Code	Three-Letter Code
TABLE 3.9 SELECTED ISO-639 TWO- AND THREE-LETTER LANGUAGE CODES		
Chinese	ZH	chi/zho
Dutch	NL	dut/nla
French	FR	fra/fre
Hindi	HI	hin
Japanese	JP	jpn
Lao	LO	lao
Norwegian	NO	nor
Sanskrit	SA	san
Thai	TH	tha
Xhosa	XH	xho

The names of the elements should cause enough confusion since they're spelled differently. However, the respective xml-lang attributes should make the spellings clearer. The country code follows the language code with a dash character separating the two parts of the xml-lang attribute's value. The country codes are based on the ISO-3166 standard, which defines two- and three-letter codes *and* a numeric code for each country. Table 3.10 lists some countries, their two- and three-letter codes, and their numeric country code. You can get more information on country codes by searching the Internet for "ISO-3166," or by visiting the book's supporting Web site or my personal Web site at http://www.designs2solutions.com/LXIAW.

 TIP You should always be aware that character encoding indicates which characters you can use in your XML documents, while the xml-lang attribute indicates which language an element's data uses. Ensure that you use the correct character encoding for your XML documents, and add the xml-lang attribute to elements residing in XML documents that use more than one language.

TABLE 3.10 SELECTED COUNTRY CODES

Country	Two-Letter Code	Three-Letter Code	Numeric Code
Canada	CA	CAN	124
Brazil	BR	BRA	076
Japan	JP	JPN	392
Philippines	PH	PHL	608
United Kingdom	GB	GBR	826
Tuvalu	TV	TUV	798
India	IN	IND	356
United States	US	USA	840
Germany	DE	DEU	276

The Fundamentals of Namespaces

All of the documents you've been working with so far have one thing in common: all of their elements reside in the default namespace. A *namespace* is a logical boundary to differentiate elements that have the same name but have different meanings. For example, consider the element name set. The word "set" has many meanings, depending on how it is used. For example, an XML document containing information about sets could define an individual set as series of numbers, letters, settings for an electronic device, or even tennis game scores.

A namespace allows XML documents to use element names that are identical but have different meanings to different applications. This allows one system to process XML documents from a variety of sources, while ensuring that similar element names do not logically overlap with each other. For example, consider the following XML document:

```
<?xml version="1.0" encoding="UTF-8"?>
<sets>
  <set>4,6,12,14,16,18,20,22</set>
  <set>3,11,17,19,23,29,31,37</set>
  <set>18,20,21,22,24,25,26,27</set>
</sets>
```

Now, consider the following XML document:

```
<?xml version="1.0" encoding="UTF-8"?>
<sets>
  <set>4-2</set>
  <set>6-0</set>
  <set>4-2</set>
</sets>
```

What do the documents represent? Based on the names of XML elements, you'd be hard-pressed to guess that the first XML document lists sets of even, prime, and non-prime numbers, and that the second XML document lists the scores of a game of tennis. An XML-aware application or XML parser would treat both documents in the same way since they happen to share identical element names. The result is that both of the documents become ambiguous since neither one refers to anything specific, as far as an XML-aware application is concerned.

XML helps to resolve ambiguous elements with namespaces. Think of a namespace as a name for a container that holds an XML document with a specific meaning. For example, the following listing describes the first XML document in its own namespace:

```
<?xml version="1.0" encoding="UTF-8"?>
<sets xmlns="interestingNumbers">
   <set>4,6,12,14,16,18,20,22</set>
   <set>3,11,17,19,23,29,31,37</set>
   <set>18,20,21,22,24,25,26,27</set>
</sets>
```

The xmlns attribute of the sets element identifies the name of the namespace in which the XML document resides. All elements that do not have their own namespace declaration and appear after an element that declares its own namespace reside in the defining element's namespace. Using the previous example, all of the set elements reside in the namespace "interestingNumbers". The namespace declaration allows XML-aware applications to unambiguously differentiate one set from another. Here's the second XML document that's been changed to reside in its own namespace:

```
<?xml version="1.0" encoding="UTF-8"?>
<sets xmlns="myTennisScores">
   <set>4-2</set>
   <set>6-0</set>
   <set>4-2</set>
</sets>
```

In this example, the sets reside in the "myTennisScores" namespace. When an XML-aware application reads the XML documents, it "sees" the elements in the context of their namespace, as shown in Figure 3.15.

Figure 3.15

Two similar XML documents in different namespaces.

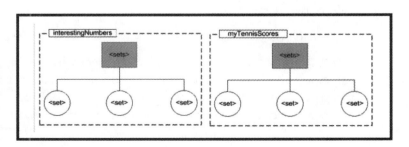

Declaring and Using Namespaces

You can declare a namespace in two ways, both of which use the special XML reserved attribute `xmlns` (in lowercase). Namespace declarations appear in the attribute list of the elements you want to affect by the namespace. Often, the root element contains namespace declarations for the entire document, making it easier to read and understand. (For the benefit of users only. XML-aware applications and parsers don't care where you put namespace declarations, as long as you declare the namespace before you use it.)

The first way of declaring a namespace is to use a *default declaration*:

```
<sets xmlns="interestingNumbers">
```

The default declaration causes all elements that appear after the declaration to reside in the defined namespace, unless you specify otherwise by providing another namespace declaration. While this approach is simple, it distributes namespaces throughout your XML documents, making them more difficult for people to understand.

The second method of declaring a namespace is called an *explicit namespace declaration*. Unlike the default declaration, which associates elements with a namespace simply by association (since elements that appear after a default declaration become associated with the namespace), the explicit namespace declaration makes it clear which elements reside in a particular namespace through direct association. Here's an example of an explicit namespace declaration:

```
<sets xmlns:myNumbers="interestingNumbers">
```

This associates an arbitrary prefix, `myNumbers`, with a namespace. The explicit syntax allows you to declare multiple namespaces in a single place in your XML document, usually the root element. For example, the following defines two namespaces:

```
<sets xmlns:myNumbers="interestingNumbers" xmlns:myScores="scores">
```

The `myNumbers` prefix associates a given element with the `interestingNumbers` namespace, and the `myScores` prefix associates an element with the `scores` namespace. So how do you use the prefixes to segregate content into different namespaces? Here's how (the numbers on the left represent line numbers):

```
<!-- 01 --> <?xml version="1.0" encoding="UTF-8"?>
<!-- 02 --> <sets xmlns:myNumbers="interestingNumbers"
            xmlns:myScores="scores">
<!-- 03 -->    <myNumbers:set>3,11,17,19,23,29,31,37</myNumbers:set>
<!-- 04 -->    <myScores:set>4-2</myScores:set>
<!-- 05 --> </sets>
```

The second line in the listing defines the two namespace prefixes, `myNumbers` and `myScores`, and assigns namespace names to them. The third line associates the `set` element that refers to a set of numbers with the `myNumbers` namespace using the naming syntax `namespacePrefix:elementName`. Note that the element's opening and closing tags must have identical names, as is the case with all XML element names. When an XML-aware application reviews line 03 of the previous document, it will "see" the `set` element in the `"interestingNumbers"` namespace. Line four associates the `myScores` prefix with the `set` element, which refers to the set of tennis scores using the same syntax as shown for line three (only the prefix and the element's content are different).

Explicit namespace declarations allow you to not only process disparate information from various sources, but also store it in the same XML document:

```
<?xml version="1.0" encoding="UTF-8"?>
<sets xmlns:myNumbers="interestingNumbers" xmlns:myScores="scores">
   <myNumbers:set>4,6,12,14,16,18,20,22</myNumbers:set>
   <myNumbers:set>3,11,17,19,23,29,31,37</myNumbers:set>
   <myNumbers:set>18,20,21,22,24,25,26,27</myNumbers:set>
   <myScores:set>4-2</myScores:set>
   <myScores:set>6-0</myScores:set>
   <myScores:set>4-2</myScores:set>
</sets>
```

This merges the two sample documents that we have been working with separately so far. The explicit namespace declaration appears in the document's root element (`sets`), and elements that are part of a specific namespace have the namespace's prefix (as defined by the explicit namespace declaration) added to the element's name. Although using explicit namespace declarations and prefixes makes the document more verbose, it also makes the document easier to work with and understand for both humans and computers.

Assuring Unique Namespace Names

The namespace names you've seen so far (the strings in quotes that appear after namespaces' default or explicit declarations) are very simplistic because they use plain English words. As a result, a *namespace name collision* is inevitable. This occurs when two or more XML documents share the same namespace name.

Namespace names use a special form called a URI (Uniform Resource Indicator) to ensure that all namespaces are unique, eliminating the possibility of a namespace collision. A URI provides a simple and extensible means of uniquely identifying resources. A *resource* is anything that you want to give an identity, be it a namespace or a Web site. However, a URI does not have to refer to a resource on the Internet. It can indirectly refer to a resource, since a URI acts only as a conceptual reference. A type of URI you'll probably be more familiar with is a URL or Uniform Resource Locator, which is more commonly known as an Internet address. For example, the URL of my Web site is http://www.designs2solutions.com. In contrast to a URI, a URL refers directly to a resource, which is usually a Web site or a specific page on a Web site.

For example, the following document is the same document as in the previous section, except that I have replaced the simple namespace names with URIs:

```
<?xml version="1.0" encoding="UTF-8"?>
<sets xmlns:myNumbers="uuid:2a837228-c59b-419f-8bfd-0692e54eac1c"
    xmlns:myScores="http://designs2solutions.com/LXW/ns/Examples">
  <myNumbers:set>4,6,12,14,16,18,20,22</myNumbers:set>
  <myNumbers:set>3,11,17,19,23,29,31,37</myNumbers:set>
  <myNumbers:set>18,20,21,22,24,25,26,27</myNumbers:set>
  <myScores:set>4-2</myScores:set>
  <myScores:set>6-0</myScores:set>
  <myScores:set>4-2</myScores:set>
</sets>
```

The first namespace name begins with uuid, Unique Universal Identifier, which is a very long number that's guaranteed to be unique. UUIDs will never match. The uuid: prefix is there by convention to make it easier for people to understand that the number represents a UUID.

> ## WHY UUIDs ARE ALWAYS UNIQUE
>
> You can generate your own UUID using a program. UUIDs are made up of several components that include some numbers based on your system's hardware, clock, and a random number. I have created a Web-based UUID generator in case you don't have access to a program to generate UUIDs. You can access the UUID generator at the following address:
>
> http://www.designs2solutions.com/redirect.asp?item=uuidgen
>
> It's been said that there are enough UUIDs to number each molecule in the universe and still have some UUIDs left over!

The second namespace (http://designs2solutions.com/LX...) looks like a URL. However, you won't find anything useful there if you type that address into your browser. Basically, the URL acts as a URI by assigning a name to a namespace based on a URL. URLs contain a Web site's address (in this example, **designs2solutions.com**) and an optional path to a specific document (everything that appears after the Web site's address). The Web site's address is guaranteed to be unique. That is, it there won't ever be more than one Web site with an address of **designs2solutions.com** because there's a governing organization to ensure that only one Web site can have a given name. As a result, it makes sense to use a URL for the name of a namespace because Web site addresses are guaranteed to be unique. Always. If there's a name collision involving the part of the URL that appears after the Web site's address (the *path*), it's up to the person who uses that name to resolve the collision by either selecting a new name or using something like a UUID.

The reason that a name collision can occur within a path is that you're using a private Web site's address to identify a resource. What you do with that address is between you and the Web site's owner. For example, if you create an XML document that uses a namespace that's based on my Web site's address and a namespace name collision occurs between your XML document and one of mine, it's up to us to resolve that situation. On the other hand, if you use a UUID and a namespace name collision occurs, your only recourse is to generate another UUID. There isn't a governing organization handing out UUIDs, as is the case with Web site addresses.

So which should you use for a namespace name, URLs or URIs (containing a UUID)? That depends on how you plan to use your XML document. If you plan to publish your XML document to a broad audience and want control over the namespace, use an address that you own or have direct control over. If you're creating an XML document whose primary consumers are computers, and you're not particularly concerned about the name of the namespace, use a UUID since it's easy to generate and is guaranteed to always be unique.

Namespaces and Their Scope

A namespace's scope refers to its effect within your XML document. For example, consider the following namespace declaration:

```
<?xml version="1.0" encoding="UTF-8"?>
<!-- 01 --> <inventory xmlns="uuid:d5fb44a9-2b7f-4d18-aaea-51066e5042fb">
```

The namespace declaration defines a default namespace that has a scope of the entire XML document. Unless you declare another namespace later in the document, all child elements (elements within the inventory root element) will reside within the same namespace.

Take a look at the following XML document. Can you tell which elements belong in which namespace? There's a twist to this question because the document also contains an attribute in the code element. Here's a hint—keep the names of the types of namespace declarations in mind as you review this document:

```
<?xml version="1.0" encoding="UTF-8"?>
<!-- 01 --> <inventory
    xmlns:inv="first"
    xmlns="second">
<!-- 02 -->    <inv:item>
<!-- 03 -->       <inv:code type="book">12345</inv:code>
<!-- 04 -->       <description>Learn XML in a Weekend</description>
<!-- 05 -->       <inv:count>21</inv:count>
<!-- 06 -->    </inv:item>
<!-- 07 --> </inventory>
```

Table 3.11 provides the answers:

TABLE 3.11 DISTRIBUTION OF NAMESPACES OVER SAMPLE XML	
Element	**Namespace**
inventory	Second
item	First
code	First
type (attribute)	Default
description	Second
count	First

The inventory element is not prefixed with a namespace annotation, so it resides in the document's default namespace. This is not a surprise (see "The Fundamentals of Namespaces" earlier in this lesson for a quick refresher). The surprise is that the inventory element does not reside in the document's default namespace, but in the second namespace. This is because it contains a default namespace declaration whose scope is for the entire document, unless otherwise specified (as described in "Declaring and Using Namespaces," earlier in this lesson).

The item, code, and count elements reside in the first namespace because each element is prefixed with the inv prefix, which is bound to the first namespace. Note how the prefix is used for both the start and end tag of each of the three elements.

The twist is the code element's type attribute, because it doesn't reside in either the first or second namespace. The XML specification is a little asymmetric with respect to unannotated elements, and attributes and elements. As Table 3.11 demonstrates, unannotated elements reside in the document's namespace, which in this example is the second one. In contrast, unannotated attributes don't get the same treatment. They end up residing in the default, nameless namespace. As a result, you must add a prefix to attributes to ensure that an attribute ends up in a specific namespace, or else it ends up in the default nameless document namespace.

Wrapping Up

You've learned a lot of new information. The key points you need to remember from this lesson are the following:

➤ Elements follow strict naming rules and are the foundation of the structure of all XML documents.

➤ Attributes add information to XML documents.

➤ Processing Instructions add application-specific information to an XML document.

➤ You need to enclose illegal characters in a CDATA section or use predefined entity references.

➤ XML documents can contain data using a variety of character encodings and languages.

➤ Remember to save XML documents in Unicode format.

➤ Namespaces address element and attribute name collisions and make XML documents easier to share with others.

It's time to take a break, because we're going to spend the rest of the afternoon on data modeling using Document Type Definitions and XML schemas. See you back here in about 20 minutes!

Document Modeling

Glad to see you again after your break. Let's jump right in and get started by understanding document modeling and how it applies to XML.

A *document model* defines a set of element names and attributes that can appear in an XML document. Recall from Friday evening's lesson that elements form an XML vocabulary, otherwise known as an *XML application*. A document model allows you to define exactly what form an XML vocabulary can assume, and to clearly convey what the vocabulary does and does not allow. For example, if you're creating an XML vocabulary that describes a `person` element, you can specify that each person must have a `firstName` and `lastName` element and may contain optional elements like `address`, `dateOfBirth`, and `citizenship`. A document model can also specify which attributes elements can or must have. For example, you could specify that all `person` elements must have a `gender` attribute and that all `citizen` elements may include an optional `countryCode` attribute that uses ISO 3166 country codes.

The rest of this lesson covers the basics of data modeling and data modeling using Document Type Declarations and XML Schemas. The pace of this lesson is a little quicker than some of the preceding lesson, so feel free to take a break whenever you feel the need. I suggest that you take a break after "Understanding and Using DTDs." Take some time to think about the new material you've just learned, and you'll be ready to work with the more advanced data modeling capabilities that XML Schemas offer.

The focus of this section is mostly theoretical, but it lays the foundation for tomorrow evening when I'll show you how to use XML Spy and Stylus Studio to create, edit, and validate XML documents.

What Is a Data Model?

A document model, more formally and generally known as a data model, describes the logical structure of a set of data. The data model specifies which information a data set contains in terms of the names of the fields, which data each field can contain, and the relationships between fields and other sets of data.

A data model becomes important in the following scenarios:

➤ You want to define an XML vocabulary, and you need to ensure that people and computers produce XML documents that conform to the vocabulary.

➤ You want to reduce the cost of creating a new XML-aware application. A data model can restrict an element's possible values, and can even go so far as to describe what form an element's data may take. An application can validate the document (compare its content to its model) using an XML parser to quickly determine if it conforms to the format that the application expects. This reduces the amount of code that needs to be written, thus reducing the cost of creating the application. This also reduces the amount of time it takes to update validation rules, because application developers work with standard XML features instead of application code that's often difficult to maintain and update.

➤ You want to ensure that XML documents meet a certain level of quality, in terms of their structure and the data that they contain. An XML data model can act as an objective measure of the quality of data that your organization or application receives, making it easier to pinpoint data-related issues.

➤ XML documents are created by people or other applications and are consumed (read) by other applications. The XML data model acts as a rules-enforcement agent, ensuring that people and applications generate XML documents that conform to a set of rules with respect to their structure and content.

Data models are also important when you want to share XML documents, when you want to ensure that they use a well-known structure, and when you want to ensure a certain level of uniformity across several similar types of documents. For example, DocBook is a well-known XML data model for creating XML documents that contain books. It contains information about how to structure XML documents that represent a book, with features like a table of contents, index, tables, figures, and a range of other elements that make up a book. Once a book is in XML format, you can transform it into any other format, such as HTML or print, based on XSL (described on Sunday afternoon).

Without a data model, XML documents can contain any elements, using any structure, and can contain any number of attributes. There aren't any restrictions on the things elements may contain, as long as the XML is well-formed. XML documents that don't use a data model are far more difficult for a computer to process.

When your XML documents use an XML data model, XML editors (software for creating and maintaining XML documents) can read the data model and ensure that an XML file contains elements and attributes that your purpose requires. When an XML document conforms to its data model, it's said to be *valid*. Unlike XML documents that are *well-formed* (implement the XML's essential rules, making it possible for them to be consumed or processed by an XML parser), valid XML documents structure their data based on a predefined *schema* (data model). When you publish a valid XML document, you make it easier to use by a broad audience, which can include people and other computers.

Types of Data Models

There are three major technologies that you can use to create a data model for your XML documents:

➤ DTD

➤ XDR Schema

➤ XML Schema

Data Modeling with a DTD

DTD, or Document Type Definition, is a technology that's part of the XML specification. This means that all *validating* XML parsers must be able to read and work with a DTD. A validating XML parser can not only read XML documents, but verify that they conform to a specific schema (data model). DTDs enjoy broad support from a variety of vendors and products. All validating XML parsers support DTDs. To give you a real example of what a DTD looks like, consider the following listing:

```
<?xml version="1.0" encoding="UTF-8"?>
<!-- The DTD follows... -->
<!DOCTYPE people
[
  <!ELEMENT people (person+)>
  <!ELEMENT person (name)>
```

```
        <!ELEMENT name (first, last)>
        <!ELEMENT first (#PCDATA)>
        <!ELEMENT last (#PCDATA)>
]>
<!-- The XML data begins here ... -->
<people>
  <person>
    <name>
      <first>Erik</first>
      <last>Westermann</last>
    </name>
  </person>
  <person>
    <name>
      <first>Tom</first>
      <last>Archer</last>
    </name>
  </person>
</people>
```

This is an XML document that describes two people. The DTD begins just after the XML declaration, with a strange-looking element called DOCTYPE. Within that element are some other ELEMENT elements, each of which describes an element that appears in the document. The DTD begins by describing that the document contains people, which are composed of one or more person elements. A person element contains a name element, which is in turn composed of first and last elements, which contain parsed character data. When you review the XML data that follows the DTD, you'll find that the XML data conforms exactly with the description in the DTD.

DTDs can become very complex. You can define the structure of elements and attributes, have mandatory and optional parts, and allow only certain data to appear in each part. Although DTDs are popular, they have some characteristics that are holding them back from widespread adoption among current and new software products:

➤ DTDs use a specialized syntax that's different from XML, making them more difficult to learn for people without a background in SGML or XML.

➤ DTDs don't allow you to specify which type of data an element can contain. As far as a DTD is concerned, all data in an XML document is considered to be simple string (text) data, even though programming languages use a range of string (text) and numeric representations.

➤ DTDs have a fixed, non-extensible content model that doesn't allow developers to create new elements and attributes.

➤ DTDs don't support namespaces. As a result, a DTD can act as a schema for an entire XML document. Sometimes it's useful to have one part of an XML document conform to one schema and another part conform to another schema.

As a result of these characteristics, and the business pressures of releasing a number of new products (such as Microsoft SQL Server 2000 and the Microsoft BizTalk framework and server), Microsoft developed the XDR Schema, and the World Wide Web Consortium developed the XML Schema.

Data Modeling with the XDR Schema

XDR, or XML Data Reduced, is an XML vocabulary invented by Microsoft that allows you to describe the schema of an XML document. The following listing represents the XDR for the document shown in the previous section:

```
<?xml version="1.0" encoding="UTF-8"?>
<Schema name="Untitled-schema"
    xmlns="urn:schemas-microsoft-com:xml-data"
    xmlns:dt="urn:schemas-microsoft-com:datatypes">
  <ElementType name="people" model="closed" content="eltOnly"
order="seq">
    <AttributeType name="xmlns" dt:type="string"/>
    <attribute type="xmlns"/>
    <element type="person" minOccurs="1" maxOccurs="*"/>
  </ElementType>
  <ElementType name="person" model="closed" content="eltOnly"
order="seq">
    <element type="name" minOccurs="1" maxOccurs="1"/>
  </ElementType>
  <ElementType name="name" model="closed" content="eltOnly"
order="seq">
    <element type="first" minOccurs="1" maxOccurs="1"/>
```

```
    <element type="last" minOccurs="1" maxOccurs="1"/>
  </ElementType>
  <ElementType name="first" model="closed" content="textOnly"
dt:type="string"/>
  <ElementType name="last" model="closed" content="textOnly"
dt:type="string"/>
</Schema>
```

The XDR describes the schema in terms of not only the document's content, but also which types of content are contained in the document's elements. For example, the XDR explicitly states that the first and last elements are string (text) types using the dt:type attribute. XDR supports other types, including dates and integers.

The primary drawback to using XDR is that it's limited to Microsoft products and technologies—other vendors don't support XDR. The W3C has created a newer standard, called XSD, which is gaining in popularity because it's not proprietary.

Data Modeling Using XSD

XSD, the XML Schema Definition, is a W3C recommendation (a standard, in practical terms) that allows you to describe XML schemas using an XML vocabulary. The following listing demonstrates the XSD for the document from the previous sections:

```
<?xml version="1.0" encoding="UTF-8"?>
<xs:schema xmlns:xs="http://www.w3.org/2001/XMLSchema"
    elementFormDefault="qualified">
  <xs:element name="first" type="xs:string"/>
  <xs:element name="last" type="xs:string"/>
  <xs:element name="name">
    <xs:complexType>
      <xs:sequence>
        <xs:element ref="first"/>
        <xs:element ref="last"/>
      </xs:sequence>
    </xs:complexType>
  </xs:element>
  <xs:element name="people">
```

```
    <xs:complexType>
      <xs:sequence>
        <xs:element ref="person" maxOccurs="unbounded"/>
      </xs:sequence>
    </xs:complexType>
  </xs:element>
  <xs:element name="person">
    <xs:complexType>
      <xs:sequence>
        <xs:element ref="name"/>
      </xs:sequence>
    </xs:complexType>
  </xs:element>
</xs:schema>
```

The XSD describes the XML document in terms of its data types. For example, the XSD describes the people type (element) as an unbounded complex type made up of person types. (*Unbounded* means that there can be any number of person types in the document.) A person type is made up of a name type, which is made up of a sequence of a first and last type, which in turn are string (text) types.

Which Data Modeling Technique Should I Use?

With three approaches to creating a data model, or *schema*, for your XML documents, a lot of people who are new to XML are confused about which approach to use.

DTDs have been around for a long time and enjoy broad support from a wide range of products and vendors. They're generally well-understood, so it's relatively easy to find someone who has been exposed to them. Your XML documents will find broad acceptance by the XML community if you use DTDs.

XDR is a Microsoft-specific technology. As a result, it has limited support in the industry. Although Microsoft products are in broad use, there's not much of a point in continuing XDR's development because XSD has the backing of the W3C. Using XDR makes sense only if you're upgrading an existing application, or you're interested only in targeting solutions and systems based on Microsoft products and technologies.

XSD is a W3C recommendation, which translates into potentially broad acceptance from vendors and the XML community at large. It's relatively new on the market, but it's gaining support because it's easier to learn than DTDs.

Depending on how strict you need to be with respect to validating your XML documents, DTDs may be all you need. They're part of the XML specification and are often the only means to gain access to useful XML vocabularies, like DocBook. For example, if you need to ensure that a document contains a `name` element, as in the `people` document featured in this lesson, a DTD will be more than sufficient. If you need to be stricter about the actual data that users put into their XML documents (for example, allowing only *positive* integers), XSD is much more suitable. It can save a lot of time in developing an application that produces documents that conform to your requirements. You shouldn't consider using XDR unless you're working with an application that already supports it. Stick with DTDs and XSD, because they're both backed by the W3C.

The following sections go into detail about using DTD and XSD. However, first you need to understand the XML declaration's `standalone` attribute and how to validate an XML document using Internet Explorer.

Understanding the XML Declaration's standalone Attribute

There's a seemingly innocuous attribute in an XML declaration called `standalone`. It's important that you understand what this attribute is for and how to use it, because it can cause some XML parsers to behave in an unusual manner.

Recall that XML documents begin with an XML declaration, as described on Friday evening. Here's an example of an XML document declaration:

```
<?xml version="1.0" encoding="UTF-8" standalone="yes"?>
```

The `standalone` attribute indicates whether the document has any external references. If you declare an XML document using the value `yes` for the `standalone` attribute, XML parsers can ignore all external references. It's rare to see `standalone="yes"` XML documents. If you don't use the `standalone` attribute in your declaration, its default value is `standalone="no"`, which causes XML parsers to honor both internal and external references.

Validating XML Documents Using Internet Explorer

This section discusses valid XML documents throughout. While it's great to say that a document is valid, it's another thing to actually *prove* that it's valid. I've created a Web page called the XML Validator that checks XML documents for validity (see Figure 4.1). If the XML Validator finds any problems with the document you're checking, it pinpoints the line number in the document and describes the error.

You can use the XML Validator by using Windows Explorer to locate where you extracted the sample code on your system's hard drive. (See the Preface for information on where to download the sample code from and how to install it.)

When you want to validate an XML document, type its name (including its directory) into the XML File box. If you don't know exactly where the file is located, click on the Browse button to browse through your system's hard disk, as shown in Figure 4.2.

Once you find the file you want to validate, double-click on its name to copy the file's name and directory into the XML File box. Click on the Check Document button to validate the file. The result of the validation is shown in the Result box, as shown in Figure 4.3.

You can use the XML Validator to validate and experiment with documents that have an internal DTD.

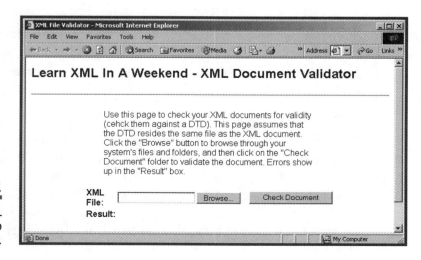

Figure 4.1

Using the XML Validator Web page.

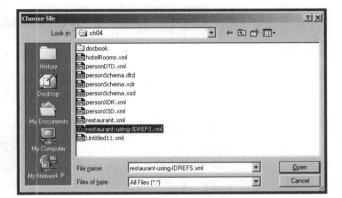

Figure 4.2

Browsing for a file on the system's hard drive.

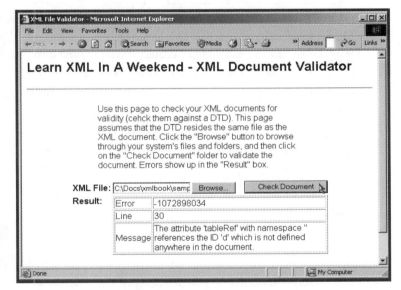

Figure 4.3

Reviewing the result of validating an XML document.

Understanding and Using DTDs

A DTD models a document by

➤ Defining a set of elements that can appear in an XML document.

➤ Defining the content model for each element. A *content model* describes what an element can contain in terms of any subelements and data. Content models are covered in more detail in the following sections.

➤ Defining a set of optional or mandatory attributes for each element. Attribute definitions include an attribute name, default value, and data type.

The following sections describe the DTD in detail.

Adding a DTD to an XML Document

Like the rest of an XML document, a DTD is simply a special section of text. However, it must appear at the very beginning of an XML document so that an XML-aware application can validate the document. A DTD can be external or internal to an XML document. An external DTD resides in another file, sometimes even on another computer. An XML document *binds* (associates) itself to an external DTD by using a special directive. An internal DTD resides in the same file as an XML document. This is sometimes referred to as a *private DTD* because it defines the data model that a specific XML document uses. In contrast, an external DTD usually defines a data model for a set of related XML documents. As a result, an external DTD is sometimes referred to as a *public* or *shared DTD*.

Whether internal or external, a DTD always appears at the beginning of an XML document, immediately following the XML declaration:

```
<?xml version="1.0" encoding="UTF-8"?>
<!-- The DTD begins here -->
<!DOCTYPE people
[
   ...
]>
<!-- The XML document's content begins here -->
<people>
  <person>
    ...
</person>
</people>
```

The ellipsis (...) isn't part of the listing. It's just there as a placeholder for content that I omitted in the listing.

As you can see, a DTD uses a unique syntax that's very different from the XML syntax. The following sections describe the syntax in detail.

Understanding the Document Type Declaration

A DTD begins with a Document Type Declaration, which contains a reference to an external DTD or declares an internal DTD. Figure 4.4 shows a complete Document Type Declaration because it includes all possibilities (two types of external DTDs and an internal DTD). Although it's possible to use this type of declaration, it's rare.

The Document Type Declaration begins with <!DOCTYPE (number 1 in the figure), which must be in all caps. If you plan to declare an internal DTD—that is, you plan to declare the XML document's structure within the XML document itself—you must provide the name of the root element, as shown in number 2 of Figure 4.4.

As previously mentioned, an external DTD is sometimes referred to as a public or shared DTD because it resides in a separate file. However, you can still declare an external DTD as being private by using the declaration shown in number 3 in Figure 4.4. When you use this type of declaration, you're indicating that the DTD resides in another file but is intended for the exclusive use of only one XML document. Although there isn't anything stopping you from reusing an external, private DTD in another XML document, this usually isn't done because it indicates that the DTD isn't intended for broad use.

You can declare a shared, publicly accessible DTD by using the syntax shown in number 4 in Figure 4.4. This type of declaration indicates, by convention, that the DTD you're referencing is a shared DTD that others

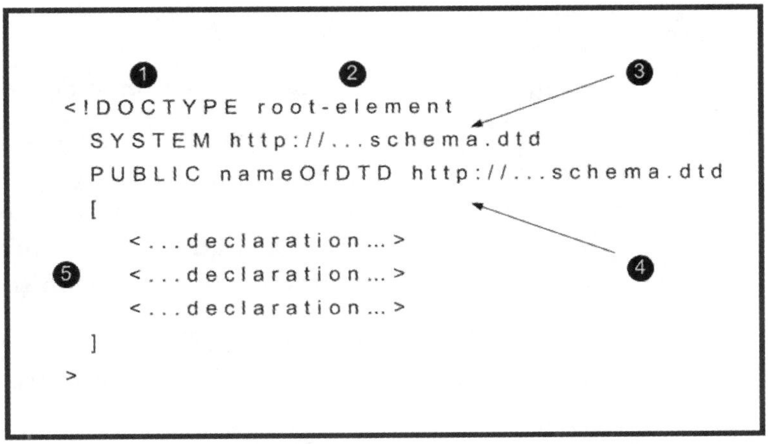

Figure 4.4

Document Type
Declaration.

probably use. You shouldn't modify a shared DTD in any way. An organization probably maintains and updates it, and changing it would make any XML documents you produce invalid because your document wouldn't conform to the shared DTD's data model. (It would conform only to your version of the modified DTD.)

Number 5 in Figure 4.4 represents an internal DTD declaration (the "...declaration..." isn't part of a DTD). This type of declaration is for the private, exclusive use of the XML document in which the declaration appears. Internal DTDs are convenient because they're easy to maintain and transport (the DTD resides in the same file as the XML document), but they're not considered to be reusable. They're usually useful when you're developing a new XML vocabulary or learning how to work with DTDs.

Here are some examples of various types of Document Type Declarations (note that the ellipsis (...) isn't part of the listing—it acts only as a placeholder):

```
<!DOCTYPE people>
<!DOCTYPE people SYSTEM ".../people.dtd">
<!DOCTYPE book PUBLIC "-//OASIS//DTD DocBook XML V4.1.2//EN"
  "http://www.oasis-open.org/docbook/xml/4.0/docbookx.dtd">
<!DOCTYPE employees SYSTEM "employees.dtd" [...]>
```

The first example represents the most minimal representation of a Document Type Declaration. The declaration only specifies the name of the document's root element—you can still validate an XML file using such a minimalist declaration!

Declaring Elements

Declare elements using the general form shown in Figure 4.5.

An element declaration begins with the <! delimiter (number 1 in the figure) immediately followed by ELMENT in uppercase (number 2 in the figure). The name of the element (number 3 in the figure) specifies which name an element must have. The content model (number 4 in the figure) allows you to declare the four different types of elements you can create using XML:

➤ **Empty elements** don't contain any data.

➤ **Element only elements** contain only other elements.

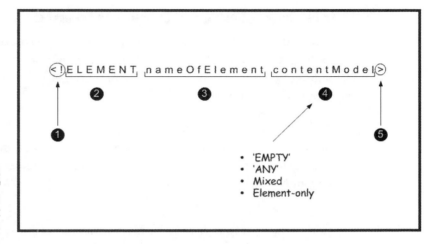

Figure 4.5

General form of an element declaration.

➤ **Mixed elements** contain text and other elements.

➤ **Any elements** can contain any permitted content.

Declaring EMPTY Elements

Empty elements don't contain any content and typically use attributes to convey data and information. The following example declares an empty element:

```
<!ELEMENT lineBreak EMPTY>
```

This is how the preceding element could appear as part of an XML document:

```
<!-- shorthand version one --> <lineBreak/>
<!-- shorthand version two --> <lineBreak />
<!-- long version -->          <lineBreak></lineBreak>
```

This shows two shorthand notations. Both of them end using the /> character sequence, but the difference is the space between the name of the element and the closing character sequence. The long version isn't as desirable as either of the first two forms. The first two make it clear that the element is empty, whereas the long version doesn't. An XML-aware application views all three shorthand notations in the same way. However, the last two notations are easier for people to read.

Declaring Element-Only Elements

Element-only elements don't contain any data, but can contain other elements. The declaration of an element-only element describes the name of the element along with the content it can contain. The general form of an element-only declaration is

```
<!ELEMENT name content>
```

The name represents the name of the element as it appears in an XML document, and the content represents what you want the element to contain. An element-only declaration can contain

➤ An ordered listing of elements

➤ One element from a listing of valid elements

➤ A repeating set of elements

➤ A mixture of all of the above

Look at an ordered list of elements first, because it's the easiest of all three types of content to understand. Assume that you're modeling an XML document that contains information about some books, and you want to make sure it contains basic information about each book, such as the publisher, publication date, ISBN, title, subtitle, author, and a comment—in that order. You can express an ordered listing of elements using the following syntax:

```
<!ELEMENT elementName
  (element1, element2, element3,...,elementN) >
```

The declaration specifies the name of the element, which contains the ordered subelements. The commas indicate that the listing is an ordered list. As a result, subelements must appear in the order specified by the listing in the brackets.

For example, the following DTD declares a collection of books. Each book element is an element-only element made up of publisher, releaseDate, isbn, title, subTitle, author, and comment elements:

```
<!DOCTYPE books
[
<!ELEMENT books (book)>
<!ELEMENT book (publisher, releaseDate,
  isbn, title, subTitle, author, comment)> ...]>
```

This specifies that each book element must contain all elements that appear in the list shown in the brackets. It doesn't show the complete DTD, so what you see here is incomplete because the DTD doesn't specify which content the publisher, releaseDate, and other elements in the listing can have. Assuming that the subelements don't contain any data (they're EMPTY elements), the complete DTD would look like this:

```
<!ELEMENT books
   (publisher, releaseDate, isbn, title, subTitle, author, comment)>
<!ELEMENT publisher EMPTY>
<!ELEMENT releaseDate EMPTY>
<!ELEMENT isbn EMPTY>
<!ELEMENT title EMPTY>
<!ELEMENT subTitle EMPTY>
<!ELEMENT author EMPTY>
<!ELEMENT comment EMPTY>
```

The following XML document would validate against the preceding DTD:

```
<?xml version="1.0"?>
<books>
   <publisher/>
   <releaseDate/>
   <isbn/>
   <title/>
   <subTitle/>
   <author/>
   <comment/>
</books>
```

If you want to include the DTD along with the XML document so that you don't have to manage two separate files, modify the XML document so that it appears as follows:

```
<?xml version="1.0"?>
<!DOCTYPE books [
   <!ELEMENT books
      (publisher, releaseDate, isbn, title, subTitle, author, comment)>
   <!ELEMENT publisher EMPTY>
   <!ELEMENT releaseDate EMPTY>
   <!ELEMENT isbn EMPTY>
```

```
    <!ELEMENT title EMPTY>
    <!ELEMENT subTitle EMPTY>
    <!ELEMENT author EMPTY>
    <!ELEMENT comment EMPTY>
]>
<books>
  <publisher/>
  <releaseDate/>
  <isbn/>
  <title/>
  <subTitle/>
  <author/>
  <comment/>
</books>
```

In contrast to an ordered list of elements, a selection element lists a series of elements that an element can contain. However, the element can contain only one of the elements in the list. Say you're modeling an inventory document that contains the retail and wholesale prices for items in a warehouse, but you don't want to have both prices appear for any given item. You want a price to appear, but only the wholesale or retail price. The following DTD models the inventory document:

```
<!ELEMENT items (item+)>
<!ELEMENT item ( wholesalePrice | retailPrice ) >
<!ELEMENT wholesalePrice EMPTY>
<!ELEMENT retailPrice EMPTY>
```

If you want to include the DTD at the beginning of an XML document, surround it using the DOCTYPE declaration:

```
<?xml version="1.0"?>
<!DOCTYPE items [
  <!ELEMENT items (item+)>
  <!ELEMENT item (wholesalePrice | retailPrice)>
  <!ELEMENT wholesalePrice EMPTY>
  <!ELEMENT retailPrice EMPTY>
]>
<items>
  <item>
    <retailPrice/>
  </item>
```

```
<item>
  <wholesalePrice/>
</item>
<item>
  <retailPrice/>
</item>
</items>
```

This introduces a repeating set of elements. Here's a closer look at the element that declares it must contain a repeating list of item elements:

```
<!ELEMENT items (item+)>
```

The element declaration looks very similar to an ordered listing that contains a single element, except that a plus symbol follows the word item. This indicates that the name of the element that precedes it must appear at least once and can appear any number of times. You can use several symbols to restrict the number of times subelements can appear, as shown in Table 4.1.

TABLE 4.1 SYMBOLS IN ELEMENT DECLARATIONS

Symbol	Name	Purpose
(no symbol)	(no symbol)	Indicates that the element must appear exactly once.
?	Question mark	Indicates that the element is optional—if you decide to use it, use it only once.
*	Asterisk	Indicates that the element can appear zero or more times (optional, but you can use it more than once).
+	Plus symbol	Indicates that an element must appear one or more times.
( )	Parenthesis	Groups a sequence or choice list.
|	Pipe	Used as part of a list of choices—you can select only one item from the list.
,	Comma	Used as part of a sequence—you can use the elements in the sequence based on their individual restrictions.

These symbols will be useful as your DTDs become more complex. For example, books usually have a dedication, preface, table of contents, and one or more chapters. Each chapter in a book has at least one heading and one paragraph, which can contain text, a figure, a table, or a listing. Rather than impose this structure on all book XML documents, you can add some flexibility using the following declaration:

```
<!ELEMENT book ((dedication?), preface, toc, (chapter+))>
<!ELEMENT chapter (heading, (paragraph+))>
<!ELEMENT paragraph (#PCDATA | figure | table | listing)*>
```

The DTD fragment states that the dedication is optional, as indicated by the ? symbol, but that there must be one preface, one table of contents (toc), and at least one chapter (followed by other optional chapters). Each chapter has one heading and one or more paragraphs that can contain some text (#PCDATA), a figure, a table, or a listing.

The following XML document conforms to the DTD fragment (assuming that all elements, except for the paragraph element, are empty):

```
<book>
  <dedication/>
  <preface/>
  <toc/>
  <chapter>
    <heading/>
    <paragraph>this is a paragraph...
      <figure/>
    </paragraph>
    <paragraph>
      <table/>
    </paragraph>
  </chapter>
  <chapter>
    <heading/>
    <paragraph>
      <listing/>
    </paragraph>
    <paragraph>
      <figure/>
```

```
    </paragraph>
  </chapter>
</book>
```

Each chapter is made up of elements that contain heading, paragraph, figure, table, and listing elements, and the elements appear several times. Note that paragraph elements, in addition to the subelements they contain, also contain the paragraph's text. This type of element is referred to as a *mixed content element.*

A DTD can model more complex structures as well:

```
<!ELEMENT author_info (biography+)>
<!ELEMENT biography (graphic?, paragraph+, siteAddress, emailAddress?,
table?)>
<!ELEMENT table (caption, number?, description, footnote?)>
```

This describes a document, made up of one or more biography elements, that contains information about an author. Each biography element contains a sequence of elements made up of an optional graphic, at least one paragraph, one siteAddress, an optional emailAddress, and an optional table. A table contains a sequence of elements made up of a caption, an optional number, a description, and an optional footnote.

Declaring Mixed Elements

A mixed element can contain data and elements. This model is an extension of element-only elements that also allows text data. The following listing declares some mixed elements:

```
<!DOCTYPE countries
[
  <!ELEMENT countries (country)>
  <!ELEMENT country (#PCDATA | location | population)
  <!ELEMENT population (#PCDATA | units)
  <!ELEMENT location (#PCDATA | region | #PCDATA)
  <!ELEMENT comment (#PCDATA)
]>
```

This declares a document containing a collection of countries. Each country is made up of some text (#PCDATA), a location, and population elements.

`#PCDATA` can appear more than once in an element's declaration, as shown in the `location` element. You can declare a text-only element using the form shown in the `comment` element.

When you declare a mixed element, you can only declare that it contains elements and text—you cannot specify how many times child elements should appear or in what order they may appear. Mixed elements are also more difficult to process using some processing techniques. It's best to stick to using these element declarations for declaring text-only elements, and use element-only elements along with attributes where appropriate.

Declaring ANY Elements

An `ANY` element can contain any content. Declare the element as shown:

```
<!ELEMENT name 'ANY'>
```

The `ANY` element doesn't have any structure. As a result, you should avoid using it in your own DTDs. Its main role is to act as a placeholder until you decide which type an element should contain.

Declaring Attributes

Elements often contain attributes, which you must declare in order for your document to be considered valid. You can declare attributes using an attribute-list declaration, which allows you to

- ➤ Name attributes
- ➤ Assign data types to attributes
- ➤ Describe if the attribute is required, optional, or has a default value

The general form of an attribute-list declaration is shown here, followed by an actual declaration:

```
<!ATTLIST elementName attributeName attributeType defaultValue>
<!ATTLIST book retailPrice CDATA #REQUIRED>
```

The example defines a `retailPrice` attribute that's associated with the `book` element. The attribute's type is `CDATA` and is `#REQUIRED`. The `defaultValue` in the general form (the first line in the listing) has a dual role, as shown in Table 4.2.

TABLE 4.2 ROLE OF defaultVALUE IN AN ATTLIST DECLARATION	
Setting	**Effect**
"some text in quotes"	Acts as the attribute's default value, if you don't specify the attribute when you use the associated element in your XML document.
#IMPLIED	The attribute is optional.
#REQUIRED	The attribute is required.
#FIXED	The attribute has a fixed value that cannot change.

Here are some examples of attribute list declarations:

```
<!-- 1 --> <!ATTLIST item retailPrice CDATA #REQUIRED
    supplierID CDATA #IMPLIED>
<!-- 2 --> <!ATTLIST door doorWidth CDATA #FIXED "30">
<!-- 3 --> <!ATTLIST drink type ( "water" | "juice" | "beer") "water">
```

The first example lists two attributes of the item element, the required retailPrice attribute and the optional supplierID attribute. The second example declares a #FIXED attribute called doorWidth, which is associated with the door element. You don't need to use #FIXED attributes in your XML documents—they are automatically included in each instance of the element that appears in the document. The last example specifies that a drink element must have one of the values that appear in the brackets for the type attribute. If the type attribute isn't specified in the XML document, its default value is water.

There are several types of attributes, as shown in Table 4.3. The details of each type appear in the following subsections.

Attributes fall into three categories: string, tokenized, and enumerated. A string attribute is one whose value appears in quotes or is a CDATA attribute type. Tokenized attributes get special treatment from XML parsers, as I'll explain in the following sections. Enumerated attributes represent a list of choices—an attribute must use one of those choices to be valid.

TABLE 4.3 TYPES OF ATTRIBUTES

Attribute Type	Description	Category
CDATA	Unparsed text data (the XML processor doesn't review CDATA)	String
ENTITY	Refers to an external, binary entity	Tokenized
ENTITIES	Refers to a list of external, binary entities	Tokenized
Enumerated	Refers to a list of text values	Enumerated
ID	A unique identifier whose value occurs only once in an XML document	Tokenized
IDREF	A reference to an ID somewhere else in the DTD	Tokenized
IDREFS	A collection of IDREF types	Tokenized
NMTOKEN	A name made up of XML token characters	Tokenized
NMTOKENS	A collection of NMTOKEN types	Tokenized

Using CDATA Attributes

String attributes are the simplest and most common types of attributes. They contain plain text and are declared using the CDATA attribute type, as shown:

```
<!ATTLIST door model CDATA #REQUIRED>
```

The declaration associates the model attribute with the door element, stating that all door elements must have a model attribute. This is how you would use the attribute in an XML document:

```
<?xml version="1.0" encoding="UTF-8"?>
<!DOCTYPE doors [
  <!ELEMENT doors (door)>
  <!ELEMENT door EMPTY>
  <!ATTLIST door model CDATA #REQUIRED>
]>
```

```
<doors>
  <door model="A14"/>
  <door model="11191992"/>
</doors>
```

Because the ATTLIST states that the model attribute is #REQUIRED, it would be an error to have a door element that doesn't have that attribute. For example, the following door element is invalid:

```
<door/>
```

Note that CDATA here represents arbitrary text. This isn't the same as a CDATA section in an XML document.

Using the ID Attribute Type

The ID attribute type is an identifier that's used to pinpoint a particular element in an XML document. For example, a hotel has many rooms, each of which is occupied by a guest. The hotel staff needs a way to refer to a particular room, regardless of which guest occupies it. The easiest way is to assign each room a unique number:

```
<rooms>
  <room number="135">Rockwell</room>
  <room number="400">Archer</room>
  <room number="800">Jones</room>
</rooms>
```

Regardless of which guest occupies a given room, the hotel staff has a way of referring to that room. Because all room numbers are unique—no two rooms can have the same number—the number attribute is said to *uniquely identify* a particular room.

The ID attribute allows you to specify that an attribute must be unique within an XML document, as shown in the following listing:

```
<?xml version="1.0" encoding="UTF-8"?>
<!DOCTYPE rooms [
  <!ELEMENT rooms (room+)>
  <!ELEMENT room (#PCDATA)>
  <!ATTLIST room  number ID #REQUIRED>
]>
```

```
<rooms>
  <room number="_135">Rockwell</room>
  <room number="_400">Archer</room>
  <room number="_800">Jones</room>
</rooms>
```

The ID attribute type requires that values conform to the XML naming rules. As a result, I had to add an underscore character to the beginning of each room number. (Recall that the first character of an XML name must be a letter or an underscore character.)

Using the IDREF Attribute Type

The IDREF attribute type refers to other unique IDs in an XML document. This is useful when you want to ensure that an element's attribute refers to another valid ID within the same XML document. For example, if a waiter in a restaurant is responsible for serving customers seated in a certain section, you could write an XML document to describe that scenario:

```
<?xml version="1.0" encoding="UTF-8"?>
<!DOCTYPE restaurant [
  <!-- restaurant element -->
  <!ELEMENT restaurant (tables, waiter)>
  <!-- tables is a collection of table elements  -->
  <!ELEMENT tables (table+)>
  <!ELEMENT table EMPTY>
  <!-- each table has a unique ref -->
  <!ATTLIST table  ref ID #REQUIRED>
  <!-- waiter element -->
  <!ELEMENT waiter (serviceTable+)>
  <!ATTLIST waiter
  name CDATA #REQUIRED>
  <!-- waiters service existing tables -->
  <!ELEMENT serviceTable EMPTY>
  <!ATTLIST serviceTable  tableRef IDREF #REQUIRED>
]>
<restaurant>
  <tables>
    <table ref="a"/>
    <table ref="b"/>
```

```
      <table ref="c"/>
    </tables>
    <waiter name="Diane">
      <serviceTable tableRef="a"/>
      <serviceTable tableRef="b"/>
      <!-- the following element is not valid...-->
      <!-- <serviceTable tableRef="f"/> -->
    </waiter>
</restaurant>
```

This example is a little more complicated than the ones you've seen so far because it uses a slightly more complex structure, but it follows all of the rules you've learned. The only exception is the comments in the DTD. You can add comments wherever you like, as long as they don't appear within an element.

Take a look at the `table` element's declaration in the DTD—it has a `ref` attribute that's an `ID` type. The final element declaration in the DTD is the `serviceTable` element, which has a `tableRef` attribute that refers to an existing table in the document. The XML document's content shows how to create and use `ID` and `IDREF` type attributes. Each `table` element has a unique `ref` attribute, while each of the `serviceTable` element's `tableRef` attributes refers to one of the existing values of a `table` element's `ref` attribute.

Using the IDREFS Attribute Type

`IDREFS` represents a collection of `IDREF` types. In other words, `IDREFS` attribute values refer to a list of other `ID` attributes. The following listing uses the previous restaurant example, but it changes how the document represents the relationship between waiters and the tables they service (the changed lines appear in bold):

```
<?xml version="1.0" encoding="UTF-8"?>
<!DOCTYPE restaurant [
  <!-- restaurant element -->
  <!ELEMENT restaurant (tables, waiter)>
  <!-- tables is a collection of table elements  -->
  <!ELEMENT tables (table+)>
  <!ELEMENT table EMPTY>
  <!-- each table has a unique ref -->
  <!ATTLIST table  ref ID #REQUIRED>
```

```
<!-- waiter element -->
<!ELEMENT waiter (serviceTable+)>
<!ATTLIST waiter
name CDATA #REQUIRED>
<!-- waiters service existing tables -->
<!ELEMENT serviceTable EMPTY>
<!ATTLIST serviceTable  tableRef IDREFS #REQUIRED>
]>
<restaurant>
  <tables>
    <table ref="a"/>
    <table ref="b"/>
    <table ref="c"/>
  </tables>
  <waiter name="Oswald">
    <serviceTable tableRef="a b c"/>
  </waiter>
</restaurant>
```

The only things that have changed are that the tableRef attribute is now an IDREFS type, and a waiter needs only one serviceTable element to represent all of the tables he serves. If you add an invalid value to the tableRef attribute and attempt to validate the document, the XML parser will generate an error, as shown in Figure 4.3.

Using the NMTOKEN and NMTOKENS Attribute Types

NMTOKEN is a value that has some restrictions on it. NMTOKEN attributes are usually used to provide processing directives or hints to XML-aware applications. These values are limited to letters, numbers, and the following characters: period, hyphen, single colon, and underscore. Here's an example of an NMTOKEN attribute declaration:

```
<!ELEMENT document EMPTY>
<!ATTLIST document location NMTOKEN #REQUIRED>
```

This following listing uses some valid and invalid values:

```
<document location="V10:S5">            <!-- Ok -->
<document location="drawer.10-file.33">   <!-- Ok -->
```

```
<document location="http://www.designs2solutions.com"> <!-- Error! -->
<document location="a5:c7:h3">                          <!-- Error! -->
```

The last two location attribute values are invalid because the first one uses slash characters (which aren't allowed), and the second uses more than one colon character.

NMTOKENS represents a list of NMTOKEN attribute values. The following demonstrates how to declare and use an NMTOKENS attribute:

```
<!ELEMENT badPasswords EMPTY>
<!ATTLIST badPasswords passwords NMTOKENS>
<!-- this is how to use the NMTOKENS type -->
<badPasswords passwords="password hello monday nothing">
```

Understanding and Using Entities

DTDs offer a way to add flexibility to your documents through *entities*, which are placeholders for some text that you want the XML parser to use when it reads an XML document. Entities are useful when you want to change some text throughout a document. For example, suppose that you run a music store that sells CDs, and you want to make sure that the XML documents that describe your inventory include the retail and wholesale (discounted) price of each CD. You could use a DTD like this (the XML document is included to clarify the DTD):

```
<?xml version="1.0" encoding="UTF-8"?>
<!DOCTYPE inventory
[
  <!ELEMENT inventory (CD+)>
  <!ELEMENT CD (retailPrice, wholesalePrice)>
  <!ATTLIST CD ref ID #REQUIRED>

  <!ELEMENT retailPrice (#PCDATA)>
  <!ELEMENT wholesalePrice (#PCDATA)>
]>
<inventory>
  <CD ref="a">
    <retailPrice>9.99</retailPrice>
    <wholesalePrice>8.99</wholesalePrice>
  </CD>
```

```
<CD ref="b">
  <retailPrice>15.99</retailPrice>
  <wholesalePrice>14.99</wholesalePrice>
</CD>
<CD ref="c">
  <retailPrice>5.00</retailPrice>
  <wholesalePrice>2.00</wholesalePrice>
</CD>
</inventory>
```

Suppose that you now want to publish your XML document, but you don't want people to know your wholesale prices. You need to change your DTD and document by removing the reference to the wholesalePrice element that resides within the CD element, and you need to remove all wholesalePrice elements from the document. Although you can go ahead and delete the reference to the wholesalePrice element from your DTD, you can use an ENTITY to do the work for you. Here's a DTD that uses an ENTITY and is functionally identical to the previous DTD (the changed lines appear in bold):

```
<!DOCTYPE inventory

[

  <!ENTITY % prices "retailPrice, wholesalePrice">

  <!ELEMENT inventory (CD+)>

  <!ELEMENT CD (%prices;)>

  <!ATTLIST CD ref ID #REQUIRED>

  <!ELEMENT retailPrice (#PCDATA)>

  <!ELEMENT wholesalePrice (#PCDATA)>

]>
```

This DTD behaves in exactly the same way as the previous DTD, because the XML parser replaces the reference to %prices with retailPrice, wholesalePrice. If you want to remove the wholesalePrice, just edit the ENTITY so that it looks like this (you also need to remove the wholesalePrice element's declaration):

```
<!ENTITY % prices "retailPrice, wholesalePrice">
```

Entities can add a lot of flexibility to your DTD because you can replace text when the parser reads your XML documents.

Tips for Designing Effective DTDs

Understanding a DTD is a lot different than designing your own DTD. Here are some tips for creating your own DTDs:

➤ Use meaningful or descriptive names for elements and attributes

➤ Arrange declarations by role or function

➤ Use lots of whitespace

➤ Use comments

➤ Review other people's DTDs

Use Meaningful Names for Elements and Attributes

You should name elements according to which concept they represent. Element and attribute names like A, text, object, and set are valid names, but they convey little information about what they represent. Remember that someone else may have to review your DTD or XML documents. Using descriptive names can convey a lot of information about what an element or attribute refers to, which can help pinpoint problems or make maintenance easier.

Arrange Declarations by Role or Function

It's common to create an XML document and then use a tool like XML Spy to generate the DTD for you. However, while computer-generated DTDs are technically correct, declarations often appear in an order that makes it difficult for a person to understand the structure of a document. You can rearrange declarations, as long as you declare elements before you use them (that is, before they appear in something like an ordered listing or choice group).

You can group declarations by role. For example, declare all entities together, and then declare elements that use those entities. Alternately, you can group declarations by function or concept. Declare a person element and related subelements in one place, and then declare an address element and its subelements in another place within the same DTD.

Use Lots of Whitespace

While the DTD syntax is strict with regards to casing (upper- and lowercase letters) and sequences of characters (such as <!), you're free to use as much or as little whitespace as you like. Use tab characters to indent related groups, and use new lines to break a long declaration into several lines to make it easier to read. Introduce some spaces into declarations to make them more visible. Using whitespace characters makes a DTD more visually appealing and easier to review.

Use Comments

While DTDs generally convey all necessary information about the structure of a document, some sections may need clarification or explanation. You can embed comments within a DTD to describe particularly complex structures, or even provide examples of how you expect XML document authors to use your structures. Ensure that your comments are always up to date as you make changes to ensure that people reading your DTD always have relevant information readily at hand.

Review Other People's DTDs

One way to learn how to create DTDs is to read those that others produce. Read through DTDs like DocBook to get an idea of how entities add a high degree of flexibility to a DTD, for example. You'll also gain a great deal of insight about how people use and interact with DTDs, and how DTD authors structure their documents to make them as efficient as possible without losing clarity. While it may sound boring at first, reading DTDs can be very interesting!

This wraps up our look at DTDs. The next section discusses XML Schemas and how to use them.

Data Modeling Using XSD

XSD, or XML Schema Definition, is an XML vocabulary that allows you to define XML documents and their content. XSD addresses the limitations of DTDs and gives developers a flexible means of describing an XML document using a familiar syntax.

DTDs are perfect for document-centric information—XML documents that describe something in terms of its content. For example, DTDs are great for describing books or Web pages, because they contain relatively simple information that doesn't have a lot of constraints on it. A DTD can constrain an XML document to ensure that a book has at least one author, one ISBN, and a table of contents, as shown in the following listing:

```
<?xml version="1.0" encoding="UTF-8"?>
<!DOCTYPE books
[
  <!ELEMENT books (book)>
  <!ELEMENT book (author+, ISBN, TableOfContents)>
  <!ELEMENT author (#PCDATA)>
  <!ELEMENT ISBN (#PCDATA)>
  <!ELEMENT TableOfContents (#PCDATA)>
]>
<books>
  <book>
    <author>...</author>
    <author>...</author>
    <ISBN>...</ISBN>
    <TableOfContents>...</TableOfContents>
  </book>
</books>
```

A DTD becomes useless if you want your data model to have an element with a string value of "yes" or "no," because a DTD doesn't allow you to define values that elements may contain. Here's an XSD document that constrains an answer element's value to yes or no:

```
<!-- yesNo.xsd -->
<xs:schema xmlns:xs="http://www.w3.org/2001/XMLSchema"
elementFormDefault="qualified">
  <xs:element name="answer">
    <xs:complexType>
      <xs:simpleContent>
        <xs:restriction base="xs:string">
          <xs:enumeration value="yes"/>
          <xs:enumeration value="no"/>
```

```
            </xs:restriction>
          </xs:simpleContent>
        </xs:complexType>
      </xs:element>
      <xs:element name="answers">
        <xs:complexType>
          <xs:sequence>
            <xs:element ref="answer" maxOccurs="unbounded"/>
          </xs:sequence>
        </xs:complexType>
      </xs:element>
    </xs:schema>

    <!-- Here's a sample XML document that the schema validates...-->
    <?xml version="1.0" encoding="UTF-8"?>
    <answers xmlns:xsi="http://www.w3.org/2001/XMLSchema-instance"
    xsi:noNamespaceSchemaLocation="yesNo.xsd">
        <answer>yes</answer>
        <answer>no</answer>
    </answers>
```

This looks rather involved at first glance, when you consider that it's simply constraining the value of an element. Even though you don't know XSD yet, chances are that you can figure out what the document is trying to describe. That's the power of XSD—it's easy to understand and work with because it uses XML. The rest of this lesson goes into detail about XSD and how you can use it to validate your XML documents.

Understanding XML Schemas

As you saw in the previous lesson, a data model describes the logical structure of a set of data. The XML Schema Definition, or XSD, is based primarily on data types, whereas DTDs are primarily based on tags.

XSD supports 19 built-in data types that represent the basic units of data you can store in an XML document. For example, you can use XSD to ensure that one element contains character data and another element contains a numeric value. An XSD-aware XML processor (an application that's not only XML-aware, but XSD-aware) can validate an XML document against its XSD and enforce any constraints it places on the document. A great example of an XSD-aware application is XML Spy, an XML editor that can validate XML documents against an XSD or a DTD, among other features. I'll discuss XML Spy later in this book (Sunday morning and Sunday afternoon).

Let's start with a simple example: I live in Canada. When I want to send a letter to someone, the address I write on the envelope must include a postal code to ensure the letter gets to where it's going. If I make a mistake in the address by writing in an incorrect city, street name, or even house number, the postal code can help to get the letter to its proper address. For example, Canada's CN Tower is a well-known landmark whose address is

> 301 Front Street West
> Toronto, Ontario, Canada
> M5V-2T6

The last line in the address is the postal code, a sequence of six letters and numbers with one dash or space character. If you want to store the postal code in an XML document, you do it like this:

```
<?xml version="1.0" encoding="UTF-8"?>
<postalCodes>
   <postalCode>M5V-2T6</postalCode>
</postalCodes>
```

The only problem with this XML document is that there aren't any restrictions on what you can store in the postalCode element. As long as you follow the rules for the #PCDATA type, you can put anything you want in the element. You could use XSD to restrict the data to the xsd:string type (one of the 19 built-in XSD data types), but that's too general because you can store just about anything in the postalCode element. XSD allows you to create your own data types that are based on its built-in data types. For example, you could create a CanadianPostalCodeType type that's an xsd:string type with some restrictions:

```
<xsd:simpleType name="CanadianPostalCodeType">
  <xsd:restriction base="xsd:string">
    <xsd:pattern value="[A-Z]\d[A-Z]-\d[A-Z]\d"/>
  </xsd:restriction>
</xsd:simpleType>
```

The XSD restricts the value you can store in it using a pattern, which is expressed using a *regular expression* (described later in this lesson). The XSD associates the `CanadianPostalCodeType` type with the `postalCode` element using the following declaration:

```
<xsd:element
  name="postalCode"
  type="CanadianPostalCodeType"
/>
```

This statement says that there's an element called `postalCode` that's a `CanadianPostalCodeType` data type. As a result, the values that the `postalCode` element can hold are restricted to those that match the expression: Letter, number, letter, dash character, number, letter, number—in that order.

Like all other XML documents, XSD documents must be well-formed and valid. Well-formed documents have a root, or document, element. This is described next.

Understanding the schema Element

All XSD documents begin with a `schema` element whose attributes define the schema's namespace. Namespaces play a key role in XSD, whereas DTDs treat namespaces rather indifferently. The XSD `schema` element resides in the http://www.w3.org/2001/XMLSchema namespace:

```
<?xml version="1.0" encoding="UTF-8"?>
<xsd:schema xmlns:xsd="http://www.w3.org/2001/XMLSchema">
   ...
</xsd:schema>
```

Recall that the `xmlns` attribute defines which namespace the XML document resides in. When the attribute is used as shown here (`xmlns:xsd="..."`), the `xsd` prefix represents a shorthand notation for the namespace (http://www.w3.org/2001/XMLSchema), making the document easier to read. The `xsd` prefix is used by convention only—you're free to use any prefix you like. In fact, some XML editors and tools use their own prefix.

XSD relies on the http://www.w3.org/2001/XMLSchema namespace to qualify all constructs that appear in XSD documents. If you use another namespace, or an incorrect one, you'll probably end up with some strange error messages from your XML parser, or you may wonder why a feature isn't working.

Because all XSD constructs reside in their own namespaces, your XML document resides in a separate namespace whether you use the default namespace or define your own. For example, consider the document in the following listing:

```
<?xml version="1.0" encoding="UTF-8"?>
<samples xmlns="http://www.designs2solutions.com/LXW/Namespaces">
  <sample>
    ...
  <sample>
</samples>
```

The namespace declaration (the xmlns attribute of the samples element) associates all elements in the document with the http://www.designs2solutions... namespace. Use the targetNamespace attribute in the XSD schema element to associate elements from your XML document that reside in a particular namespace with an XSD, as shown:

```
<?xml version="1.0" encoding="UTF-8"?>
<xsd:schema xmlns:xsd="http://www.w3.org/2001/XMLSchema"
  targetNamespace="http://www.designs2solutions.com/LXW/Namespaces">
  ...
</xsd:schema>
```

When you use a declaration like this, the declarations in the XSD become bound to the elements that reside in the http://www.designs2solutions.com/LXW/Namespaces namespace. If you don't include a targetNamespace attribute in the schema element, the XSD declarations associate themselves with the XML document's default namespace.

Associating an XSD with an XML Document

XSD documents usually reside in a file of their own because they contain a lot of content and are often shared between related XML documents. As a result, XML documents associate themselves with an XSD using a special declaration, usually contained in the document's root element. The following listing demonstrates how to associate an XSD with an XML document:

```
<?xml version="1.0" encoding="UTF-8"?>
<addresses xmlns = "http://www.designs2solutions.com/LXW/Namespaces"
    xmlns:xsi = "http://www.w3c.org/2001/XMLSchema-instance"
```

```
     xsi:schemaLocation = "c:\samples\sampleSchema.xsd">
  <address>
    <!-- ... -->
  </address>
</addresses>
```

The root element, addresses, has two new attributes that work together to associate the XML with the XSD document. The xmlns:xsi = "..." namespace declaration associates the xsi prefix with the http://www.w3c.org/ 2001/XMLSchema-instance namespace. The xsi:schemaLocation attribute associates an XSD with the XML document.

If your XML document requires more than one XSD, just add entries to the xsi:schemaLocation attribute by separating each location with a space. The following listing demonstrates how to use two XSD documents with one XML document:

```
<?xml version="1.0" encoding="UTF-8"?>
<addresses xmlns = "http://www.designs2solutions.com/LXW/Namespaces"
    xmlns:xsi = "http://www.w3c.org/2001/XMLSchema-instance"
    xsi:schemaLocation =
      "c:\samples\sampleSchema.xsd c:\xml\anotherSchema.xsd">
  <address>
    <!-- ... -->
  </address>
</addresses>
```

Understanding XSD Data Types

XSD supports more than 40 data types that fall into four major categories:

➤ String types
➤ DTD-compatible types
➤ Numeric types
➤ Time types

You should become familiar with these types, because tools that generate XSD for you tend to use data types that closely match the data that elements hold. Often this is not what you want. For example, consider the following XML document:

```
<sample>
  <name>Erik Westermann</name>
  <someNumber>10</someNumber>
  <aDecimalNumber>5.0</aDecimalNumber>
  <aNegativeInteger>-6</aNegativeInteger>
</sample>
```

When you use a tool like XML Spy to generate the XSD for you based on the document's content, it looks like this:

```
<?xml version="1.0" encoding="UTF-8"?>
<xs:schema xmlns:xs="http://www.w3.org/2001/XMLSchema"
    elementFormDefault="qualified">
  <xs:element name="aDecimalNumber"
    type="xs:decimal"/>
  <xs:element name="aNegativeInteger"
    type="xs:byte"/>
  <xs:element name="name"
    type="xs:string"/>
  <xs:element name="someNumber"
    type="xs:byte"/>
  <xs:element name="sample">
    <xs:complexType>
      <xs:sequence>
        <xs:element ref="name"/>
        <xs:element ref="someNumber"/>
        <xs:element ref="aDecimalNumber"/>
        <xs:element ref="aNegativeInteger"/>
      </xs:sequence>
    </xs:complexType>
  </xs:element>
</xs:schema>
```

The bold line highlights the most relevant part of the listing. XML Spy correctly selected the xs:decimal type for the aDecimalNumber element and xs:string for the name element. When it considered the someNumber and aNegativeInteger elements, XML Spy chose the xs:byte type, which has a range between -127 and +128. XML Spy selects the data type based on the values of the respective elements. As a result, it selects the closest matching type. In most cases, this will suffice. However, more specific types add flexibility.

Here's a modified version of the previous XSD that uses more specific data types for the someNumber and aNegativeInteger elements (the text in bold highlights the changes):

```
<?xml version="1.0" encoding="UTF-8"?>
<xs:schema xmlns:xs="http://www.w3.org/2001/XMLSchema"
    elementFormDefault="qualified">
  <xs:element name="aDecimalNumber" type="xs:decimal"/>
  <xs:element name="aNegativeInteger"
    type="xs:negativeInteger"/>
  <xs:element name="name"
    type="xs:string"/>
  <xs:element name="someNumber"
    type="xs:positiveInteger"/>
  <xs:element name="sample">
    <xs:complexType>
      <xs:sequence>
        <xs:element ref="name"/>
        <xs:element ref="someNumber"/>
        <xs:element ref="aDecimalNumber"/>
        <xs:element ref="aNegativeInteger"/>
      </xs:sequence>
    </xs:complexType>
  </xs:element>
</xs:schema>
```

When you use the data types in your own XSD documents, prefix each type with the XSD namespace. For example, the following XSD document uses the xs prefix for the XSD namespace:

```
<?xml version="1.0" encoding="UTF-8"?>
<xs:schema xmlns:xs="http://www.w3.org/2001/XMLSchema">

   ...
</xs:schema>
```

If you want to use the positiveInteger type in your XSD, prefix it with the xs: prefix like this: xs:positiveInteger.

The next four sections discuss each XSD data type category in detail and provide examples of each data type.

Understanding String Data Types

String data types are the simplest, most general, and therefore most pervasive of all XSD data types. A string contains a sequence of Unicode characters of any length. Table 4.4 describes the string data types.

Understanding DTD-Compatible Types

DTD-compatible types are almost identical to their actual DTD counterparts, with one exception. While you can use DTD types for attributes only, you can use XSD DTD-compatible types with attributes *and* elements. Table 4.5 describes each DTD-compatible type.

Table 4.6 describes four additional types in this category: language, Name, QName, and NCName.

Understanding XSD Numeric Types

XSD defines a broad range of numeric types because it tries to be as compatible with as many programming languages as possible. It does this because software is the most common consumer of XML data, and people benefit from the information that the XML data conveys.

Table 4.7 describes the XSD numeric types that are available for you to use. In practice, however, only a small subset of the entire group is ever used in a particular group of related XSD documents. The types you use depend on the capabilities of the programming languages that the developers in your organization plan to use.

TABLE 4.4 XSD STRING DATA TYPES

Data Type	Description	Example
string	Any Unicode string	This is some text; E & W Accessories
normalizedString	A string that doesn't contain any whitespace characters	Hello World; this is some more text
token	A string made up of tokens separated by not more than one space	This is a tokenized string; day-to-day responsibilities

TABLE 4.5 XSD DTD-COMPATIBLE TYPES

Data Type	Description	Examples
ID	Identical to the XML ID attribute type—represents a unique value	a123, b456, yyz
IDREF	Identical to the XML IDREF attribute type—the value must refer to an ID type elsewhere in the XML document	a123, b456, yyz
IDREFS	Identical to the XML IDREFS attribute type—the value represents a listing of ID values elsewhere in the XML document	a123 b456 yyz
ENTITY	Identical to the XML ENTITY attribute type—refers to an external, binary entity using a string token	IMG1, IMG2
ENTITIES	Identical to the XML ENTITIES attribute type—refers to a list of external, binary entities using string tokens	IMG1 IMG2
NMTOKEN	Identical to the XML NMTOKEN attribute type—the value is made up of XML token characters	e1:w2, valid.text, Hello-World
NMTOKENS	Identical to the XML NMTOKENS attribute type—the value is a list of NMTOKEN values	e1:w2 valid.text Hello-World

TABLE 4.6 ADDITIONAL XSD DTD-COMPATIBLE TYPES

Data Type	Description	Examples
language	Represents a language code, as defined by the XML specification	en, en-US
Name	Represents an XML Name—see Appendix C, Table C.2	a_bcd, a-bcd, abcd
QName	Represents a qualified name (a name with a prefix)	xs:string, d2s:types
NCName	A name without a prefix (the colon character isn't allowed)	table-5.3, a-bcd, abcd

TABLE 4.7 XSD NUMERIC TYPES

Data Type	Description	Examples
unsignedByte	A positive number having a range of 0 to 255	0,2,7,11,23
byte	A signed number having a range of –127 to +127	-100, 100
unsignedShort	A positive number having a range of 0 to 65535	1, 5, 7, 2000
short	A signed number having a range of –32767 to 32768	-1, 1, 3000
unsignedInt	A positive number having a range of 0 to 4.294e9	0, 2, 7, 11
int	A signed number having a range of –2.147e9 to 2.147e9	-300, 0, 300
integer	A signed number having a range of –4.567e27 to 4.567e27	-300, 0, 300
positiveInteger	An unsigned number having a range of 0 to 4.567e27	0, 300, 3000
nonPositiveInteger	A signed number having a range of 0 to –4.567e27	0, -1, -2
negativeInteger	A signed number having a range of –1 to –4.567e27	-1, -2, -3
nonNegativeInteger	An unsigned number having a range of 0 to 4.567e27	0, 300, 3000
unsignedLong	An unsigned number having a range of 0 to 18.446e18	0, 300, 3000
long	A signed number having a range of –9.223e18 to 9.223e18	-300, 0, 300
decimal	A signed number with variable precision	-0.72, 1.0, 1e1024
float	A signed, floating point number (32-bits)	-100.1, 0.0, 104.5
double	A signed floating point number (64-bits) ranging from –infinity to infinity	-0.1, 0, 100.2

The last three types (decimal, float, and double) can represent very large and very small numbers. The reference to infinity is based on a standard representation of infinity using the IEEE 754 standard.

Understanding XSD Time Types

People around the world represent times and dates according to local and cultural standards, or just whatever seems convenient. XSD defines a standardized way of representing times and dates based on an international standard. Table 4.8 describes the XSD time types.

TABLE 4.8 XSD TIME TYPES

Data Type	Description	Example
timeInstant	Represents a specific date and time in UTC (Coordinated Universal Time, also known as GMT)	1992-03-12T16:30:30.500-05:00
duration	Represents a beginning or ending of a span of time	P1996Y11M19D18H29M20.2S
date	An exact date without reference to time	1997-06-07
time	A specific time of day without reference to the date	08:45:30.500
gYear	A year	0001, 9999
gMonth	A month	—01—, —12—
gYearMonth	A month in a year	1992-03, 1996-11
gMonthDay	A date in a month without regard to the year	—03-03, —06-04
recurringDay	A date without regard to the month or year	—01, —31

There's another type I haven't discussed: `boolean`. A `boolean` value represents only two values, which are analogous to on and off. You can assign a value to the `boolean` type using either `true` or `false` or the numbers 1 and 0, which represent `true` and `false`, respectively.

Defining Your Own Data Types

While XSD offers diverse data types, the most useful feature of XSD is that it allows you to define your *own* data types. XSD supports two categories of named type definitions (data types): simple types and complex types.

A *simple type* is analogous to a text-only element, which doesn't have any attributes and contains only text. You define a simple type using the `simpleType` construct described in the following section.

A *complex type* is analogous to an element that has a mixed-content model. It describes an element, its attributes, and its children. A complex type can describe itself and its children using a local declaration (described later in this lesson), which overrides any global declarations (also described later) that may be in effect.

Defining Your Own Simple Data Types

Simple data types are based on existing data types. When you define your own simple type, you give the type a name and introduce new restrictions to an existing type. Think of a credit card. You can spend as much as you like, as long as you stay within your credit limit. You're not concerned about how *others* use their credit cards. You're just concerned with your own spending limit. Here's one way to express a set of credit card transactions, each of which has a spending limit of $500:

```
<?xml version="1.0" encoding="UTF-8"?>
<!-- Note: this is a fragment of a complete XSD document -->
<xs:schema xmlns:xs="http://www.w3.org/2001/XMLSchema">
  <xs:element name="transactionAmount">
    <xs:simpleType >
      <xs:restriction base="xs:unsignedInt">
        <xs:minInclusive value="0"/>
        <xs:maxInclusive value="500"/>
```

```
        </xs:restriction>
      </xs:simpleType>
    </xs:element>
</xs:schema>
```

The XSD defines an element called `transactionAmount` that's based on the `unsignedInt` type (described earlier under "Understanding XSD Numeric Types"). The new data type has a `restriction` that limits its minimum value (`minInclusive`) to 0 and its maximum value (`maxInclusive`) to 500. The XML document that validates against the schema fragment would look like this:

```
<?xml version="1.0" encoding="UTF-8"?>
<statement
    xmlns:xsi="http://www.w3.org/2001/XMLSchema-instance"
    xsi:noNamespaceSchemaLocation="ccStatement.xsd">
  <transactionAmount>100</transactionAmount>
  <transactionAmount>200</transactionAmount>
  <transactionAmount>300</transactionAmount>
  <transactionAmount>400</transactionAmount>
  <transactionAmount>499</transactionAmount>
</statement>
```

The constraints you place on the built-in XSD data types are referred to as *constraining facets*, or more commonly just *facets*. For example, `minInclusive` and `maxInclusive` are both facets of the `unsignedInt` XSD data type. Table 4.9 describes the facets that are applicable to all XSD data types.

The last three items (`whiteSpace`, `enumeration`, and `pattern`) are explained in detail in the following sections.

Understanding the whiteSpace Facet

The `whiteSpace` facet is a little different from the other facets because it doesn't constrain data in any way. Instead, it describes how an XML processor handles whitespace characters (spaces, tabs, line feeds, and carriage return characters) that appear in the data. The `whiteSpace` facet has three possible values, which have different effects on string data types, as shown in Table 4.10.

If you don't specify a value for the `whiteSpace` facet, its default is `collapse`. The `collapse` setting is the only valid setting for non-string types.

TABLE 4.9 CONSTRAINING FACETS

Facet	Description	Use for
minInclusive	Value of the data must be equal to or greater than the value of the facet	Numeric, date, and time types
maxInclusive	Value of the data must be equal to or less than the value of the facet	Numeric, date, and time types
minExclusive	Value of the data must be greater than the value of the facet	Numeric, date, and time types
maxExclusive	Value of the data must be less than the value of the facet	Numeric, date, and time types
minLength	Minimum number of characters the data may have	String
maxLength	Maximum number of characters the data may have	String
length	Required number of characters the data must have	String
totalDigits	Maximum number of digits the data may have	Numeric types
whiteSpace	Determines how the XML processor handles whitespace characters	All types
enumeration	Constrains data to a list of values	All types
pattern	Constrains data to certain literal values	All types

TABLE 4.10 whiteSpace Facet Setting and Effect on String Types	
Setting	**Effect on a string type**
preserve	Whitespace characters aren't modified in any way
replace	Each whitespace character is replaced with a single space character
collapse	Removes all leading and trailing whitespace characters and converts all remaining whitespace characters into single spaces, as described in the replace setting

Understanding the enumeration Facet

The enumeration facet defines an element's permitted values. A simple example is documenting the state of a light switch, which has two valid states: on and off. You can create an enumeration of the two states, as shown in the following XSD fragment:

```
<xsd:simpleType name="switchState">
  <xsd:restriction base="xsd:string">
    <xsd:enumeration value="on"/>
    <xsd:enumeration value="off"/>
  </xsd:restriction>
</xsd:simpleType>
```

The declaration creates a simpleType based on a string that's restricted to the two values specified in each of the enumeration element's value attributes (on and off). You can create enumerations based on any XSD data type, as shown in the following listing:

```
<xsd:simpleType name="primeNumbers">
  <xsd:restriction base="xsd:unsignedInt">
    <xsd:enumeration value="2"/>
    <xsd:enumeration value="149"/>
```

```
    <xsd:enumeration value="233"/>
    <xsd:enumeration value="1123"/>
  </xsd:restriction>
</xsd:simpleType>
```

The declaration creates a `simpleType` called `primeNumbers` that's based on the `unsignedInt` type. The `restriction` limits possible values to a few prime numbers, as specified by each `enumeration`'s `value` attribute. Note that even though the declaration uses numeric types, the values must still appear in quotes.

Understanding the pattern Facet

The `pattern` facet acts as a template for `simpleType`'s literal values. You saw an example of the `pattern` facet at work earlier in this lesson, where it restricted the characters that a `postalCode` element could hold. Here's the XSD fragment again (the `pattern` facet appears in bold):

```
<xsd:simpleType name="CanadianPostalCodeType">
  <xsd:restriction base="xsd:string">
    <xsd:pattern value="[A-Z]\d[A-Z]-\d[A-Z]\d"/>
  </xsd:restriction>
</xsd:simpleType>
<xsd:element name="postalCode" type="CanadianPostalCodeType"/>
```

The pattern restricts the possible values a `postalCode` element can have to the following sequence of characters, in this order: letter, number, letter, dash character, number, letter, number. This pattern uses a special notation, called a *regular expression*, that uses a set of symbols to define a template and perform string manipulations. Regular expressions can get very complex, but the basics are easy to understand. Table 4.11 describes some common regular expressions.

Going back to the `CanadianPostalCodeType`, the pattern `[A-Z]\d[A-Z]-\d[A-Z]\d` matches a sequence of characters that contains letters (`[A-Z]`), numbers (`\d`), and a dash character in the specified order.

You can restrict simple types in three other ways, using enumerations, lists, and unions, all of which are discussed in the following sections.

TABLE 4.11 COMMON COMPONENTS OF REGULAR EXPRESSIONS

Expression	Description	Example
. (period)	Matches anything except a newline character	The expression a.c matches a sequence of three characters starting with a and ending with c, having any character between them (for example, abc, a1c, and acc)
*	Matches the character or pattern that appears before it one or more times	The expression yipe* matches yi'pee' and 'yipeeee', but doesn't match just 'yip'
+	Matches the character or pattern that appears before it one or more times	The expression mo+d matches 'mood' and 'moood', but doesn't match 'mod'
?	Matches the preceding character or pattern zero or one times	The expression st?ill matches 'still' and 'sill'
[...]	Defines a set of characters; matches any one of the characters in the set	The expression m[ai]ll matches 'mall' and 'mill'
[a-z]	Defines a range of characters in a set and matches any one of the characters in the set	The expression [a-d] is equivalent to the set [abcd] and matches any one character in the set (a, b, c, or d)
[^a-z]	Defines a range of characters in a set and matches characters that aren't in the set	The expression [^a-d] is equivalent to any one character that is *not* in the set (a, b, c, or d)
| (pipe)	Defines an alternative	The pattern a|b matches the letter a or b
^	Matches characters at the beginning of a line	The expression ^cat matches 'cat' only if it's the beginning of the line

TABLE 4.11 COMMON COMPONENTS OF REGULAR EXPRESSIONS (CONTINUED)

Expression	Description	Example
$	Matches characters at the end of a line	The expression $at matches 'This is a cat' and 'That is a hat', but doesn't match 'Meet me at 5'
\	Escapes the special characters \, ^, $, *, +, ., and ?—you can use these characters only if you prefix them with a \ character	The expression $\? matches anything that ends in a question mark
\b	Matches characters appearing at word boundaries	The expression \bok matches 'book', but doesn't match 'Ok, there you go'
\B	Matches characters appearing within words only, not at word boundaries	The expression \Bea matches 'care', but doesn't match 'wear'
{n}	Matches the preceding character or pattern exactly n times	The expression .e{2} matches 'see' and 'tee', but doesn't match 'me'
{n,}	Matches the preceding character or pattern at least n times	The expression ab{2,} matches 'abb' and 'abbb', but doesn't match 'ab'
{n,m}	Matches the preceding character or pattern between n and m times	The expression e{1,2} matches 'feet' and 'heal'
(...)*digit*	Matches and locates the characters or pattern in brackets and retains the matching value, which you can refer to later using the *digit* expression (regular expressions can retain up to nine matches, which you can address using the expression \1, \2,...,\9)	The expression (.+)\1 matches a string that has two identical halves, as in 'byebye'; the expression (.+) matches any string and retains it in the \1 position; the \1 expression matches the first retained string again (in this case, the string 'bye')

Using an enumeration to Restrict a Type's Possible Values

An enumeration allows you to define a set of valid values that an element may have. For example, the following XSD fragment restricts the value of an element to "yes" or "no":

```
<xs:simpleType name="yesNoType">
  <xs:restriction base="xs:string">
    <xs:enumeration value="yes"/>
    <xs:enumeration value="no"/>
  </xs:restriction>
</xs:simpleType>
```

The listing uses the string type. However, you can use any XSD type as long as the enumeration's types match the restriction's type. For example, you cannot restrict a date type using the name of a month, which is a string.

Using a list to Restrict a Type's Possible Values

A list is similar to an enumeration because it allows you to define a range of possible values an element may have. The difference, however, is that a list represents a space-separated listing of values within a single element. For example, consider the following XSD document:

```
<xsd:schema xmlns:xsd="http://www.w3.org/2001/XMLSchema">
  <xsd:simpleType name="floats">
    <xsd:list itemType="xsd:float"/>
  </xsd:simpleType>
  <xsd:element name="item" type="floats"/>
</xsd:schema>
```

The XSD defines a simpleType that's made up of a list of floating point numbers (the float type). The following XML validates against the XSD:

```
<?xml version="1.0" encoding="UTF-8"?>
  <item xmlns:xsi="http://www.w3.org/2001/XMLSchema-instance"
    xsi:noNamespaceSchemaLocation="...">1 2 3 4.5 9.99</item>
```

The list in the XML document's item element represents a list of floating point numbers. All numbers in the list are considered floating point numbers, regardless of whether they have decimal points.

Using a union to Restrict a Type's Values

A union represents a combination of restrictions on a type. For example, you could limit a list of numbers to string or integer types:

```
<xs:simpleType name="numberNumber">
  <xs:list itemType="xs:integer">
</xs:simpleType>


<xs:simpleType name="stringNumber">
  <xs:list itemType="xs:string">
</xs:simpleType>


<xs:simpleType name="NumericOrStringNumber">
  <xs:union memberTypes="numberNumber stringNumber"/>
</xs:simpleType>
```

The union type combines the restrictions of both the numberNumber and stringNumber types, making the following XML fragment valid:

```
<amount>1 2 3</amount>
<amount>one two three</amount>
```

Defining Complex Types

One of the best features of XSD is that you can define your own data types. While a simple type allows you to define only what an element can contain, a complex type allows you to define elements that have attributes, and that contain text and other elements. You define complex types using particles within a complexType declaration. A *particle* is a part of a complexType declaration that defines

➤ A local element
➤ Reference to a global element
➤ A sequence, choice, or all compositor
➤ Reference to a group

Complex types can also use the constraining facets, as described in Table 4.9. Constraining facets allow you to restrict data, such as limiting its length. Using constraints can make complex types more useful in a much broader range of applications.

The following sections describe how to use particles to declare complex types. The information will help you interpret existing XSD documents, and will also help you create an XSD that's best for your XML documents.

Understanding Element Declarations

Elements are the foundation of XML documents. As a result, they're an essential part of complex types. Element declarations allow you to provide a detailed description of the elements you can have within an XML document. You define an element using the element tag, as shown in the following listing:

```
<!-- 01 --> <xs:schema xmlns:xs="http://www.w3.org/2001/XMLSchema">
<!-- 02 -->    <xs:element name="units" .../>
<!-- 03 -->    <xs:element name="amount" .../>
<!-- 04 -->       ...
<!-- 05 --> </xs:schema>
```

Lines 02 and 03 declare two elements: units and amount. The name attribute defines the name of the element as you want it to appear in an XML document. There are several other attributes you can use within an element's declaration, as shown in the following declaration:

```
<xs:element
   name="..."
   type="..."
   minOccurs="..."
   maxOccurs="..."
   default="..."
   fixed="..."
   nillable="..."
/>
```

The type attribute defines the element's data type. You can use the name of an XSD data type (as described earlier in "Understanding XSD Data Types"), the name of a simpleType, or the name of a complexType.

Simple types support only mandatory content. In contrast, complex types support optional and mandatory elements using two facets: minOccurs and maxOccurs. The minOccurs attribute describes the minimum number of times an element can occur within a complex type, while the maxOccurs attribute describes the maximum number of occurrences. Both attributes have default values, so that you don't have to use them for all element declarations within your complex types. The default value of the minOccurs attribute is always 1, and the default value of the maxOccurs attribute is 1 *or* the same value as the minOccurs attribute, whichever is greater.

The value of minOccurs and maxOccurs must be an unsigned integer (a positive number), with one exception: you can use the term unbounded to describe an unlimited value. Using these attributes together allows you to create optional or mandatory elements, as shown in Table 4.12.

The default attribute allows you to define an element's default value. The only restriction is that you can define a default only for elements whose type attribute is one of the XSD data types.

The fixed attribute allows you to define an unchanging value based on one of the XSD data types. This attribute is useful when you want to add infor-

TABLE 4.12 COMBINATIONS OF MINOCCURS AND MAXOCCURS		
minOccurs	**maxOccurs**	**Effect**
unspecified	unspecified	minOccurs=1, maxOccurs=1
unspecified	1	minOccurs=1, maxOccurs=1
1	unspecified	minOccurs=1, maxOccurs=1
0	1	Defines an optional element that can appear only once
1	0	Invalid setting
1	1	Defines a mandatory element that can appear only once
0	unbounded	Defines an optional element that you can repeat as many times as you like
1	unbounded	Defines a mandatory element that you can repeat as many times as you like

mation to an XML document without having users or other applications add it to the document.

The `nillable` attribute allows you to define an element that's present but doesn't have a value. This is in contrast to an element whose `minOccurs` attribute is 0, because that defines an optional element, not an element that's present but doesn't have a value. The `nillable` attribute has two valid values: `true` or `false`. Its default value is `false`. The following listing demonstrates how to define the `nillable` attribute:

```
<!-- 01 --> <?xml version="1.0" encoding="UTF-8"?>
<!-- 02 --> <xsd:schema xmlns:xsd="http://www.w3.org/2001/XMLSchema">
<!-- 03 -->   <xsd:complexType name="sampleComplexType">
<!-- 04 -->     <xsd:sequence>
<!-- 05 -->       <xsd:element name="a"
                       type="xs:string"
                       nillable="true/>
<!-- 06 -->       <xsd:element name="b" type="xs:integer" />
<!-- 07 -->     </xsd:sequence>
<!-- 08 -->   </xsd:complexType>
<!-- 09 --> </xsd:schema>
```

Line 05 demonstrates the `nillable` attribute. When you want to declare an element without a value in your XML document, use the following syntax:

```
<!-- 01 --> <?xml version="1.0" encoding="UTF-8"?>
<!-- 02 --> <sampleComplexType
                 xmlns:xsi="http://www.w3.org/2001/XMLSchema-instance">
<!-- 03 -->   <a xsi:nil="1"></a>
<!-- 04 -->   <b>100000</b>
<!-- 05 --> </sampleComplexType>
```

Line 03 shows how to use the `nil` attribute to describe that an element is present but doesn't have a value. You'll notice that the `nil` attribute has an `xsi` namespace prefix. This refers to a special namespace that allows you to use attributes like `nil`. You can use the namespace only within XML documents, not within XSD documents.

There are some other attributes of an element's declaration that I haven't discussed yet because they apply to features like global and local element declarations, which are discussed next. I'll describe the additional attributes throughout the rest of this lesson.

Global Element Declarations

There are two ways of describing an element that appears as part of a complex type's declaration: a global declaration and a local declaration. This section describes global declarations, and the following section describes local declarations and how to refer to globally defined elements within local declarations.

Consider the following XML document:

```
<?xml version="1.0" encoding="UTF-8"?>
<person>
  <firstName>Vikranth</firstName >
  <age>10</age>
</person>
```

This describes a person with two elements: firstName and age. Both elements are useful to the person element but can also be useful elsewhere in the same document. A global element declaration allows you to reuse an element's declaration in other parts of an XSD document. The following listing demonstrates how to define two global elements and then refer to them within a complex type:

```
<!-- 01 --> <xs:schema xmlns:xs="http://www.w3.org/2001/XMLSchema">
<!-- 02 -->     <xs:element name="age" type="xs:byte"/>
<!-- 03 -->     <xs:element name=" firstName" type="xs:string"/>
<!-- 04 -->     <xs:element name="person">
<!-- 05 -->        <xs:complexType>
<!-- 06 -->          <xs:sequence>
<!-- 07 -->            <xs:element ref="name"/>
<!-- 08 -->            <xs:element ref="age"/>
<!-- 09 -->          </xs:sequence>
<!-- 10 -->        </xs:complexType>
<!-- 11 -->     </xs:element>
<!-- 12 --> </xs:schema>
```

The global element declarations for the firstName and age elements are on lines 02 and 03. The declarations are considered global to the XSD document because both elements are outside of any other elements (except the schema element). The XSD refers to the global elements on lines 07 and 08, which are within a complexType declaration, using element tags. The difference is that the elements use a `ref` attribute instead of using the `name` and `type` attributes, as in lines 02 and 03.

Local Element Declarations

Local element declarations are usable only within the context they appear in. When you define a local element, you need to declare its `type` and other attributes within the element's declaration. This is in contrast to using a global element with a `ref` attribute. The following listing defines two local element declarations:

```
<!-- 01 --> <?xml version="1.0"?>
<!-- 02 --> <xsd:schema xmlns:xsd="http://www.w3.org/2001/XMLSchema">
<!-- 03 -->    <xsd:complexType name="sampleComplexType">
<!-- 04 -->      <xsd:sequence>
<!-- 05 -->        <xsd:element name="a" type="xs:string" />
<!-- 06 -->        <xsd:element name="b" type="xs:integer" />
<!-- 07 -->      </xsd:sequence>
<!-- 08 -->    </xsd:complexType>
<!-- 09 --> </xsd:schema>
```

Lines 05 and 06 define two elements that can appear only within the complex type, `sampleComplexType`. It would be an error to reference the elements outside of the complex type, as shown in the following listing:

```
<!-- 01 --> <?xml version="1.0"?>
<!-- 02 --> <xsd:schema xmlns:xsd="http://www.w3.org/2001/XMLSchema">
<!-- 03 -->    <xsd:complexType name="sampleComplexType">
<!-- 04 -->      <xsd:sequence>
<!-- 05 -->        <xsd:element name="a"
                        type="xs:string" />
<!-- 06 -->        <xsd:element name="b"
                        type="xs:integer" />
<!-- 07 -->      </xsd:sequence>
<!-- 08 -->    </xsd:complexType>
<!-- 09 -->    <xsd:element ref="a" />   <!-- ERROR! -->
<!-- 10 --> </xsd:schema>
```

Line 09 attempts to refer to the `a` element using a `ref` attribute. This is an error because `a` is a local element declaration. As a result, you cannot reuse the local element outside of the complex type that declares it.

Composing Elements Using Compositors

As previously described, elements have a content model that describes which kinds of content they can have (see Table 3.2 for a refresher). While the three content models are useful, XSD allows you to get much more specific. You can describe exactly how you want an element's content to appear in an XML document. You define an element's content using three types of compositors: sequence, choice, or all.

Using the sequence Compositor

A sequence compositor allows you to define an element that contains a sequence of other elements. The syntax of the sequence compositor is as follows:

```
<xsd:sequence minOccurs="..." maxOccurs="...">

   ...
</xsd:sequence>
```

The minOccurs and maxOccurs attributes limit the number of times a sequence can appear in the XML document. You can make a sequence mandatory or optional based on the settings shown in Table 4.2.

The elements in the XML document must appear in the same order as defined by the XSD document. The following listing demonstrates how to create a sequence:

```
<?xml version="1.0"?>
<xsd:schema xmlns:xsd="http://www.w3.org/2001/XMLSchema">
  <xsd:complexType name="sequenceDemo">
    <xsd:sequence>
      <xsd:element name="item" type="xs:string" />
      <xsd:element name="value" type="xs:int" />
    </xsd:sequence>
  </xsd:complexType>
  <xsd:element name="items" type="sequenceDemo"/>
</xsd:schema>
```

The XSD defines an items element, which is a sequenceDemo type. The sequenceDemo type defines a sequence of two elements: item and value. The following XML document demonstrates how to use the sequence:

```
<?xml version="1.0" encoding="UTF-8"?>
<items>
```

```
<item>hammer</item><value>5</value>
<item>nails</item><value>1</value>
</items>
```

The sequence is valid because the `item` and `value` elements appear in the same order as defined by the XSD and have the correct data types.

You can combine a `sequence` with another `sequence` or a `choice`, which is described next.

Using the choice Compositor

The `choice` compositor defines a set of elements where you can pick one element from a group of available elements. The syntax of the `choice` compositor is as follows:

```
<xsd:choice minOccurs="..." maxOccurs="...">
    ...
</xsd:choice>
```

The `minOccurs` and `maxOccurs` attributes limit the number of times a choice can appear in the XML document (you can only still choose only one element). You can make a choice mandatory or optional based on the settings shown in Table 4.2.

The following listing demonstrates a simple use of the `choice` compositor:

```
<?xml version="1.0"?>
<xsd:schema xmlns:xsd="http://www.w3.org/2001/XMLSchema">
  <xsd:complexType name="choiceDemo">
    <xsd:choice>
      <xsd:element name="item" type="xs:string" />
      <xsd:element name="value" type="xs:int" />
    </xsd:choice>
  </xsd:complexType>
  <xsd:element name="items" type=" choiceDemo"/>
</xsd:schema>
```

The following XML document conforms to the XSD:

```
<?xml version="1.0" encoding="UTF-8"?>
<items>
  <item>hammer</item>
</items>
```

The choice compositor is more useful when you're mixing simple types and other compositors. Consider the following XSD:

```
<!-- 01 --> <?xml version="1.0"?>
<!-- 02 --> <xsd:schema xmlns:xsd="http://www.w3.org/2001/XMLSchema">
<!-- 03 -->   <xsd:complexType name="choiceDemo">
<!-- 04 -->     <xsd:choice>
<!-- 05 -->       <xsd:sequence>
<!-- 06 -->         <xsd:element name="countryName"
                         type="xsd:string" />
<!-- 07 -->         <xsd:element name="countryCode"
                         type="xsd:string" />
<!-- 08 -->       <xsd:sequence>
<!-- 09 -->       <xsd:element name="nameOfCountry"
                       type="xsd:string"/>
<!-- 10 -->     </xsd:choice>
<!-- 11 -->   </xsd:complexType>
<!-- 12 -->   </xsd:element name="countries"
                    type="choiceDemo">
<!-- 13 --> </xsd:schema>
```

The XSD creates a complex type called choiceDemo that contains a choice of a sequence (declared between lines 05 and 08) or an element (declared on line 09). The following two XML documents validate against the XSD:

```
<?xml version="1.0" encoding="UTF-8"?>
<countries>
  <countryName>Canada</countryName>
  <countryCode>CA</countryCode>
</countries>

<!-- the following document is also valid... -->

<?xml version="1.0" encoding="UTF-8"?>
<countries>
  <nameOfCountry>Canada</nameOfCountry >
</countries>
```

Note that because the choice element contains a sequence and an element, an XML document can contain only one of them.

You can combine a choice with another choice or sequence.

Using the all Compositor

The all compositor defines a set of elements that can appear in any order. The syntax of the all compositor is as follows:

```
<xsd:all minOccurs="..." maxOccurs="...">
   ...
</xsd:all>
```

There are some restrictions on how you can use this compositor:

➤ The all compositor can only appear within a complexType declaration—you cannot include it in a choice or a sequence.

➤ The all compositor can contain only element particles.

➤ Elements within an all compositor can have a maxOccurs attribute value of 1.

➤ Elements within an all compositor may have a minOccurs attribute value of 0 (to make the element optional).

Consider the following XSD:

```
<?xml version="1.0"?>
<xsd:schema xmlns:xsd="http://www.w3.org/2001/XMLSchema">
  <xsd:complexType name="allDemo">
    <xsd:all>
      <xsd:element name="a" type="xs:string" />
      <xsd:element name="b" type="xs:string" />
      <xsd:element name="c" type="xs:string" />
      <xsd:element name="d" type="xs:string" minOccurs="0" />
    </xsd:choice>
  </xsd:complexType>
  <xsd:element name="items" type=" allDemo"/>
</xsd:schema>
```

The following XML document is considered to be valid when validated against the preceding XSD:

```
<?xml version="1.0"?>
<items>
  <c>...</c>
  <a>...</a>
  <b>...</b>
</items>
```

Note that the a, b, and c elements don't appear in the same order as they appear in the XSD, while the d element doesn't appear at all because it's optional.

Understanding the group Element

A group element defines a set of elements that you can reuse throughout your XSD documents. The syntax for a group declaration is as follows:

```
<xsd:group minOccurs="..." maxOccurs="...">

  ...

</xsd:group>
```

The minOccurs and maxOccurs attributes allow you to define how many times a group can appear within an element. You can define a group as a global just as you would define a global element, making it usable throughout the XSD. A group usually contains other compositors, including choice, sequence, and all. For example, consider the following XML document:

```
<?xml version="1.0" encoding="UTF-8"?>
<person xmlns:xsi="http://www.w3.org/2001/XMLSchema-instance"
        xsi:noNamespaceSchemaLocation="personalInformation.xsd">
        <firstName>Erik</firstName>
        <lastName>Westermann</lastName>
        <buildingNumber>301</buildingNumber>
        <streetName>Front Street West</streetName>
        <mailCode>M5V-2T6</mailCode>
</person>
```

This document describes a person and an address. (That's not my address, by the way—it's the address of Canada's CN Tower that was used earlier in this lesson.) The information contains elements, like buildingNumber and streetName, that could be useful elsewhere in an XML document. The following XSD validates the preceding XML document:

```
<?xml version="1.0"?>
<xsd:schema xmlns:xsd="http://www.w3.org/2001/XMLSchema">
  <xsd:group name="detailedStreetAddress">
    <xsd:all>
      <xsd:element name="buildingNumber"
        type="xsd:positiveInteger"/>
      <xsd:element name="apartment"
        type="xsd:positiveInteger"
```

```
                minOccurs="0"/>
            <xsd:element name="streetName"
               type="xsd:string"/>
            <xsd:element name="mailCode"
               type="xsd:string"/>
          </xsd:all>
        </xsd:group>
        <xsd:group name="identification">
          <xsd:sequence>
            <xsd:element name="firstName"
               type="xsd:string"/>
            <xsd:element name="lastName"
               type="xsd:string"/>
            <xsd:group ref="detailedStreetAddress"/>
          </xsd:sequence>
        </xsd:group>
        <xsd:complexType name="personalIdentification">
          <xsd:group ref="identification"/>
        </xsd:complexType>
        <xsd:element name="person"
           type="personalIdentification"/>
      </xsd:schema>
```

The XSD looks a little involved at first, but it's very straightforward. The trick is to read it as if it appears upside-down, from the bottom to the top. The document has a root element called person, which is composed of a firstName, a lastName, and a detailedStreetAddress through a reference to the identification group. Note that when you reference a group within a complex type, refer to it using the ref attribute.

The detailedStreetAddress, which is a group, is made up of an all compositor containing the buildingNumber, optional apartment (it's optional because minOccurs is 0), streetName, and mailCode elements.

Complex Types with Attributes

Complex types also support attributes. In fact, you must use a complex type if you want to define elements that have attributes (using XSD). The syntax for declaring an attribute is shown here:

```
<xsd:attribute
  name="..."
  type="..."
  use="..."
  default="..."
  value="..."
  ref="..."
>
```

The `name` attribute defines an `attribute`'s name.

The `type` attribute defines the `attribute`'s data type. You can use any XSD data type, or a `simpleType` that you define elsewhere in the XSD document.

The `use` attribute combines with the `value` attribute to define how XML documents can use an attribute. There are six different settings, as described in Table 4.13.

The following listing demonstrates how to define an attribute within a complex type:

```
<?xml version="1.0" encoding="UTF-8"?>
<xsd:schema xmlns:xsd="http://www.w3.org/2001/XMLSchema">
  <xs:element name="attributeSampleOne">
    <xs:complexType>
      <xs:attribute name="attributeA"
        type="xs:NMTOKEN"
        use="required"/>
    </xs:complexType>
  </xs:element>
</xs:schema>
```

The XSD defines a local element called `attributeSampleOne`. The element has an attribute called `attributeA` that's an `NMTOKEN` type (see Table 5.2 for a definition of this type). The following XML document validates against the preceding schema:

```
<?xml version="1.0" encoding="UTF-8"?>
<attributeSampleOne
  attributeA="LearnXMLInAWeekend"
/>
```

TABLE 4.13   SETTINGS FOR THE USE ATTRIBUTE

Setting	Description
use='default' value='default value'	The attribute is optional. If you don't use the attribute, it becomes part of the XML document as if you provided it with the value as defined by the value attribute.
use='fixed' value='fixed value'	The attribute is optional. If you use it, the attribute must have the value as defined by the value attribute. If you don't use the attribute, it becomes part of the XML document as if you provided it with the value specified in the value attribute.
use='optional'	The attribute is optional and can have any value that's compatible with the attribute's type.
use='prohibited'	The attribute isn't allowed.
use='required' value='required value'	The attribute is required and must have the value as defined by the value attribute.
use='required'	The attribute is required. It can have any value that's compatible with the attribute's type.

Recall that you can define elements in two ways, using global and local element declarations. You can define global and local attributes in the same way that you define global and local elements. The preceding example uses a local element declaration. The following example demonstrates how to create and use global attributes:

```
<?xml version="1.0" encoding="UTF-8"?>
<xs:schema xmlns:xs="http://www.w3.org/2001/XMLSchema">
  <xs:attribute
    name="globalAttributeA"
    type="xs:int"
    use="required"/>
  <xs:attribute
    name="globalAttributeB"
```

```
      type="xs:string"
      use="required"/>
    <xs:element name="attributeSampleTwo">
      <xs:complexType>
        <xs:attribute ref="globalAttributeA"/>
        <xs:attribute ref="globalAttributeB"/>
        <xs:attribute
          name="localAttributeA"
          use="required"/>
      </xs:complexType>
    </xs:element>
</xs:schema>
```

The XSD defines two required, global attributes immediately following the
schema element. The attributeSampleTwo element has three attributes. Two
of them refer to the global attribute declarations using the ref attribute, and
one is a local attribute. The following XML document validates against the
preceding XSD:

```
<?xml version="1.0" encoding="UTF-8"?>
<attributeSampleTwo
  globalAttributeA="0"
  globalAttributeB="String"
  localAttributeA="Text"
/>
```

A global attribute declaration allows you to reuse the attribute anywhere else
in an XSD. However, there are cases when a related group of attributes is
more useful. An attributeGroup represents a named grouping of attributes
that you can refer to anywhere in an XSD. The only restriction on an
attributeGroup is that it can't appear outside the schema element—
attributeGroup declarations cannot be members of complexType or any
other declarations. The following listing demonstrates how to create and use
an attributeGroup:

```
<?xml version="1.0" encoding="UTF-8"?>
<xs:schema xmlns:xs="http://www.w3.org/2001/XMLSchema">
<xs:attributeGroup name="groupA">
  <xs:attribute name="attributeA"
    type="xs:int"
```

```
        use="required"/>
    <xs:attribute name="attributeB"
      type="xs:string"
      use="required"/>
    </xs:attributeGroup>
    <xs:element name="attributeSampleThree">
      <xs:complexType>
        <xs:attributeGroup ref="groupA"/>
      </xs:complexType>
    </xs:element>
</xs:schema>
```

The following XML document validates against the preceding XSD:

```
<?xml version="1.0" encoding="UTF-8"?>
<attributeSampleThree
  attributeA="0"
  attributeB="String"
/>
```

Extending XSD

The *X* in *XSD* stands for *extensible*, which we've touched upon. In the previous lesson, you extended the `simpleType` using a `restriction` to limit the possible values of an element. Later in the lesson, you looked at creating your own data types using the `complexType`, which added more expressive capabilities to XSD. Extending a `simpleType` by restriction is one form of extending XSD. This lesson discusses how you can allow XML documents to contain other elements you didn't anticipate when you designed your XSD, and other ways you can extend existing XSD documents or data types.

While it may be possible to define data types that are perfect for your needs, eventually you'll need to redefine an existing type or extend it in some way to address an unanticipated need or requirement. For example, assume you have an XSD that defines the basic traits of an address in your country. The following XSD represents a generic address:

```
<?xml version="1.0" encoding-"UTF-8"?>
<xs:schema xmlns:xs="http://www.w3.org/2001/XMLSchema">
```

```
<xs:complexType name="address">
  <xs:sequence>
    <xs:element name="street"
      type="xs:string"/>
    <xs:element name="city"
      type="xs:string" />
  </xs:sequence>
</xs:complexType>
<xs:element name="myAddress"
  type="address"/>
</xs:schema>
```

The XSD captures two essential elements of an address: `street` and `city`. Using the `address` type yields the following XML document:

```
<?xml version="1.0" encoding-"UTF-8"?>
<myAddress>
  <street>Front Street West</street>
  <city>Toronto</city>
</myAddress>
```

The problem with this XML document is that it doesn't capture all elements that make up a valid address (in this case, Canadian). As the designer of the XSD document, it's your role to either capture all possible types of addresses from around the world in your specification, or provide a means of extending your definition of an address so others can customize it to their needs. Defining all possible types of addresses from around the world is a long and difficult task, because there isn't a uniform method of specifying an address for all countries. For example, an address in India could look something like this:

> 1 Entrenchment Road
> Near St. Ann's College
> West Marredpaly, Secunderabad
> AP, 500026, India

Whereas an address in Poland could look like this:

> UI. Bosmanska 1
> 81-116 Gdynia
> Poland

Allowing Any Elements to Appear as Part of a Choice or Sequence

One approach to capturing address formats and styles in your XSD could be to require basic information using some elements, while allowing XML documents to contain other elements yet still be considered valid against your XSD. You can create an XSD using the any element, which allows XML documents to contain any elements as long as they conform to the requirements the XSD sets out. For example, consider the following XSD:

```
<?xml version="1.0" encoding="UTF-8"?>
<!-- 01 --> <xs:schema xmlns:xs="http://www.w3.org/2001/XMLSchema">
<!-- 02 -->   <xs:complexType name="address">
<!-- 03 -->     <xs:sequence>
<!-- 04 -->       <xs:element name="street"
                      type="xs:string"
                      minOccurs="1"/>
<!-- 05 -->       <xs:element name="city"
                      type="xs:string"
                      minOccurs="1"/>
<!-- 06 -->       <xs:any/>
<!-- 07 -->     </xs:sequence>
<!-- 08 -->   </xs:complexType>
<!-- 09 -->   <xs:element name="myAddress"
                    type="address"/>
<!-- 10 --> </xs:schema>
```

This XSD specifies that an address must have at least a street and a city (both elements have minOccurs=1), as shown on lines 04 and 05. XML documents can contain *one* element that doesn't appear in the XSD, as shown in line 06. The any element acts as a wild card, allowing any XML content as long as it's well-formed XML. For example, the following XML validates against the preceding XSD:

```
<?xml version="1.0" encoding="UTF-8"?>
<myAddress>
   <buildingNumber>301</buildingNumber >
   <street>Front Street West</street>
   <city>Toronto</city>
</myAddress>
```

You can use the minOccurs and maxOccurs attributes to specify how many unde-clared elements an XML document can contain. Use maxOccurs='unbounded' to allow any number of undeclared elements in an XML document.

The any element has a processContent attribute that defines how strict an XML processor will be when validating an XML document against an XSD containing the any element. There are three settings you can use with the processContent attribute:

➤ strict: An XML processor validates any elements that appear in place of an any element.

➤ lax: An XML processor will try to validate any elements that appear in place of an any attribute. However, if it cannot validate the elements, it won't consider them invalid.

➤ skip: An XML processor won't attempt to validate any elements that appear in place of an any element.

The only restriction on using an any element is that it can appear only as part of a choice or sequence element.

Extending XSD Through Extension

XSD supports a hierarchy of data types in which one data type can derive from another data type. For example, the address type in the previous sec-tion describes a basic address. You could derive from that type to create a new type, as shown in Figure 4.6.

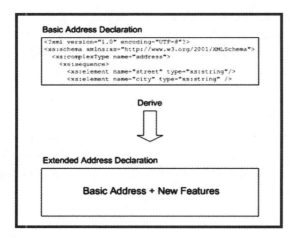

Figure 4.6

Creating a new type through extension.

When you derive one type from another, you create a new type by extending an existing type to suit your needs. For example, Figure 4.6 shows an extended address declaration that's made up of a basic address plus some new features. The extended address is said to *inherit* all of the features of the basic address, as well as adding its own new features to suit the new type's purpose.

Extending a data type through extension is different than extending a data type through restriction. When you restrict a data type, you limit the value it can have based on a sequence, choice, or enumeration. When you derive one type from another, the new type takes on the characteristics of the type you're deriving from in addition to adding its own new features.

Extending a simpleType

You can create a new type based on an existing XSD type, a simpleType, or a complexType. The address type we looked at earlier is a complexType. We'll return to that example shortly. Consider the following XSD fragment:

```
<xs:simpleType name="size">
  <xs:restriction base="xs:string">
    <xs:enumeration value="small"/>
    <xs:enumeration value="medium"/>
    <xs:enumeration value="large"/>
  </xs:restriction>
</xs:simpleType>
```

The XSD fragment defines a simpleType element that's restricted to the values "small," "medium," and "large." I want to use this type to define a list of menu items in an XSD that I plan to use for a restaurant. I want to capture what customers order in an attribute and store the size of the item using the size element defined by the preceding XSD fragment. Here's what I want the XML document to look like:

```
<?xml version="1.0" encoding="UTF-8"?>
<order item="drink">large</order>
```

This is an excellent candidate for deriving a new type from an existing type, because the existing type already suits most of my needs. I just need to add a new attribute called item and restrict its possible value to items on the menu.

When you create a new type by extension, you must use the `complexType` element, regardless of whether the type is actually complex. Here's an XSD fragment that adds the `item` attribute to the `size` element:

```
<!-- 01 --> <xs:complexType name="menu">
<!-- 02 -->   <xs:simpleContent>
<!-- 03 -->     <xs:extension base="size">
<!-- 04 -->       <xs:attribute name="item">
<!-- 05 -->         <xs:simpleType>
<!-- 06 -->           <xs:restriction base="xs:string">
<!-- 07 -->             <xs:enumeration value="drink"/>
<!-- 08 -->             <xs:enumeration value="sandwich"/>
<!-- 09 -->             <xs:enumeration value="soup"/>
<!-- 10 -->           </xs:restriction>
<!-- 11 -->         </xs:simpleType>
<!-- 12 -->       </xs:attribute>
<!-- 13 -->     </xs:extension>
<!-- 14 -->   </xs:simpleContent>
<!-- 15 --> </xs:complexType>
```

The fragment introduces a new element, `simpleContent`, on line 02. A `simpleContent` element allows you to extend either a `complexType` or a `simpleType`, with only one restriction: You cannot create a new element. You can only add new attributes because, by definition, a `simpleType` doesn't have any child elements. Line 03 introduces another new element: `extension`. This element defines what type it's extending using the `base` attribute. In this example, the `extension` element defines its `base` as the `size` element from the preceding listing. Line 04 begins the description of the new attribute, called `item`. The new attribute is a `simpleType` that's a restriction of the XSD `string` type. The restriction limits the possible values that the new attribute can have to "drink," "sandwich," and "soup." Lines 10 to 15 close all of the parent elements. The end result of the combined declarations is that I reused the existing `size` element and customized it to suit my needs. If you want the sample to be a little more realistic and allow multiple orders in an XML document, add the following:

```
<xs:element name="orders">
  <xs:complexType>
    <xs:sequence minOccurs="1" maxOccurs="unbounded">
```

```
        <xs:element name="order" type="menu"/>
    </xs:sequence>
  </xs:complexType>
</xs:element>
```

The resulting XML document looks like this:

```
<?xml version="1.0" encoding="UTF-8"?>
<orders xsi:noNamespaceSchemaLocation="orders.xsd">
  <order item="drink">small</order>
  <order item="sandwich">large</order>
</orders>
```

Extending a complexType

Complex types grant you more freedom when you extend types. Not only can you add new attributes, but you can add new elements to them. Consider the following XSD from earlier in this lesson:

```
<xs:schema xmlns:xs="http://www.w3.org/2001/XMLSchema">
<xs:complexType name="address">
  <xs:sequence>
    <xs:element name="street"
      type="xs:string"
      minOccurs="1"/>
    <xs:element name="city"
      type="xs:string"
      minOccurs="1"/>
  </xs:sequence>
</xs:complexType>
```

I want to extend this type to accommodate a Canadian address so that the final XML document looks like this:

```
<?xml version="1.0" encoding-"UTF-8"?>
<myAddress>
  <buildingNumber>301</buildingNumber>
  <street>Front Street West</street>
  <city>Toronto</city>
  <province>Ontario</province>
  <postalCode>M5V-2T6</postalCode>
</myAddress>
```

Take this one step at a time, and begin by creating a new type based on the existing address type:

```
<xs:complexType name="canadianAddress">
  <xs:complexContent>
    <xs:extension base="address">
```

The second line in the listing declares the content of the new type as complexContent because you will add new elements to the existing type. As a result, you must use the complexContent element. The third line defines the data type you're extending—the address type. The next thing to do is to look at which type of information you want to capture. Is it a list, sequence, choice, or group? A sequence or an all element is good in this case, because the order doesn't really matter as long as all the information is present. The first elements to add to the address are the building number and optional apartment number, as shown in the following listing:

```
<xs:element name="buildingNumber"
  type="xs:positiveInteger"
  minOccurs="1"
  maxOccurs="1"/>


<xs:element name="apartment"
  type="xs:positiveInteger"
  minOccurs="0"
  maxOccurs="1"/>
```

The buildingNumber is required, must be a positive number, and can appear only once in an address. As a result, its minOccurs and maxOccurs attributes are both 1. The apartment number is an optional element, because not all addresses have apartment numbers. As a result, its minOccurs is 0, while the maxOccurs attribute is 1. Define the province element next, and restrict its possible values to valid Canadian provinces. The following listing demonstrates how to declare the province element:

```
<xs:element name="province" minOccurs="1" maxOccurs="1">
  <xs:complexType>
    <xs:simpleContent>
      <xs:restriction base="xs:string">
        <xs:enumeration value="Alberta"/>
        <xs:enumeration value="British Columbia"/>
```

```
            <xs:enumeration value="Manitoba"/>
            <xs:enumeration value="New Brunswick"/>
            <xs:enumeration value="Newfoundland and Labrador"/>
            <xs:enumeration value="Northwest Territories"/>
            <xs:enumeration value="Nova Scotia"/>
            <xs:enumeration value="Nunavit"/>
            <xs:enumeration value="Prince Edward Island"/>
            <xs:enumeration value="Saskatchewan"/>
            <xs:enumeration value="Quebec"/>
            <xs:enumeration value="Yukon"/>
          </xs:restriction>
        </xs:simpleContent>
      </xs:complexType>
    </xs:element>
```

The province element is very straightforward. It's an XSD string type that's restricted to a list of possible provinces, and it's a mandatory element (based on the values of an element's minOccurs and maxOccurs attributes).

The Canadian postal code is next. Here's its declaration:

```
<xs:element name="postalCode" minOccurs="1" maxOccurs="1">
  <xs:complexType>
    <xs:simpleContent>
      <xs:restriction base="xs:string">
        <xs:pattern value="[A-Z]\d[A-Z]-\d[A-Z]\d"/>
      </xs:restriction>
    </xs:simpleContent>
  </xs:complexType>
</xs:element>
```

Recall that the pattern of a Canadian postal code consists of a letter, number, letter, dash or space, number, letter, and number. The postalCode element uses a regular expression to define the pattern and indicates that the element is mandatory through its minOccurs and maxOccurs attributes. Now you need to close all of the remaining elements, as shown:

```
        </xs:sequence>
      </xs:extension>
    </xs:complexContent>
  </xs:complexType>
```

Now the only thing left to do is to define the root element, as shown in the following listing:

```
<xs:element name="addresses">
  <xs:complexType>
    <xs:all minOccurs="1" maxOccurs="unbounded">
      <xs:element name="address" type="canadianAddress"/>
    </xs:all>
  </xs:complexType>
</xs:element>
```

This listing uses an all element to enclose a list of address elements within the root addresses element. The resulting XML document can contain an unlimited number of address elements, but must contain at least one. As a result, the minOccurs attribute is 1 and the maxOccurs attribute is unbounded. I used the all element to enclose the address elements. That makes more sense than using a sequence element, because there's only one element in the list.

The thing to notice in that listing is the simplicity of declaring a canadianAddress type. The single line declaration encompasses all of the functionality that we've discussed up to this point. Here's what the resulting XML document looks like:

```
<?xml version="1.0" encoding="UTF-8"?>
<addresses xsi:noNamespaceSchemaLocation="canadianAddress.xsd">
  <address>
    <street>Front Street West</street>
    <city>Toronto</city>
    <buildingNumber>301</buildingNumber>
    <province>Ontario</province>
    <postalCode>M5V-2T6</postalCode>
  </address>
  <address>
    <street>Queen Street</street>
    <city>Charlottetown</city>
    <buildingNumber>479</buildingNumber>
    <province>Prince Edward Island</province>
    <postalCode>C1A-5C6</postalCode>
  </address>
</addresses>
```

This XML file has all the relevant information in it, but it appears to be out of order because the street and city elements appear first for each address. This is a result of how the canadianAddress type is composed: canadianAddress extends the address type. As a result, the address type must appear first, followed by the canadianAddress-specific features. The order of the elements isn't important, because most XML-aware applications will query an XML file for specific elements and attributes whenever necessary. The important thing is that all of the required information is present.

Here's the complete listing of the XSD document:

```
<?xml version="1.0" encoding="UTF-8"?>
<xs:schema xmlns:xs="http://www.w3.org/2001/XMLSchema">
  <xs:complexType name="address">
    <xs:sequence>
      <xs:element name="street"
        type="xs:string" minOccurs="1"/>
      <xs:element name="city"
        type="xs:string" minOccurs="1"/>
    </xs:sequence>
  </xs:complexType>
  <xs:complexType name="canadianAddress">
    <xs:complexContent>
      <xs:extension base="address">
        <xs:sequence>
          <xs:element name="buildingNumber"
            type="xs:positiveInteger"
            minOccurs="1" maxOccurs="1"/>
          <xs:element name="apartment"
            type="xs:positiveInteger"
            minOccurs="0" maxOccurs="1"/>
          <xs:element name="province"
            minOccurs="1" maxOccurs="1">
            <xs:complexType>
              <xs:simpleContent>
                <xs:restriction base="xs:string">
                  <xs:enumeration value="Alberta"/>
                  <xs:enumeration value="British Columbia"/>
                  <xs:enumeration value="Manitoba"/>
```

```
                            <xs:enumeration value="New Brunswick"/>
                            <xs:enumeration value="Newfoundland and Labrador"/>
                            <xs:enumeration value="Northwest Territories"/>
                            <xs:enumeration value="Nova Scotia"/>
                            <xs:enumeration value="Nunavit"/>
                            <xs:enumeration value="Prince Edward Island"/>
                            <xs:enumeration value="Saskatchewan"/>
                            <xs:enumeration value="Quebec"/>
                            <xs:enumeration value="Yukon"/>
                         </xs:restriction>
                      </xs:simpleContent>
                   </xs:complexType>
                </xs:element>
                <xs:element name="postalCode" minOccurs="1" maxOccurs="1">
                   <xs:complexType>
                      <xs:simpleContent>
                         <xs:restriction base="xs:string">
                            <xs:pattern value="[A-Z]\d[A-Z]-\d[A-Z]\d"/>
                         </xs:restriction>
                      </xs:simpleContent>
                   </xs:complexType>
                </xs:element>
             </xs:sequence>
          </xs:extension>
       </xs:complexContent>
    </xs:complexType>
    <xs:element name="addresses">
       <xs:complexType>
          <xs:all minOccurs="1" maxOccurs="unbounded">
             <xs:element name="address" type="canadianAddress"/>
          </xs:all>
       </xs:complexType>
    </xs:element>
</xs:schema>
```

This just scratches the surface. There's an amazing array of potential solutions. Using the skills you've gained so far will enable you to build and analyze complex and useful systems using just XSD and XML.

Identity Constraints

Sometimes you'll want to ensure that an item of data is unique to a data set whose role is to uniquely identify one particular item. For example, people in most countries have some type of government-issued identification. This identification usually distinguishes one person from another not by name, but by some other aspect, such as a unique number or sequence of letters and numbers. Another example is the license plate of a car. Most countries require that no two vehicles have identical license numbers or plates, to help identify a particular car from all the others. This type of unique identification is referred to in the database world as an *identity constraint*, or a *key*.

An identity constraint limits the possible values that a particular field of data can have, ensuring that each instance of the field has a unique (different) value. Let's say you want to store the license numbers of a number of cars, along with the names of the people who own the cars. While it's possible for one person to own more than one car (or for more than one person to have the same name), you want to ensure that all of the cars' license numbers are different. This is what the XML document looks like:

```
<?xml version="1.0" encoding="UTF-8"?>
<licenseNumbers xmlns:xsi="http://www.w3.org/2001/XMLSchema-instance"
    xsi:noNamespaceSchemaLocation="licenseNumbers.xsd">
  <license licenseNumber="292DAD" ownerName="Essam Ahmed"/>
  <license licenseNumber="TRAN582" ownerName="Tom Archer"/>
  <license licenseNumber="CP2002" ownerName="Chris Maunder"/>
  <license licenseNumber="AUK7NZ" ownerName="Colin Davies"/>
  <license licenseNumber="DEVCOM1" ownerName="Brad Jones"/>
</licenseNumbers>
```

You could create an XSD document that validates the document's structure:

```
<xs:complexType name="license_t">
  <xs:simpleContent>
    <xs:extension base="xs:string">
      <xs:attribute name="licenseNumber" type="xs:string"/>
      <xs:attribute name="ownerName" type="xs:string"/>
    </xs:extension>
  </xs:simpleContent>
</xs:complexType>
```

This XSD doesn't limit the value that the licenseNumber attribute can have, however. XSD provides a unique construct, which specifies a different value for each instance of a particular element or attribute. You can use a unique element to limit the value of the license_t type's licenseNumber attribute to unique values.

The XSD's unique element allows you to define which identity constraints to place on a data set. The syntax of the element is shown here:

```
<xs:unique
  name="..."
</xs:unique>
```

The name attribute declares the name of the constraint, which must not match any other names in the XSD document. There are some limits on how you can use this element:

➤ The unique element can appear only at the end of a type's declaration.

➤ A type can have only one unique declaration.

➤ The name is a required attribute and may not contain any colon (:) characters.

➤ The unique element can contain only selector and field elements (described next).

Here's an example of what a complete unique element looks like:

```
<xs:unique name="nameOfKey">
  <xs:selector xpath="expression"/>
  <xs:field xpath="expression"/>
</xs:unique>
```

The selector and field elements work together to define which data in an XML document must be unique. Both elements have an xpath attribute that represents a range of elements or attributes in an existing XML document. The xpath attribute uses a special XML vocabulary (syntax) called XPath, or XML Path (discussed in detail later on Sunday afternoon). For example, the following XPath expression returns a list of all license elements that reside within the licenseNumbers element:

```
/licenseNumbers/license
```

The easiest way to understand XPath is to think of an XML document as a hierarchy of information. For example, Figure 4.7 shows a conceptual view of the licenseNumbers XML document.

If you want to refer to all licenseNumbers children, start at the root, select the licenseNumbers element (the root node), and describe what you're interested in—license elements, in this example. Figure 4.8 shows what the previous XPath expression looks like when you break it down.

The selector element, in conjunction with its xpath attribute, selects the overall parts of an XML document that should contain unique data. In other words, the selector element defines a range that should contain some unique data. You can define more than one XPath expression in the xpath

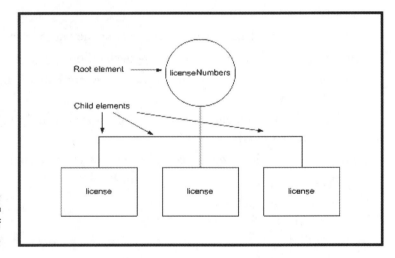

Figure 4.7

Hierarchical view of an XML document.

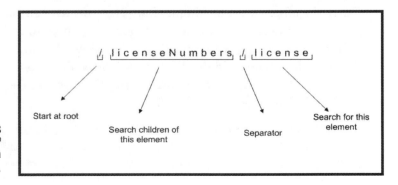

Figure 4.8

Detailed view of an XPath expression.

attribute. Just separate each XPath expression using a single space. When you use more than one XPath expression with a selector, the element works by selecting all of the ranges your XPath expressions identify, and then combines them into a single set of elements.

The field element's xpath attribute also contains an XPath expression. However, the field element represents which part of the range defined by the selector element must contain unique data. Returning to the licenses example, the selector should select all license elements, and the field that must contain unique data is the licenseNumber attribute. Here's what the unique element looks like so far:

```
<xs:unique name="license_pk">
  <xs:selector xpath="license"/>
  <xs:field xpath="@licenseNumber"/>
</xs:unique>
```

Earlier I mentioned that the unique element has some restrictions related to how you can use it. Here's the XSD that declares the licenceNumbers root element, the license element, and its unique element:

```
<xs:element name="licenseNumbers">
  <xs:complexType>
    <xs:sequence>
      <xs:element
        name="license"
        type="license_t"
        maxOccurs="unbounded"/>
    </xs:sequence>
  </xs:complexType>
  <xs:unique name="license_pk">
    <xs:selector xpath="license"/>
    <xs:field xpath="@licenseNumber"/>
  </xs:unique>
</xs:element>
```

This listing shows that the unique element is at the end of the licenseNumbers element's declaration. In addition, notice that the field element's xpath attribute has an expression that begins with an @ symbol. In the XPath syntax, this indicates that the expression represents the name of an attribute. In this case, the field refers to the license element's licenseNumber attribute.

If you're following closely, you'll notice that the listing has a reference to a license_t type. Here's its declaration as part of the entire XSD document:

```xml
<?xml version="1.0" encoding="UTF-8"?>
<xs:schema xmlns:xs="http://www.w3.org/2001/XMLSchema">
  <xs:complexType name="license_t">
    <xs:simpleContent>
      <xs:extension base="xs:string">
        <xs:attribute name="licenseNumber" type="xs:string"/>
        <xs:attribute name="ownerName" type="xs:string"/>
      </xs:extension>
    </xs:simpleContent>
  </xs:complexType>
  <xs:element name="licenseNumbers">
    <xs:complexType>
      <xs:sequence>
        <xs:element name="license" type="license_t" maxOccurs="unbounded"/>
      </xs:sequence>
    </xs:complexType>
    <xs:unique name="license_pk">
      <xs:selector xpath="license"/>
      <xs:field xpath="@licenseNumber"/>
    </xs:unique>
  </xs:element>
</xs:schema>
```

The license_t type is a complexType that defines two attributes through extension, and it's a global declaration. The license element appears later in the XSD, within the licenseNumbers element declaration.

Referential Integrity Using keyref

Identity constraints are very useful. They ensure that an XML document allows other applications to uniquely identify some or all of its data in a way that's similar to commercial database systems. Another aspect of uniqueness is *referential integrity*.

Referential integrity has two parts: a reference and a check. A *reference* is a reference to a unique part of a data set (the value of a licenseNumber attribute in the previous example), and a *check* confirms that the reference refers to an existing value. If the reference refers to a nonexistent value, it's considered to be invalid and an XML processor will raise an error. Referential integrity is important in large data sets, where data from one data set refers to data in another data set. Commercial database systems even go so far as to maintain a link between related data sets (those that refer to each other). When a unique item of data is deleted from one data set, its corresponding reference in the other data set also gets deleted.

XSD implements referential integrity using the keyref construct. Its syntax looks like this:

```
<keyref name="..." refer="...">
  <selector xpath="..."/>
  <field xpath="..."/>
</keyref>
```

The name attribute should be familiar to you by now. It's a required attribute that defines the reference's name. The refer attribute is the name of an existing unique element, defining which part of the data must reference an existing unique value. The keyref element must have two child elements: selector and field. As with the unique element (described in the preceding section), both elements have an xpath attribute which must contain an XPath expression. The difference in this case is that the selector and field elements define which part of the data actually contains the reference. When combined, the entire keyref element relates a value in one part of a data set with an existing value in another part of the same data set.

The discussion has been a little abstract so far. Time for an example. Let's say you want to have an XML document that contains information about customers and how much they buy. You decide that you want a structure that looks something like the one shown in Figure 4.9. The boxes represent tables, or sets of data. The customer table has two important pieces of information about each of your customers: identification number and name. You decide that this structure suits your needs, because you plan to reuse the customer type in some other way in the future. The customerSales table contains information on how much you sell to each customer. Because you want to make sure that you have the right sales figure for each customer, you also have a customerID field, which represents the customer's identification number.

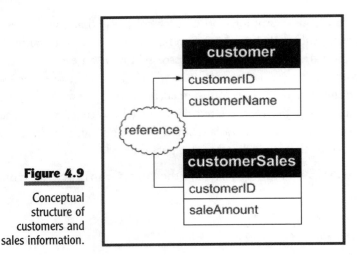

Figure 4.9

Conceptual
structure of
customers and
sales information.

The `customerSales` table is said to reference the `customers` table using the value of the `customerID` field, because that field must refer to an existing `customer`. If a `customerSale` becomes disassociated with a customer, it's said to become *orphaned*. Orphaned information isn't useful because you have no way of determining what the orphan originally referred to.

When you use the structure in Figure 4.9 as a model for an XML document, you end up with a document that looks like this:

```
<?xml version="1.0" encoding="UTF-8"?>
<!--Sample XML file generated by XML Spy v4.3 U
(http://www.xmlspy.com)-->
<salesInformation>
  <customers>
    <customer customerName="Essam Ahmed" customerID="1"/>
    <customer customerName="Stephen Lee" customerID="2"/>
    <customer customerName="John Schoep" customerID="3"/>
  </customers>
  <customerSales>
    <sale saleAmount="100" customerID="1"/>
    <sale saleAmount="200" customerID="2"/>
    <sale saleAmount="300" customerID="3"/>
  </customerSales>
</salesInformation>
```

The only deviation from the original model is that I enclosed the document in the salesInformation root element. The document is valid as it is at the moment, because all sale elements' customerID attributes refer to existing customer elements' customerID attributes. You can invalidate the document by adding a new sale element that looks similar to the following:

```
<sale saleAmount="400" customerID="4"/>
```

The new sale invalidates the document because its customerID attribute refers to a nonexistent customer. As a result, the new sale element is considered to be an orphan. You can use XSD to ensure that all sale elements have a customerID attribute that refers to an existing customer element's customerID attribute.

Let's design a new XSD document! The best place to begin is by designing the two tables shown in Figure 4.9. Instead of composing each table out of a single element, define the fields in each table as attributes of a new type. The following listing defines the fields that appear in both the customers and customerSales tables by creating two new data types:

```
<xs:complexType name="customer_t">
  <xs:simpleContent>
    <xs:extension base="xs:string">
      <xs:attribute name="customerName"
        type="xs:string"/>
      <xs:attribute name="customerID"
        type="xs:positiveInteger"/>
    </xs:extension>
  </xs:simpleContent>
</xs:complexType>

<xs:complexType name="sale_t">
  <xs:simpleContent>
    <xs:extension base="xs:string">
      <xs:attribute name="saleAmount"
        type="xs:positiveInteger"/>
      <xs:attribute name="customerID"
        type="xs:positiveInteger"/>
    </xs:extension>
  </xs:simpleContent>
</xs:complexType>
```

This listing creates two global definitions for two new types: customer_t and sale_t (the _t stands for "type"). The next step is to associate the fields with their respective tables. The customers table is straightforward because it has a unique constraint—something you're already familiar with. Here's how to define the customers table and associate it with the customer_t type:

```
<xs:element name="customers">
  <xs:complexType>
    <xs:sequence>
      <xs:element name="customer" type="customer_t"
maxOccurs="unbounded"/>
    </xs:sequence>
  </xs:complexType>
  <xs:unique name="customer_pk">
    <xs:selector xpath="customer"/>
    <xs:field xpath="@customerID"/>
  </xs:unique>
</xs:element>
```

The customers table contains an unlimited number of customer elements, each of which represents one of your customers. The unique constraint declares that the values of all customer elements' customerID attributes must be unique. You cannot have two identical customerID values. The customerSales table introduces the keyref element. Here's its declaration:

```
<xs:element name="customerSales">

  <xs:complexType>
    <xs:sequence>
      <xs:element name="sale"
        type="sale_t"
        maxOccurs="unbounded"/>
    </xs:sequence>
  </xs:complexType>

  <xs:keyref name="custSale" refer="customer_pk">
    <xs:selector xpath="sale"/>
    <xs:field xpath="@customerID"/>
```

```
    </xs:keyref>
```

```
</xs:element>
```

The customerSales element contains the sale element, which has information about each customer's sales. The sale element's maxOccurs is unbounded, to allow an unlimited number of sale elements. The keyref element's refer attribute is set to reference the customer element's customerID attribute through the customer_pk unique constraint, indicating that the value that the selector and field element's xpath members refer to is constrained to existing customer elements' customerID attributes.

The very last thing to do is declare the salesInformation element, which encloses the entire XML document. Here's the declaration for the salesInformation element:

```
<xs:element name="salesInformation">
  <xs:complexType>
    <xs:sequence>
      <xs:element ref="customers"/>
      <xs:element ref="customerSales"/>
    </xs:sequence>
  </xs:complexType>
</xs:element>
```

The salesInformation element is simple when you compare it to the rest of the XSD, because its elements just refer to the customer and customerSales global element declarations. Later on, I'll show you how to use XML Spy to validate the XSD and XML documents. For your reference, here's the entire XSD:

```
<?xml version="1.0" encoding="UTF-8"?>
<xs:schema xmlns:xs="http://www.w3.org/2001/XMLSchema"
elementFormDefault="qualified" attributeFormDefault="unqualified">
  <xs:complexType name="customer_t">
    <xs:simpleContent>
      <xs:extension base="xs:string">
        <xs:attribute name="customerName"
          type="xs:string"/>
        <xs:attribute name="customerID"
```

```
                type="xs:positiveInteger"/>
          </xs:extension>
        </xs:simpleContent>
      </xs:complexType>
      <xs:complexType name="sale_t">
        <xs:simpleContent>
          <xs:extension base="xs:string">
            <xs:attribute name="saleAmount"
              type="xs:positiveInteger"/>
            <xs:attribute name="customerID"
              type="xs:positiveInteger"/>
          </xs:extension>
        </xs:simpleContent>
      </xs:complexType>
      <xs:element name="customers">
        <xs:complexType>
          <xs:sequence>
            <xs:element name="customer"
              type="customer_t"
              maxOccurs="unbounded"/>
          </xs:sequence>
        </xs:complexType>
        <xs:unique name="customer_pk">
          <xs:selector xpath="customer"/>
          <xs:field xpath="@customerID"/>
        </xs:unique>
      </xs:element>
      <xs:element name="customerSales">
        <xs:complexType>
          <xs:sequence>
            <xs:element name="sale"
              type="sale_t"
              maxOccurs="unbounded"/>
          </xs:sequence>
        </xs:complexType>
  <xs:keyref name="custSale"
    refer="customer_pk">
        <xs:selector xpath="sale"/>
```

```
        <xs:field xpath="@customerID"/>
     </xs:keyref>
   </xs:element>
   <xs:element name="salesInformation">
     <xs:complexType>
       <xs:sequence>
         <xs:element ref="customers"/>
         <xs:element ref="customerSales"/>
       </xs:sequence>
     </xs:complexType>
   </xs:element>
</xs:schema>
```

What's Next?

Congratulations, you've just finished learning the essential components of XML! With this strong foundation in place, it's time to start using some tools to create, validate, and work with XML documents, DTDs, and XML Schemas. It's Saturday evening. Take a break and come back tomorrow morning. We'll begin with an overview of two XML editors, Stylus Studio and XML Spy. You'll download trial versions of both products, so you'll need your Internet connection.

XML Tools

➤ **Understanding XML Editors**
➤ **XML Spy**
➤ **Stylus Studio**
➤ **How XML Tools Relate to Microsoft's XML Technologies**

Glad to see you back after your break. It's Sunday morning, and it's time to get your mind going. You'll start by working with some XML tools, in the afternoon you'll learn how to present XML on the Web by transforming it into HTML (the publishing language of the Internet), and you'll round out the day by looking at how XML integrates with technologies like Microsoft's Active Server Pages (ASP), the Microsoft .NET Framework, and other technologies.

The last two lessons covered core XML concepts: syntax and data modeling. Now you're ready to put those skills to use with XML tools. There are three types of tools you use to work with XML, and the first two are essential:

➤ XML parsers

➤ XSL parsers

➤ XML editors

As you've learned, an XML parser is software that interprets XML elements, ensures that an XML document is well-formed, and validates an XML document against its schema. You've had only a cursory introduction to XSL so far, but there's plenty more information in this afternoon's session. XSL is an XML vocabulary that allows you to transform an XML document into new formats, like HTML. The focus of this lesson is XML editors and development tools.

Understanding XML Editors

The underlying theme of the book so far is that XML is very accessible to both computers and people, because XML documents are just simple text files that you can create and edit using an application as simple as Windows Notepad. XML editors and development tools provide a number of benefits and features, including

➤ Integration with XML parsers

➤ Graphical and structured editing

➤ Integrated well-formedness checking

➤ Validation of XML documents as they're edited or created

➤ Automatic generation of XML schemas (DTD, XSD, XDR, etc.)

➤ Auto-completion (text entry shortcuts)

➤ XPath expression testing and validation

➤ Integration with source code control systems

➤ Project management features

➤ Visual XSLT design

➤ Graphical schema design

➤ Integration with database systems for easy data migration

➤ XSL debugging

Benefit: Integration with XML Parsers

Because XML is a standards-backed specification, it enjoys broad acceptance from a number of software tools and operating system vendors. As a result, XML is said to be *cross-platform* because vendors implement their XML-aware software or XML parsers based on the official W3C specification. Recall that XML documents by themselves aren't that interesting because they only contain marked-up text. They're useful in the context of systems that generate, manipulate, and otherwise work with, present, and exchange information using XML documents.

Because XML is an open, cross-platform standard, there are many types of XML parsers available, most of which are free. XML parsers don't have a standard implementation. That is, software vendors and individual developers are free to design their own XML parser as long as it processes XML documents as described by the W3C specification. As a result, some XML parsers may have a friendly, graphical interface that you can work with, while others may not have an interface at all and require programmers to work with them using special programming approaches. Popular XML parsers include Xerces, from the Apache XML Project, and Microsoft XML Core Services 4.0 (the parser formerly known as the "Microsoft XML Parser"), both of which are implemented very differently yet perform similar functions. XML editors bridge the gap between the various parsers by integrating with the more popular parsers, providing their own internal parser as well as allowing you to use a custom XML parser. Figure 5.1 shows a screen from eXcelon Stylus Studio, an XML editor that allows you to select a specific parser that you want Stylus Studio to work with.

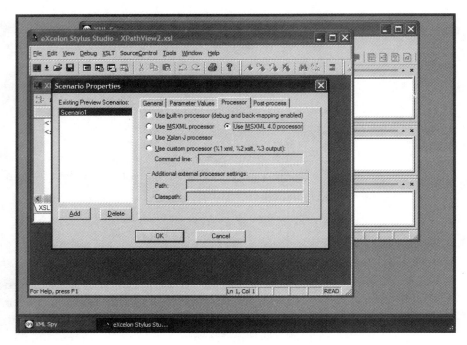

Figure 5.1

Selecting an XML parser in eXcelon Stylus Studio.

XML Spy provides a similar means of integrating with XML parsers, as shown in Figure 5.2.

Benefit: Graphical and Structured Editing

Working with plain text documents can be difficult because they look very uniform when looked at as a whole. For example, Figure 5.3 shows an XML document that describes the features of a compact disc, as viewed using Windows Notepad on Windows XP.

If you look really closely, you might be able to discern some XML tags within the text. The document is indented in an attempt to make it easier to read. Although indenting tags does help, it could be better. Figure 5.4 shows the same part of the document shown in Figure 5.3, using XML Spy's editor in enhanced grid view mode.

The grid view looks a little different at first glance, but it does logically present the XML document and allows you to make changes without having to be exposed to the underlying XML tags. The grid view structures the data

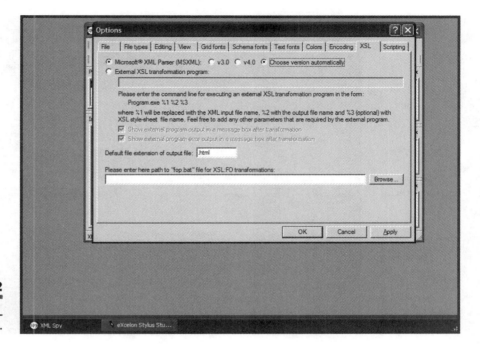

Figure 5.2

XML Spy's XML parser options.

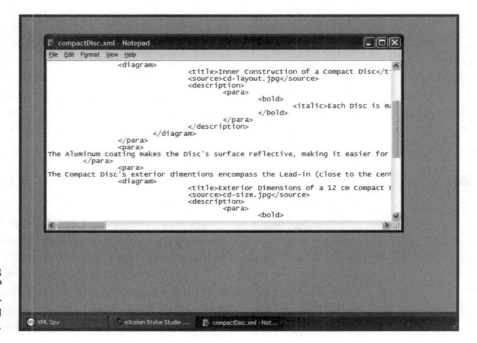

Figure 5.3

Viewing an XML document using Windows Notepad.

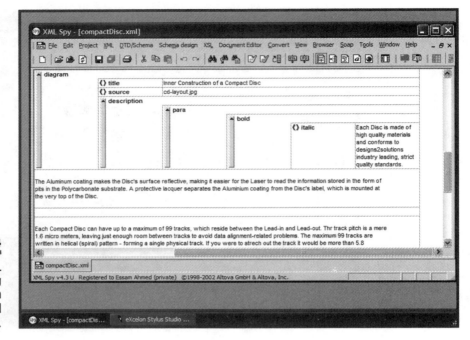

Figure 5.4

Viewing an XML document using XML Spy in enhanced grid view mode.

and allows you to "drill down" into the details by expanding elements that contain subelements. The diagram, description, para, bold, and italic elements have all been expanded in Figure 5.4.

Stylus Studio also introduces a tree-based view. It structures an XML document in the same way that the grid view does, but presents the document as a hierarchy of nodes. Figure 5.5 shows the same part of the document from the preceding two figures, viewed this time using the tree view.

Benefit: Integrated Well-Formedness Checking

It's a valuable exercise to check the well-formedness of your XML documents, confirming that their content conforms to the essential syntax that was described on Saturday afternoon. However, this can become tedious when you're already familiar with the rules and just want to know where you may have made a typing mistake. XML editors use various approaches to prevent a document from being badly formed in the first place. For example, when you create a new element in XML Spy using the text editor, typing the greater-than symbol at the end of the element's opening tag automatically

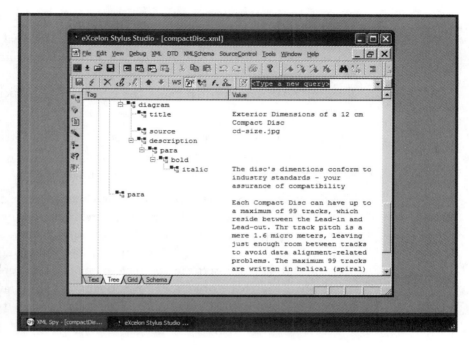

Figure 5.5

Viewing an XML document Stylus Studio's tree view mode.

creates the closing tag. Stylus Studio's text editor takes another approach. It doesn't close the tag for you right away, and instead allows you to continue editing the document. The moment you type the </ character sequence to begin a closing tag, Stylus Studio completes the tag for you by inserting the most recently opened tag. It's an interesting approach and surprises most people the first time they see it at work.

XML editors can also check the well-formedness of existing documents. Both XML Spy and Stylus Studio allow you to perform on-demand well-formedness checks, and both products pinpoint exactly where the problem is and suggest a solution. This feature can save a lot of time figuring out if a document is well-formed.

Benefit: XML Documents Are Validated as They're Edited or Created

The role of XML schemas (DTDs, XSDs) is to ensure that XML documents, more formally referred to as *instance documents*, comply with a given structure and vocabulary. It would be tedious, although not impossible, to manually validate an XML document against its schema. This is because a schema allows a degree of flexibility with regard to optional and mandatory elements and attributes. Not only can an XML editor validate an instance document against its schema, but it can also assist you when editing or creating an XML document because the editor knows which elements and attributes you can use.

Figure 5.6 shows an XML document as viewed using Stylus Studio's text view. The drop-down menu displays a listing of valid elements based on where the user positions the cursor in the document.

The figure shows that the only valid element in the context is the part element. If there are other valid elements or attributes, Stylus Studio displays them in the pop-up menu as well. When you want to add a valid element or attribute, you can type the first few letters of its name to select it and then press the Tab key to insert the complete name. This feature improves your speed when you create or edit an XML document (you have fewer keys to type), and it also dramatically improves accuracy because it's less likely that you'll type in an invalid element or attribute name.

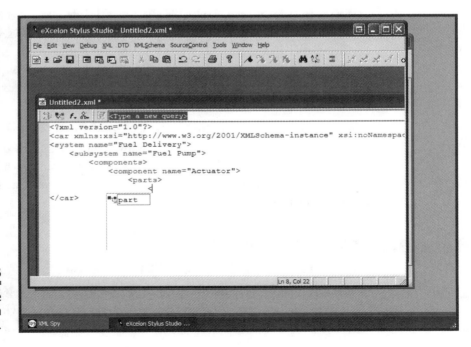

Figure 5.6

Editing an instance document based on a schema.

Benefit: XML Schemas Are Generated Based on an Instance Document

Saturday evening covered the details of understanding, writing, and working with XML schemas (DTDs and XSDs). Sometimes it's more convenient to start with an instance document and work backward to generate the schema. Some people find it easier to visualize a document's structure by expressing it directly using an instance document, as opposed to creating a schema first. You can use XML Spy to create a schema based on an instance document. XML Spy can create DTDs, W3C Schemas (XSD), and several other types of schema documents based on the content of an instance document. It generates the schema document by analyzing the document's structure, reviewing the values of elements and attributes, and determining if those elements and attributes are mandatory based on how they're used throughout the document. Then it generates the schema based on options you select.

The schemas that XML Spy produces are very accurate and are often all you need to validate new instance documents. You can also use these schemas as a starting point for creating a more specialized XML schema, such as one that includes identity constraints or requires instance documents to use specific numeric types.

Benefit: Auto-Complete Text Editing

Because XML documents are essentially text documents, a lot of people prefer to edit the text directly instead of using a graphical editor. *Auto-complete* is an innovation that's pervasive in document-editing applications. The auto-complete feature anticipates what you may type next by reviewing the text surrounding the cursor and combining that information with the keystrokes you type. When the auto-complete feature determines that it can anticipate what you're going to type, it presents an in-line pop-up menu that contains the text that it anticipates you want to type. You can either select from the list, if it guessed correctly, or simply continue to type. The auto-complete feature can increase speed and accuracy while reducing the repetitive nature of typing XML element tags.

Benefit: XPath Expression Testing and Validation

XPath expressions, covered in Sunday afternoon's lesson and in the second half of Appendix A, not only can add a high degree of flexibility to XML document transformations using XSL, but also can provide a means of querying XML data in an XML document without having to review the whole document. Getting XPath expressions correct can be difficult, especially when you're just starting to work with them. XML editors offer a means of creating, editing, and testing XPath expressions against an XML document, making XPath more accessible and easier to work with.

Benefit: Integration with Source Code Control Systems

Most professional developers rely on source code control systems to effectively manage changes to applications' instructions. Like XML, applications are usually written in plain text, using a special syntax that other applications are capable of interpreting. A source code control system allows developers to work with individual text files, much the same way you and I would check a book out of a library. When you go to a library, you can browse for books, borrow them, and return them. A source code control system works on the same basic principle. Developers can browse for code that they want to change, check out the file that contains the code they want to change, and return the file by checking it in. When a file is checked out, other developers cannot check it out. Once a file is returned, a developer can easily determine which changes have been made to the file by comparing the code that was checked out with the code that was checked in. Source code control systems are useful because they allow developers to easily manage a large number of changes to many files while ensuring that each change can be traced, undone, or merged with other code.

XML editors are capable of integrating with source code control systems to make it easier to manage XML files that are under development. A popular source code control system for Windows is Microsoft's Visual Source Safe. Both XML Spy and Stylus Studio integrate with Visual Source Safe, allowing you to manage your XML files directly from within the XML editor. You don't need to use another application to work with Visual Source Safe.

Benefit: Project Management Features

XML editors usually support *projects*, which are groups of related XML files. A project allows you to place XML documents, schemas, XSL files, and other types of files into a logical group that the editor manages for you. Files within a project can be located in any folder on a system, so you can store your files wherever it makes sense to you while maintaining the logical grouping between files in the project. Projects are sometimes the basis for working with source code control systems.

Benefit: Visual XSLT Design

XSL allows you to present XML documents in various forms, including HTML and other XML documents. XSL is very versatile, but it's completely text-based. This makes it difficult to visualize the end result as you design an XSL document. XML tools like XML Spy feature an XSLT Designer, which allows you to create an XSL document using drag-and-drop editing and makes it easy to preview the results. The key benefit of visual XSLT design is that you don't need to know a lot of XSL and HTML, which can save you a lot of time as a result of fewer errors and quick availability of results.

You can use XSL to transform an XML document by adding or removing content, combining several XML documents into a single document, or changing the overall structure to accommodate a new application. Stylus Studio can help you create this type of transformation using its XML-to-XML mapping feature, which also uses a drag-and-drop approach to creating the underlying XSL document.

Benefit: Graphical Schema Design

XML schemas (DTD, XSD) enable XML document designers to describe and enforce relationships, constraints, and other defining features of XML documents. Schemas are text-based documents that can be difficult to work with, given that most data models are designed using graphical editors. Many people are used to describing what an XML document may contain conceptually, but they have difficulty making the transition from the concept to implementation. XML editors support visual schema design, making it easier to visualize the relationships between elements, constraints on data, and the overall structure of an XML document. Graphical XML schema editors help document designers create high-fidelity schemas that model all aspects of an XML document's structure and content, without having to directly edit the underlying schema document.

Benefit: Integration with Database Systems

Because XML is an easily accessible format, it's quickly being adopted by the industry as a simple, portable database system. Database systems usually require that you access their contents using specialized software tools. In contrast, you can view and edit the contents of XML documents using any text editor, such as Windows Notepad. This makes XML documents very accessible. When you think of XML documents in the context of a system that accesses XML documents using an XML parser, it's easy to visualize both elements as a simple database system. As a result, a lot of people are expressing interest in migrating data from databases into XML documents and from XML documents to databases.

XML editors can integrate with database systems like Microsoft Access and Microsoft SQL Server to facilitate quick and easy migration from one data storage medium to another (XML to database and database to XML). This feature saves time because you don't have to purchase specialized software or hire a programmer to create a migration application for you.

Benefit: XSL Debugging

XSL documents can quickly become very complex because they offer so much flexibility in manipulating and transforming XML documents. (This is covered in detail in Sunday afternoon's lesson.) Given that a large part of XSL's functionality is based on XPath and the context node, it's easy to make a mistake that causes your transformations to produce incorrect or unexpected results, or not produce any output at all. While programmers working with programming languages like Visual Basic and Visual C++ have long had access to debuggers that allow them to interactively track down bugs in their code, XSL developers haven't been so lucky.

Until recently. Stylus Studio includes an integrated XSL debugger that allows you to stop a transformation at a given point and then interactively inspect the state of the transformation, which can help in finding XSL coding errors. The debugger also produces intermediate XSL transformation output as you step through XSL code (execute instructions one by one and on your command). It also updates the value of the very important context node, making it easier to find out where the transformation is going wrong.

Now that you know about the benefits that XML editors provide, it's time to delve further into XML Spy and Stylus Studio. The next few sections describe how to install and work with each product, followed by a demonstration of working with an XML solution.

XML Spy

Altova's XML Spy is a comprehensive suite of applications that features an XML Integrated Development Environment, a graphical XSLT Designer, and other applications to make it easier to create and manage XML solutions. Figure 5.7 demonstrates a relatively simple XML-based solution that was created entirely using the XML Integrated Development Environment and the XSLT Designer.

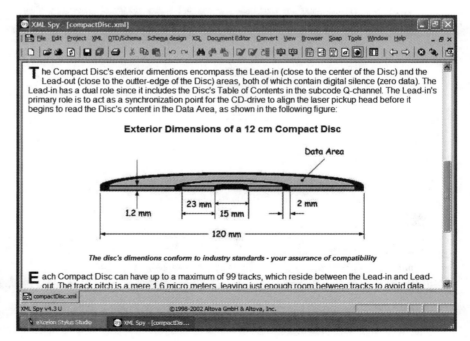

Figure 5.7

XML solution as viewed using XML Spy.

The figure demonstrates XML Spy's browser view, which allows you to preview XML documents in Internet Explorer without having to open a new IE browser. It's integrated into the editor. XML solutions often use a range of techniques to present data to end users. This solution uses XSL in conjunction with CSS to change the document's font, change the formatting of some cells of a table that appears later in the document, and create the drop-cap effect (the large, bold capital letter at the beginning of each paragraph).

The solution features an XML document, a schema, and an XSL document, all of which were created using XML Spy. The graphical schema editor shown in Figure 5.8 makes it easy to visualize the relationships between elements and understand the structure of the overall document.

The document's root element is shown on the left side of the graphical view (the `datasheet` element), and all contained elements are shown to the right. In Saturday evening's lesson, you learned how to model complex types that

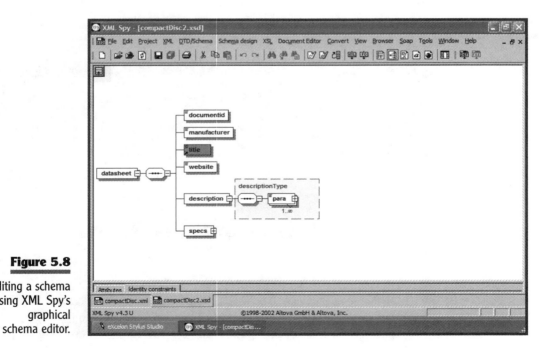

Figure 5.8

Editing a schema using XML Spy's graphical schema editor.

include a sequence of elements. The box with the dotted line in Figure 5.8 represents such a sequence. The para element within the box demonstrates how XML Spy represents a constraint, where an element must appear at least once but can appear an unlimited number of times within the sequence. The title element in the upper part of the diagram is defined using a global element declaration, as indicated by the arrow that appears at the bottom-left corner of the title element's box.

Sunday afternoon's lesson describes how to use XML Spy to work with a solution to create a schema, transform an XML document into HTML, and gain a practical understanding of XPath. Please see the Preface for important information on how to obtain and install an evaluation version of XML Spy.

Stylus Studio

eXcelon's Stylus Studio is an integrated development environment that helps XML developers create and validate XML documents, debug XSL style sheets, and perform XML-to-XML transformations to repurpose XML documents. The product includes a text-based editor that provides context-sensitive statement-completion assistance, in addition to graphical editors that give XML document designers alternate views of an XML document. Stylus Studio's XPath expression evaluator provides context-sensitive statement completion, making it easier to create, test, and evaluate XPath expressions.

Stylus Studio also includes an interactive, source-level XSL debugger that can help XML document designers find and eliminate problems that occur as a result of XSL coding errors. The debugger allows you to set multiple breakpoints so you can halt the XSL transformation at any point during the transformation process. Once transformation is stopped, you can check the state of the context node, review the state of the partial output generated up to the point where the transformation stopped, and continue on a line-by-line basis or continue processing until the debugger reaches the next breakpoint. Figure 5.9 shows the XSL debugger at a breakpoint (the large dot in the margin).

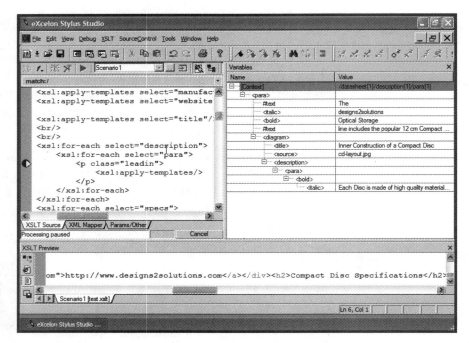

Figure 5.9

Debugging an XSL
style sheet using
Stylus Studio.

The left side of the window shows the XSL source, the right side of the window shows the value of the context node using a tree view, and the bottom of the window contains the partial output of the transformation up to the point where the debugger reached the breakpoint. The following is a listing of the partial output:

```
<html xmlns:xs="http://www.w3.org/2001/XMLSchema">
  <head>
  <META http-equiv="Content-Type" content="text/html">
  <style type="text/css">
    BODY {font-family="arial";}
    TD.desc {background-color:#c0c0c0;}
    p.leadin:first-letter {
      font-size: 200%;
      font-weight: bold;
      float:   left ;
      padding-right:5px;
    }
```

```
  </style>
  <title>Compact Disc Specifications</title>
  </head>
  <body>
    <div align="right">
    <font size="+2" color="red">designs2solutions Optical
Storage</font></div>
    <div align="right">
      <a target="_blank" href="http://www.designs2solutions.com">
        http://www.designs2solutions.com</a>
    </div>
    <h2>Compact Disc Specifications</h2>
    <br>
    <br>
```

What's interesting about this listing is that it's a partial HTML document. It's incomplete because the XSL debugger encountered a breakpoint as it carried out the document's instructions, and Stylus Studio generated the results up to that point. This is a unique feature that makes debugging easier because not only can you analyze the XSL document, but also its output, even before the transformation is complete. Sunday afternoon's lesson includes a complete debugging session and a look at XML-to-XML mapping using Stylus Studio.

How XML Tools Relate to Microsoft's XML Technologies

In Friday evening's lesson, you learned that one of XML's main benefits is that it separates data from presentation. The XML specification purposely doesn't mention anything about how to present data in an XML document because XML defines the basic syntax and rules for structuring and storing information. When you want to present data in an XML document, you format it using CSS or XSL, as shown in Figure 5.10.

The figure shows four components: an XML document, a formatting specification, transformation software, and the resulting document. The transformation software is actually made up of two parts: an XML parser and XSLT transformation software. Non-Microsoft operating systems don't have XML

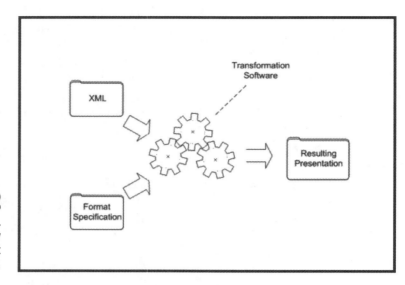

Figure 5.10

Presenting an XML document by applying a format specification.

tightly integrated, so usually you'll have to use additional software to parse and transform XML documents. Microsoft has integrated XML into its operating systems, making it a lot easier to work with and implement XML-based solutions.

The problem with using an XML parser is that each parser supports the XML specification to varying degrees. Some parsers may conform much more closely than others. Because XML-aware applications rely on the underlying parser to perform a lot of work on their behalf, the XML parser becomes a critical component of an XML-based solution.

Altova's XML Spy and eXcelon's Stylus Studio both use their own built-in XML parser and XSLT transformation software, and both provide support for integrating other parsers, including Microsoft's. The reason both products each use a built-in parser instead of an existing one is that both products also provide a certain level of support for the XML standard. This means that their own parsers must reflect that corresponding level of support. Both products enable users to use alternate parsers, such as Microsoft's, that are designed to support a wider range of software. For example, when you use Internet Explorer to view an XML document, it actually uses Microsoft's XML parser to open, read, and transform the XML document and then presents the result to you in Internet Explorer's window.

Because each parser provides a certain level of conformity to the XML standard, there's a chance that a transformation will work one way with one parser and another way using another parser. That's why the XML parser is a critical piece of software in an XML-based system. To mitigate the risk that a transformation will work differently on systems with different versions of the Microsoft XML parser, you can ensure that the system where you're creating your XML solution has the same version of the parser installed as the one on the systems where you'll deploy your solution. Another approach is to ensure that you always have the latest version of the parser available on your system, and to upgrade systems where you'll deploy your solution to have the latest version installed as well.

Microsoft integrated its XML parser into Windows operating systems years ago. However, as standards evolved, Microsoft released updated versions of its parser. Some updates are integrated directly into the operating system's initial installation process, where you get an updated version when you install, say, Windows XP. While upgrading the version of Windows you have on your system is also a great way of updating the XML parser, it's not practical in most scenarios. Microsoft also releases updates through its Web site, allowing users to download and install an updated version of the XML parser.

One of the problems associated with updating only the XML parser is that it can introduce incompatibilities with software that uses and relies on an older version. Microsoft attempted to transparently support older software by essentially replacing the parser with the updated version, while older software still continued to function as if the older version were still operational. Microsoft's attempt paved the way for systems to always have the most up-to-date version of the parser installed (which often included performance enhancements) while maintaining compatibility with older applications. The problem with this approach is that it often made the parser difficult to install, and also made it difficult for developers to figure out which version was installed on a particular system. Developers and end users faced so many difficulties that some of them were compelled to provide unofficial installation instructions and utilities on the Internet. Often that was the only way to figure out which features a system's XML parser implemented and to determine which version was installed.

Microsoft departed from this approach by issuing an update that installed a newer version of the parser, in addition to the parser that was already on the system. The advantages of this approach are that it makes installation easier, and several versions of the parser can coexist on the same system. The key disadvantage is that existing software *must* be updated to take advantage of a parser's newer features and closer conformance to XML standards.

The recommended approach to updating your system's XML parser is to install the latest update from Microsoft's XML developer center. If you don't download and update your system with interim releases, also known as *technology preview releases*, you should be able to simply download and install the updated parser from the XML developer center at Microsoft's Web site. The setup program should be able to configure your system and install the update automatically. If you've installed technology preview releases or reconfigured your system using a tool called `xmlinst.exe`, you may have to take some steps *before* you install the update to ensure that the installation program can accurately and automatically reconfigure your system. The Microsoft XML developer center's Internet address is http://msdn.microsoft.com/xml. If that's not available (Web addresses can change over time), try searching Microsoft's Web site at http://www.microsoft.com, or use a search engine such as Google at http://www.google.com. If you're having problems locating or installing the latest update, refer to the section of my Web site (http://www.designs2solutions.com/LXIAW) that supports this book. My site includes a special page that determines which version of the XML parser is installed on your system, provides information on which updates were available in the past, and tells you which operating system's default installation configuration supports which version of the XML parser.

What's Next?

This lesson introduced the basics of two excellent tools, XMP Spy and Stylus Studio. The next lesson is long, so I suggest that you thumb through it—perhaps even scan over all of it—to get an idea of how long you think it will take you to get through the lesson. You may have to start a little early to complete the lesson in one afternoon, but it's very interesting and features several demonstrations.

Presenting Data on the Web

- ➤ The Style Files
- ➤ More CSS
- ➤ Understanding and Using XSL
- ➤ Repurposing XML Documents with XSL

219

The focus of the book so far has been to get you familiar with XML from the ground up. You started by learning the basic syntax and rules, and then rapidly advanced to data modeling with DTDs and XSDs. You've come a long way in a short time, and it's time to show off a little.

One thing that XML does *not* do is define how to display data. Instead of being a weakness, XML's lack of direct support for displaying data actually strengthens its appeal because the data is completely independent of its presentation. This independence makes XML ideal when you don't know how the data will be used or displayed: It could be printed, read aloud by a reader application for the visually impaired, or displayed in a browser like Microsoft Internet Explorer.

When you want to present XML data, you can associate it with a style sheet that contains directions on how to format or present it. There are two types of style sheets: Cascading Style Sheets and the Extensible Stylesheet Language. Both are introduced in this lesson, along with suggestions on when it's appropriate to use each one. This lesson also contains a lot of sample code and demonstrations.

The Style Files

Cascading Style Sheets (CSS) and the Extensible Stylesheet Language (XSL) are two flexible and powerful means of formatting XML documents. CSS allows you to format an XML document in a variety of ways on systems that can process XML with CSS. XSL allows you to perform much more complex formatting. You can actually transform an XML document into a Web page, a binary formatted document like the popular PDF format, or even an entirely new XML document based on the existing XML document. Both formatting techniques have their benefits and drawbacks, but they share a simple trait: CSS and XSL are broadly accepted and supported industry standards. The one you choose will be based on your needs and supporting technologies, or those of your clients.

This section provides an overview of both formatting techniques and discusses the benefits and drawbacks of both. That discussion is followed by detailed discussions of CSS and XSL. I encourage you to review the material in this entire lesson, even if you don't think it applies in your particular circumstances today. You may find that you're using the wrong approach or aren't taking enough advantage of the features an approach offers.

Overview of CSS

CSS, Cascading Style Sheets, was originally designed to make it easier to control the display of Web pages in a browser like Microsoft Internet Explorer. However, CSS is also useful for displaying XML data. CSS is easiest to understand if you think of it as a set of simple instructions that describe how to draw, read, display, or otherwise present information, otherwise known as *rendering*. Figure 6.1 shows how CSS relates to information and controls how it's rendered.

Figure 6.1 shows how CSS combines a document's content with formatting instructions. CSS formatting instructions reside in their own file. You provide a link between the document and the CSS formatting instructions using a special syntax (described shortly). A rendering engine, such as Internet Explorer or other software that's capable of rendering CSS, reviews the formatting instructions and applies them to the content. Then it sends the formatted information to the user or output device (screen, speaker, etc.).

CSS is extremely flexible because it works by matching document markup tag names with CSS statements. When CSS makes a match, it reviews

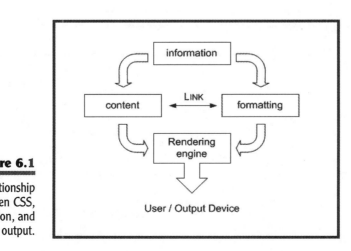

Figure 6.1

The relationship between CSS, information, and output.

property assignments that provide information on how to render the tag. Once CSS reviews the entire document, it combines all of the formatting properties it's matched and renders the final output. The CSS syntax is very easy to understand because it's made up of statements and property-value pairs, as shown in Figure 6.2.

CSS statements have two parts:

➤ The selector declares which tags the CSS formatting affects.

➤ The declaration defines the tag's format.

Figure 6.3 depicts a CSS statement in detail.

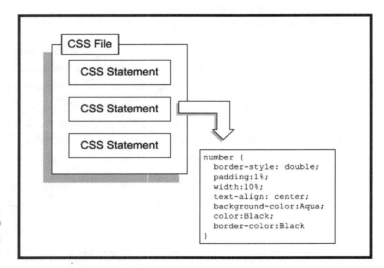

Figure 6.2

The structure of a CSS file.

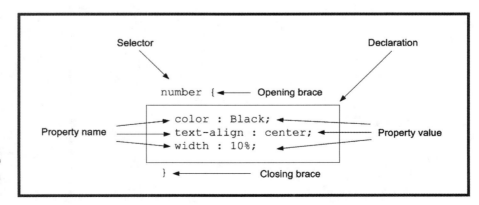

Figure 6.3

The structure of a CSS statement.

You can use CSS to format an XML document and view it using Internet Explorer. It's shown onscreen using a default set of formatting rules that add some color and interactivity. While this default formatting is useful, it's far from friendly because you can see all of the XML document's elements. Consider the following listing:

```
<?xml version="1.0" encoding="UTF-8"?>
<paragraphs>
  <paragraph>
    The diagram describes how CSS combines a document's
    content with formatting instructions. CSS formatting
    instructions reside in their own file; as a result,
    you provide a link between the document and the CSS
    formatting instructions using a special syntax
    (described shortly). A rendering engine, a software
    component such as Internet Explorer or other software
    that's capable of rendering CSS, reviews the formatting
    instructions and applies them to the content. Once
    the rendering engine formats the information, it
    sends it to the user or output device (screen,
    speaker, etc).
  </paragraph>
<paragraphs>
```

When you use Internet Explorer to view the document, you get the output shown in Figure 6.4. The pointer is in the shape of a hand, indicating that you can click on the minus sign. When you do, the document collapses to show just the paragraphs element, and the minus sign becomes a plus sign. When you click again, the document expands to the way it appeared when you first loaded it.

Some CSS statements can make a dramatic difference. Figure 6.5 shows what the previous XML document looks like in Internet Explorer. The file is called sampleParagraph.xml and is located in the samples folder. (See the Preface for directions on how to obtain the sample files that accompany this book, and how to work with the samples.)

The document has some subtle characteristics. Resize Internet Explorer's window so that it looks similar to the one in the figure, and then drag the

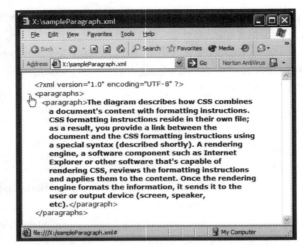

Figure 6.4

Viewing an XML document using Internet Explorer.

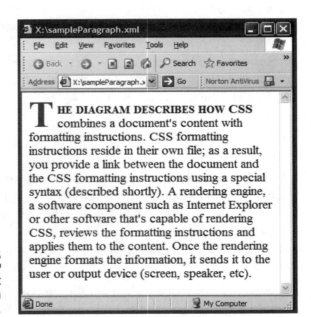

Figure 6.5

An XML document formatted with CSS.

right side of the window to the left and right and note what happens to the first line of text. You should see the words in the first line in uppercase, and as you drag the right border of Internet Explorer's window, words that move up onto the first line should also appear in uppercase. Also note that the relative space between the large letter T and the adjacent words remains the same as you resize the window.

So how do you accomplish such an effect? Here's the CSS that formats the document:

```
paragraph   {
  width: 100%;
  font-family: serif;
  font-size: 14pt;
}


paragraph:first-letter {
  font-size: 300%;
  color: Red;
  font-weight: bold;
  float:   left ;
  padding-right: 5px;
}


paragraph:first-line {
  font-variant: small-caps;
  font-weight: bold;
}
```

To understand how the CSS formats the document, you also need to consider the names of the original XML document's elements. The first formatting selector affects all paragraph elements. Note that you simply indicate which element you want to affect by name. You don't have to use a special syntax, which makes CSS easy to work with. However, it also limits CSS to formatting uniquely named elements. For example, you cannot distinguish between a paragraph element that appears as part of a paragraphs element and some other element. All paragraph elements have the same formatting. The paragraph selector sets the width property to 100%, which means that a paragraph can use the entire width of Internet Explorer's window for itself. The font-family property's value is serif, which means that Internet Explorer can pick whatever font it wants, as long as it's a serif font. (Serif fonts have fine lines that finish off the main strokes of each letter.) The last property that the paragraph selector sets is the font-size property, which sets the size of each letter. The setting in this example uses a unit called points, or pt. There are several other units of measure available, including percent and pixels. The paragraph selector declares the basic appearance of all paragraph elements, while the selectors that follow it specialize the appearance of other aspects of the paragraph.

The next two selectors use the same paragraph selector, except that they add another selector after it called a *pseudo-element*. A pseudo-element doesn't appear among a document's tags. It represents a part of a document that is otherwise inaccessible by CSS. For example, the paragraph:first-letter pseudo-element allows CSS to manipulate the properties of the first letter of the document's paragraph element, and the paragraph:first-line pseudo-element allows CSS to manipulate the first line of the paragraph element, regardless of how many words may be in the first line. CSS supports a number of useful pseudo-elements, which I'll explain in the more advanced section on Sunday evening, "Programming with XML."

Associating a CSS file with an XML document is straightforward. You just add a directive to the second line of your XML document. The following listing is from the first few lines of the sampleParagraph.xml file:

```
<?xml version="1.0" encoding="UTF-8"?>
<?xml-stylesheet type="text/css" href="sampleCSS.css"?>
<paragraphs>
   <paragraph>
```

The second line of the listing is the one that associates the CSS file with the XML document. <?xml-stylesheet... ?> is a special XML tag that informs an XML processor, like Internet Explorer, where to find the style sheet. The href attribute pinpoints the location of the style sheet file. You can provide the location of a file on your local system, or an address on a Web server on the Internet.

Here's another example that uses some more CSS properties to format a longer XML document. Consider the following XML document:

```
<?xml version="1.0"?>
<periodicTable xmlns:xsi="http://www.w3.org/2001/XMLSchema-instance">
   <atom>
```

```
        <name>Actinium</name>
        <number>89</number>
        <symbol>Ac</symbol>
      </atom>
      <atom>
        <name>Aluminum</name>
        <number>13</number>
        <symbol>Al</symbol>
      </atom>
      <atom>
        <name>Americium</name>
        <number>95</number>
        <symbol>Am</symbol>
      </atom>

<!--- etc... --->

      <atom>
        <name>Zinc</name>
        <number>30</number>
        <symbol>Zn</symbol>
      </atom>
      <atom>
        <name>Zirconium</name>
        <number>40</number>
        <symbol>Zr</symbol>
      </atom>
</periodicTable>
```

This listing shows an XML document that describes the properties of the atoms in the periodic table of elements. When you view the document in Internet Explorer, you can see each element. However, the default formatting makes it difficult to see where one atom ends and another begins. I created a CSS that formats the elements so that they're easier to read, as shown in Figure 6.6.

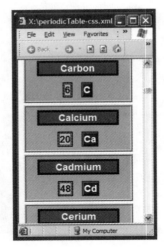

Figure 6.6

Formatting an
XML document
with CSS.

The CSS that formats the document is shown in the following listing:

```
atom {
  display: block;
  width: 200px;
  border-style: ridge;
  text-align: center;
  background-color: Silver;
  margin-bottom: 2%;
}
name, number, symbol {
  display: inline;
  font-weight: bold;
  margin: 3%;
  font-family: Arial,Verdana;
  font-size: medium;
}

name {
  border-style: solid;
  border-width: thin;
  width: 150px;
```

```
    text-align: center;
    background-color: Green;
    color: White;
    border-color: Black;
}

number {
    border-style: double;
    padding: 1%;
    width: 10%;
    text-align: center;
    background-color: Aqua;
    color: Black;
    border-color: Black;
}

symbol {
    border-style: outset;
    padding: 2%;
    width: 10%;
    text-align: center;
    background-color: Blue;
    color: White;
    border-color: Teal;
}
```

What's different about this CSS is that it uses a feature called *inheritance*, where the formatting "flows" from one element to another. For example, the second declaration (the one that begins with `name`, `number`, `symbol`) defines the basic appearance of the `name`, `number` and `symbol` elements. The declarations that follow inherit the formatting that the previous declaration specified and add new properties. For example, the `name` element's basic formatting makes the text appear in bold using either the Arial or Verdana fonts. A `name` declaration appears in the third declaration of the CSS and adds a border, changes the font's color, and aligns the text.

CSS provides a quick and easy way to format XML documents. However, it has some limitations that can make it impractical. For example, if your XML documents have elements that contain attributes and you want to be able to format those attributes, you're out of luck because some browsers, like Internet Explorer, implement an earlier version of CSS that isn't capable of accessing attributes. It's sometimes necessary to restructure XML data for a new purpose by adding or removing elements, or restructuring the entire document. Because CSS was designed as a presentation technology, it's not capable of producing new XML documents.

The Extensible Stylesheet Language, XSL, is a technology that's capable of performing advanced formatting, including producing documents in different formats like HTML (the publishing language of the Internet) and XML. The next section introduces XSL.

Overview of XSL

XSL has two goals: displaying XML and transforming XML. Displaying XML is similar to the role of CSS in that you can use it to format XML documents. Transforming XML is unique to XSL. XSL Transformations (XSLT) produces new output formats based on an XML document, along with formatting instructions that you provide. Using XSLT, you can produce an HTML document (a Web page), another XML document, or even another type of document that's unique to your application.

XSL is an XML vocabulary, which means that you write XSL using the same rules that you use for XML. You work with XSL in a way that's similar to how you work with CSS. You create an XSL file, associate it with an XML document using a special instruction, and then produce the output by viewing the resulting document in a browser or using another application. Let's take a look at a practical example.

In the last section, I showed you an XML document that describes some of the properties of atoms in the periodic table of elements. While CSS is capable of formatting the XML document, you cannot add new content to the resulting document. For example, you cannot use CSS to create a table with headings and add specific elements to certain cells of the table. Figure 6.7 shows what the XML file looks like when it's formatted using some basic XSL and viewed using Internet Explorer.

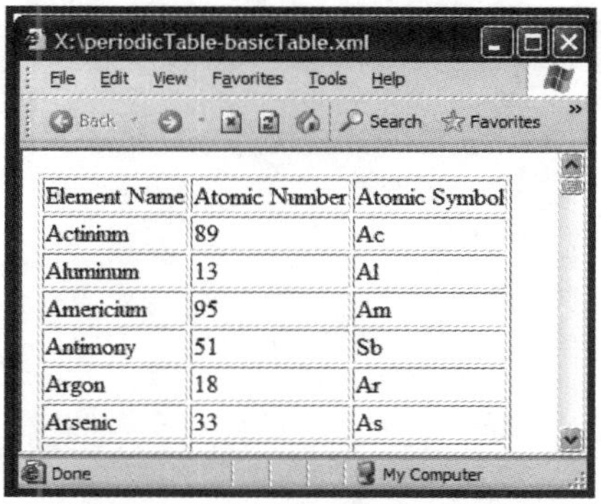

Figure 6.7

Formatting an
XML document
with XSL.

The document contains a table with three columns: Element Name, Atomic
Number, and Atomic Symbol. Here's the XSL that defines the document's presentation:

```
<?xml version="1.0" encoding="UTF-8"?>
<xsl:stylesheet version="1.0"
    xmlns:xsl="http://www.w3.org/1999/XSL/Transform"
    xmlns:xs="http://www.w3.org/2001/XMLSchema">

    <xsl:template match="/">
      <html>
        <head>
        </head>
        <body>
          <table border="1">
            <tr>
              <td>Element Name</td>
              <td>Atomic Number</td>
              <td>Atomic Symbol</td>
            </tr>
            <xsl:apply-templates select="periodicTable/atom"/>
          </table>
        </body>
      </html>
    </xsl:template>
```

```
    <xsl:template match="atom">
      <tr>
        <td>
          <xsl:value-of select="name"/>
        </td>
        <td>
          <xsl:value-of select="number"/>
        </td>
        <td>
          <xsl:value-of select="symbol"/>
        </td>
      </tr>
    </xsl:template>


</xsl:stylesheet>
```

The first thing you may notice is that XSL is XML using a special namespace (http://www.w3.org/1999/XSL/Transform) and special elements. This listing begins by declaring that the document is indeed XSL using the `stylesheet` element. This element encloses all elements in the document. Like other elements in XSL, the `stylesheet` element has an `xsl` prefix that associates it with the XSL namespace. The closing `stylesheet` element appears at the end of the listing.

XSL uses a declarative approach to locating and manipulating elements in the source XML document and manipulating them to produce the resulting document. In this example, the resulting document is an HTML page, as shown in the following listing:

```
<html xmlns:xs="http://www.w3.org/2001/XMLSchema">
  <head>
    <META http-equiv="Content-Type" content="text/html; charset=UTF-
16">
  </head>
  <body>
    <table border="1">
      <tr>
        <td>Element Name</td>
        <td>Atomic Number</td>
        <td>Atomic Symbol</td>
```

```
        </tr>
        <tr>
          <td>Actinium</td>
          <td>89</td>
          <td>Ac</td>
        </tr>
        <tr>
          <td>Aluminum</td>
          <td>13</td>
          <td>Al</td>
        </tr>
        <!-- etc... -->
        <tr>
          <td>Zinc</td>
          <td>30</td>
          <td>Zn</td>
        </tr>
        <tr>
          <td>Zirconium</td>
          <td>40</td>
          <td>Zr</td>
        </tr>
      </table>
    </body>
</html>
```

The first XSL element in the XSL file is the template element, which defines what element in the source document to manipulate. The template element's match attribute uses an XPath expression to match elements in the source document. In this example, the XPath expression "/" causes the XSL processor to match the root element of the source document. The declaration essentially says, "Produce the following output for each root element in the source document."

The source document's root element is periodicTable. So, the XSL processor generates the document fragment that appears between the beginning and ending template tags, as the following listing shows:

```
<html>
  <head>
  </head>
```

```
<body>
  <table border="1">
    <tr>
      <td>Element Name</td>
      <td>Atomic Number</td>
      <td>Atomic Symbol</td>
    </tr>
```

HTML is a very straightforward markup language. If you're not familiar with it, it's relatively easy to learn. All HTML documents begin with an HTML tag, and the entire document is enclosed in a body element. The table element encloses a table, the tr element encloses a table's row, and td elements enclose individual table cells. The XSL document generated the document fragment based on the contents of the xsl:template match="/" element. Another XSL declaration appears just after the closing tr tag, as shown in the following listing:

```
      <xsl:apply-templates select="periodicTable/atom"/>
    </table>
  </body>
</html>
```

The xsl:apply-templates element tells the XSL processor to read through the rest of the XSL file, searching for an xsl:template element that's capable of matching the expression defined by the select attribute. The select attribute contains an XPath expression. The element as a whole says, in this case, "Find a template element to generate the output for atom elements in the source document."

The XSL processor looks for and finds another xsl:template element whose match XPath expression is atom. The XSL processor looks through the source XML document and finds a lot of atom elements. It repeatedly applies the template to each atom element it finds in the source document.

Here's what happens: The following listing has the xsl:template element on the left and the source document on the right. This listing shows in detail how the XSL processor locates elements based on their names:

```
<xsl:template match="atom">                    -->      <atom>
  <tr>
    <td>
```

```
      <xsl:value-of select="name"/>        -->      <name>Carbon</name>
    </td>
    <td>
      <xsl:value-of select="number"/>      -->      <number>6</number>
    </td>
    <td>
      <xsl:value-of select="symbol"/>      -->      <symbol>C</symbol>
    </td>
  </tr>
</xsl:template>                              -->      </atom>
```

The xsl:value-of element extracts the value of the XPath expression in the element's select attribute. Because the XSL processor is able to match everything in the xsl:template element, it produces the following document fragment and appends it to the preceding document fragment:

```
<tr>
  <td>
    Carbon
  </td>
  <td>
    6
  </td>
  <td>
    C
  </td>
</tr>
```

This document fragment represents a single row (the tr element) of the table from the preceding HTML document fragment, which contains three columns (the td elements). The XSL processor continues to generate output by applying the xsl:template element that matches atom elements in the source document until it cannot match any more atom elements. Once the XSL processor reaches the end of the list of atoms, it picks up where it left off in the first xsl:template element by producing the following output and appending it to the fragments it has generated so far:

```
    </table>
  </body>
</html>
```

The fragment closes the HTML `table`, `body`, and `html` elements. The very last thing the XSL processor does is pass the formatted document in the computer's memory to Internet Explorer, which displays it on your system's screen.

While the output is interesting and useful, it can be much better. The XSL and HTML I've shown you so far uses only basic features. A more useful presentation could be to sort the atomic elements by atomic number, and shade alternating lines in a darker color to make the whole table easier to read, as shown in Figure 6.8.

The XSL that formats the enhanced version of the output is a little more involved, as is the HTML. However, it's easy to at least figure out what's happening. Here's the XSL that produces the enhanced table:

```
<?xml version="1.0" encoding="UTF-8"?>
<xsl:stylesheet version="1.0"
xmlns:xsl="http://www.w3.org/1999/XSL/Transform"
xmlns:xs="http://www.w3.org/2001/XMLSchema">
  <xsl:template match="/">
    <html>
      <head>
      </head>
      <body>
        <table border="1">
          <thead>
            <tr bgcolor="black" style="color:white;font-weight:bold;">
              <td>Element Name</td>
              <td>Atomic Number</td>
              <td>Atomic Symbol</td>
            </tr>
          </thead>
          <tbody>
            <xsl:apply-templates select="periodicTable/atom">
              <xsl:sort select="number" data-type="number"/>
            </xsl:apply-templates>
          </tbody>
        </table>
      </body>
```

```
      </html>
    </xsl:template>


    <xsl:template match="atom">
      <xsl:element name="tr">
        <xsl:choose>
          <xsl:when test="position() mod 2 = 0">
            <xsl:attribute name="bgcolor">silver</xsl:attribute>
          </xsl:when>
        </xsl:choose>
        <td>
          <xsl:value-of select="name"/>
        </td>
        <td>
          <xsl:value-of select="number"/>
        </td>
        <td>
          <xsl:value-of select="symbol"/>
        </td>
      </xsl:element>
    </xsl:template>
</xsl:stylesheet>
```

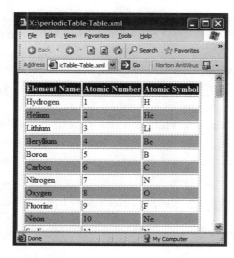

Figure 6.8

Using more XSL
features to format
an XML document.

This listing introduces a number of features in XSL and HTML. Don't be too concerned about that, because this is just an introduction to XSL. For the moment, ignore the HTML features you don't immediately recognize and just focus on the XSL. The first bold line in the listing introduces the `xsl:sort` element, which is capable of sorting an XML document in any order you specify. In this example, the XSL sorts the periodic table XML document based on the value of the `number` element (the atomic number of each atom).

The second bold set of lines in the listing handles the details of highlighting every other line in silver. XSL is capable of not only matching elements in a document, but also making decisions based on the results of a calculation (as in this example), the value of an element or attribute, or any number of other factors. If you compare this listing with the previous version of the same template, you'll notice that there isn't an opening or closing `tr` tag, which encloses an individual row of a table. The regular `tr` element (`<tr>` and `</tr>` tags) has been replaced with an `xsl:element` element just before the second block of bold XSL code. The `xsl:element` lets you manipulate the attributes of certain tags that you wouldn't be able to otherwise.

This concludes the introduction to XSL. You may be asking which is better to use, CSS or XSL?

Which One Do I Use, CSS or XSL?

CSS allows you to choose what sorts of formatting to apply to an XML document without affecting the XML document itself. This feature allows you to maintain a uniform look and feel in all of your XML documents. Its direct support for alternate output formats, such as reading a document aloud for visually impaired people, makes it possible to easily accommodate people with special needs. The primary drawback to using CSS is that it doesn't consistently work with a variety of browsers. Some browsers support an early version of CSS, others support a later version of CSS, while still others don't recognize CSS at all. As a result, a lot of Web sites purposely don't use CSS, ensuring that their content reaches the broadest possible audience. The cost is less flexible formatting capabilities.

XSL is much more complex but provides you with enormous power to render XML documents. As with CSS, major browsers currently on the market provide various levels of support for both XML and XSL. The complexity of XSL makes it the tool of choice among specialists seeking to deliver very flexible and powerful solutions. However, I believe XSL is useful for the rest of us too. One feature I haven't discussed yet is that you perform XSL-based formatting on a Web server and deliver documents in plain HTML, which ensures that the broadest possible audience can work with your content. Even the oldest browsers on the market are capable of working with plain HTML. You cannot do this type of processing with CSS.

Chances are that you'll end up working with CSS at some level for the foreseeable future, because XSL is considered to be much more complicated. In contrast, XSL has many more capabilities, as well as Web server support, making it useful in a variety of situations where using CSS isn't practical.

The driving factor in your choice of approach should be how many people you want to reach. Assuming that you want to reach visitors accessing a Web site using a browser, you should base your decision on what types of browsers most users use to access the site. If you find that users use only current versions of major browsers, and you don't want fine-grained control over the formatting of XML documents, CSS is probably the best option. If you want to reach users who use all types and versions of major and minor browsers, formatting XML documents on the Web server using XSL is likely the best option because the documents are delivered to end users in plain HTML.

More CSS

So far you've only had an introduction to CSS. Now it's time to do some exploring with CSS and discuss some of its advanced functionality. As previously mentioned, CSS is useful when you want to provide XML documents directly to end users and have all of the formatting occur when a user wants to view a document. Figure 6.9 presents a typical Web-based scenario.

The process begins when a user requests a page from a Web site using a browser like Internet Explorer. It works the same way whether the user requests an XML file directly from a Web site by typing in the Web site's address and the name of an XML file (as shown in number 1 in Figure 6.9), or the Web site provides the user with an XML file on its own. In both cases, the Web site locates an XML file (number 2).

You indicate that you want to format an XML file using CSS by linking the XML document with a CSS document (number 3). The Web site sends the XML file back to the user's browser (number 4). Reviewing the contents

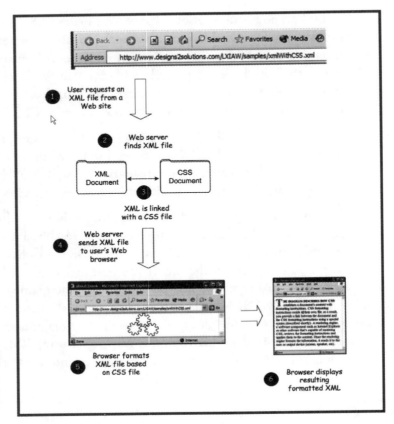

Figure 6.9

Using CSS with
XML to display
content to a user.

of the XML file, the browser finds a reference to a CSS file and downloads it too. The browser then formats the XML based on the CSS directives it finds (number 5) and renders the resulting document on the user's screen (number 6).

Your role in all of this is to author the XML document, author the CSS, and link both files together. You should be familiar with creating XML documents by now, so let's jump right into formatting XML documents using CSS.

Be aware that most CSS editors assume that you plan to write CSS for use with HTML pages. As a result, some CSS editors try to restrict you to formatting HTML elements. CSS is relatively forgiving with respect to the rules you have to follow when you create CSS documents. I suggest that you use Notepad to author CSS documents until you're comfortable with CSS and better understand your needs.

Linking CSS with XML

The most fundamental aspect of working with XML and CSS is to establish a link between both documents. You establish such a link using a special Processing Instruction (PI) in the XML document, as shown in the following listing:

```
<?xml version="1.0" encoding="UTF-8"?>
<?xml-stylesheet type="text/css" href="nameOfYourCssFileGoesHere.css"?>
<!-- Rest of XML file would appear here... -->
```

If you need a refresher course on PIs, refer to Saturday afternoon's lesson, "Marking Up Isn't Just for Graffiti Artists," under the heading "Using Processing Instructions."

Like all PIs, the style sheet PI appears after the XML declaration (the listing's first line). It begins with the `xml-stylesheet` target keyword and has two name-value pairs. The first name-value pair describes the style sheet's `type` as `text/css`, which indicates that the XML document uses CSS for its formatting. The second name-value pair is `href`, which refers to the actual location and name of a CSS file that contains the directives for formatting the XML document. `href` can take on any form that's convenient or suitable for your application, as shown in the following listing:

```
<?xml version="1.0" encoding="UTF-8"?>
<!-- Some examples of valid href values -->
<!-- CSS file resides in same location as XML file -->
<?xml-stylesheet
   type="text/css"
   href="formatUsingTables.css"?>
<!-- CSS file resides in another folder  -->
<?xml-stylesheet
   type="text/css"
   href="../styleFiles/formatUsingTables.css"?>
<!-- CSS resides on another Web site -->
<?xml-stylesheet
   type="text/css"

href="http://designs2solutions.com/styleFiles/formatUsingTables.css"?>
<!-- Rest of XML file would appear here... -->
```

This listing demonstrates three ways of referencing a CSS file. The first reference is to a file that resides in the same folder as the XML file, the second reference is to a CSS file that resides in another folder but is on the same Web site, and the last reference is to a CSS file on another Web site.

If you make a mistake in referring to a CSS file using the xml-stylesheet PI, the XML file will be formatted using the default view shown earlier in Figure 6.4. You should always test your XML files before you make them available to end users to ensure that you have the correct reference to the CSS file.

One thing that the preceding listing highlights is that it's possible to have more than one reference to a CSS file in an XML document. The only catch to doing this is that you must create a reference to each XML file at the very beginning of the document. Although PIs can appear anywhere in an XML document, the xml-stylesheet PI can appear only at the very beginning of the document (after the XML declaration, and before any XML elements).

IS THAT REFERENCE LOCAL OR REMOTE?

When you refer to a CSS document from an XML document using an xml-stylesheet Processing Instruction, you can use a complete Web address that starts with http:// or a partial address. When you start an address with http://, you must provide the complete address of the site along with the folder that the CSS document resides in, even if you end up referring to the same Web site that the XML file is on. You don't have to start the address with http:// if you plan to have your XML documents reside at the same Web site, even if the CSS document resides in another folder.

When you refer to a CSS document using a partial address, the user's browser assumes that the CSS document refers to the same site it got the XML document from. So the quickest way of figuring out if an href refers to a local or remote CSS document is to look at the first few characters of the address. An address refers to a remote CSS document when it starts with http://. Otherwise, the CSS document refers to the site on which the XML document resides.

Commenting CSS

CSS can sometimes become complicated and difficult for others to review, so it supports comments that allow you to annotate your declarations. The following listing demonstrates some ways you can add comments to your CSS (they appear in bold):

```
/* This is a single-line comment */
paragraph { width: 100%; font-family: Serif; font-size: 14pt; }


/*
This is a comment that covers
a few lines. Note that
you cannot place comments
within comments!
*/


name { border-style: solid; }     /* This comment is in
number { border-style: double; }   the wrong place, can you
symbol { border-style: outset; }   tell why? */
```

Comments always begin with the /* character sequence and end with the */ character sequence, which come from the C and C++ programming languages. They can appear on a single line, or may span multiple lines. You're free to do as you like, as long as the comment text appears between the /* and */ characters.

The last comment in the preceding listing has a question in it. Can you see what's wrong with the comment? At first glance it appears to be a simple multi-line comment. But take a look at the location of the /* character sequence and the */ character sequence, keeping in mind that a comment begins and ends with those sequences. Which lines are affected by the comment? It encloses the comment text, but it also encloses the last two CSS declarations in the listing. This can lead to some time wasted trying to figure out why the number and symbol elements aren't being formatted as specified in the CSS declarations. Be careful where you put your comments. You could accidentally enclose CSS declarations within your comments, leading to a mistake that's difficult to track down.

Taking a Closer Look at CSS Selectors

Earlier in this lesson, you learned how to construct a CSS statement. A CSS statement is made up of two major parts, a selector and a declaration, as shown in Figure 6.3. The CSS declaration is further divided into properties and values.

CSS selectors can take on a simple form, as shown in Figure 6.3. However, you can come across variations like those in the following listing:

```
/* Note the colon in the selector */
title:first-lettter { ... }


/* Note the use of commas in the selector */
paragraph, figureTitle, exercise { ... }


/* Note the use of . (dot) characters in the selector */
paragraph.highlight, listItem.important { ... }


/* Note that the selector begins with a . (dot)character */
.smallCaps { ... }
```

I'll explain how to use these selectors in detail later. You just need to be aware of their existence for now. In general, selectors specify which XML element you want the CSS declaration to affect.

CSS declarations use the format shown in Figure 6.10.

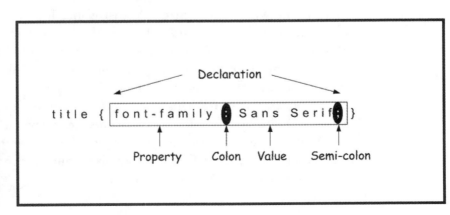

Figure 6.10

The detailed structure of a CSS statement.

As previously discussed, a CSS declaration is made up of property-value pairs. The name of the property represents a valid CSS property, such as `font-family`, `color`, and `text-align`. The property's value represents the value that you want to assign to the property. A colon separates a property and its value, and an individual declaration ends in a semicolon.

Some properties can have more than one value, as shown in the following CSS statement:

```
paragraph {
  font : normal small-caps 120%/150% serif;
  margin : 2% 5% 2% 5%;
}
```

The important aspect of this statement is that spaces separate some property values while slashes or commas separate others. There's no rule that describes when to use a space, comma, or slash, because property values vary. You'll learn which properties use separators as you gain experience working with CSS. The other option is to consult the CSS reference that's available in Appendix A, "HTML and XPath Reference."

CSS is very forgiving with respect to declarations. If you misspell a property or value, CSS ignores only the errant property, as opposed to the entire declaration. If you use a multi-valued property and make a mistake with one of the values, most browsers will ignore the entire list (in other words, they ignore the property's value) and move on to the next declaration within the statement.

Understanding Units of Measure

You configure (set the value of a specific property of) a lot of CSS properties, like margins and widths, using a numeric value and a unit of measure. CSS supports two types of units, absolute and relative.

Absolute units represent actual units like inches and centimeters, which makes them useful for positioning an element without regard to the capabilities of the output device. *Relative* units take into consideration the relative position of surrounding elements and the output device. To understand the capabilities of a device, you need to understand a few basic concepts, as shown in Figure 6.11.

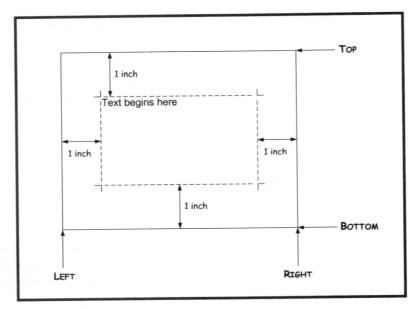

Figure 6.11

The basic layout of
an output device.

The figure shows an exaggerated view of some text ("Text begins here"), either onscreen or printed on a piece of paper. The solid border indicates the outer boundaries of the screen or the paper, and the top, left, bottom, and right solid borders are highlighted at the edges. The margins are one inch each from the border of the screen or the paper. The area in which text can reside is indicated by the dotted lines. It's easy to format the text using something like Microsoft Word. You simply set the document's margins to one inch using Microsoft Word's menu options, and then you print the document. Microsoft Word knows how to format the document when it's printed. However, placing the same text in the same position onscreen is more difficult. Unlike a printed page that you can measure using inches or centimeters, your computer measures the screen's width and height using pixels.

A *pixel* is a single dot on your computer's screen. (You can see the individual pixels if you look closely enough.) The number of pixels on your screen depends on the size of the monitor and its resolution, or capability to display information onscreen. Common computer display resolution is 800 x 600. However, computers are capable of other resolutions, including 1024 x 768 and 1552 x 864 . When you increase the screen's resolution, you also increase the amount of information you can display onscreen because the number of pixels also increases. While the physical number of dots on the screen doesn't change, the elements onscreen become smaller as the resolution increases. The smaller the elements on the screen become, the more of them you can put on the screen.

So what does all of this have to with absolute and relative measurements? Going back to Figure 6.11, you can imagine how difficult it would be to measure one inch at 800 x 600 resolution while measuring that same one inch at 1024 x 768 resolution. As you change the screen's resolution, you also change how large one inch appears to be on the screen. One inch at 800 x 600 resolution would look a lot different than one inch at 1024 x 768 resolution. CSS addresses this problem using absolute and relative measurement units. Table 6.1 lists all of the absolute measurements available to you when you use CSS.

The units in Table 6.1 are useful if your computer knows how to display them on your monitor. However, not all users' systems know how to do this, because the computer needs to understand the capabilities of the monitor that's attached to it. As a result, most developers stay away from using absolute units of measure when using CSS to format XML documents. CSS provides another set of measures called relative units, as shown in Table 6.2.

TABLE 6.1 ABSOLUTE UNITS OF MEASUREMENT IN CSS

Name	Description
inches (in)	Represents a number of inches (one inch equals about 2.2 centimeters).
centimeters (cm)	Represents a number of centimeters.
millimeters (mm)	Represents a number of mm (there are 10 mm in 1 cm).
points (pt)	A point is a standard typographical measure, and there are 72 points per inch.
picas (pc)	A pica is equal to 12 points, which means there are six picas to one inch.
pixel (px)	Represents one pixel.

TABLE 6.2 RELATIVE UNITS OF MEASUREMENT IN CSS	
Name	**Description**
em	Represents a unit of measure that is equal to the number of points that the font size is set to. For example, if the font size is 12, one em is equal to 12.
ex	Represents the height of a lowercase letter x. For example, a lowercase x in the Arial font isn't the same size as a lowercase x in the Courier font.

Relative units of measure take into consideration the size of the screen, as well as the size of the browser on an element screen. (Not all users have their browsers take up all available screen space.) Using relative units of measure can make formatting XML documents a little tricky, however. You give up a degree of control by letting the user's system decide where to place elements onscreen based on the screen's resolution.

Take a look at a concrete example before we move on. Figure 6.12 shows what the periodic table XML document looks like when it's formatted using pixels to define the width of each box.

The following listing shows the relevant CSS statement that was used to generate the document in Figure 6.12:

```
atom {
    display: inline;
    width: 200px;
    border-style: ridge;
    text-align: center;
    background-color: Silver;
    margin-bottom: 2%;
    border-bottom: double;
}
```

The bold line indicates that each atom element in the periodic table should be 200px (pixels) wide. The document would look a lot different if you changed the units from pixels to em units, as shown in Figure 6.13.

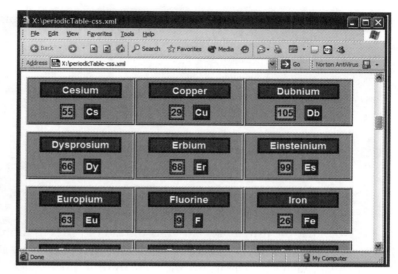

Figure 6.12

Formatting the periodic table XML document using pixels as the units of measure.

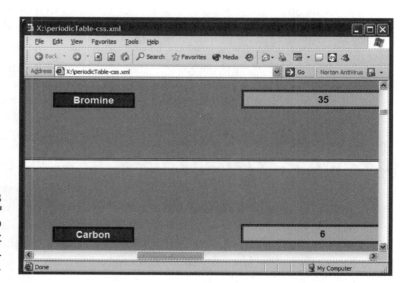

Figure 6.13

Using em units to format the periodic table XML document.

The following listing shows the relevant CSS used to format the document in Figure 6.13:

```
atom {
    display: inline;
    width: 200em;
    border-style: ridge;
    text-align: center;
    background-color: Silver;
    margin-bottom: 2%;
    border-bottom: double;
}
```

Note that the listing uses em units instead of pixels to format each atom element. As you can see, there's a significant difference between pixels and em units. (Each atom element is too wide to fit in the browser window.)

In several places, the listing uses pixel units to describe the size of the atom elements box. The W3C specification for CSS says that one inch contains 90 pixels, but most browsers don't implement that part of the specification. Generally, it's up to the browser to determine how wide an individual pixel will be. Most developers stay away from using pixel units of measure because users' screen resolutions can vary, which affects the number of pixels per inch on the users' displays. Many developers end up using percentage units of measure, which are described in the next section.

Understanding Percentage Units of Measure

Percentage units are a relative unit of measure, which are very easy to understand. These units are always relative to the surrounding element. For example, you can create a new table with a width of 50 percent. The table's width is relative to the browser's width on the user's screen. As the user makes the browser window larger or smaller, the table's size changes so that it always uses 50 percent of the available space within the browser window. Figure 6.14 shows a variation of the periodic table XML document formatted such that each atom element uses 30% of the browser's window.

Figure 6.15 shows the same document. This time the browser takes up more space on the screen, so each atom element stretches along with the browser window because the browser window is wider.

Figure 6.14

Using percentage units to format an XML document.

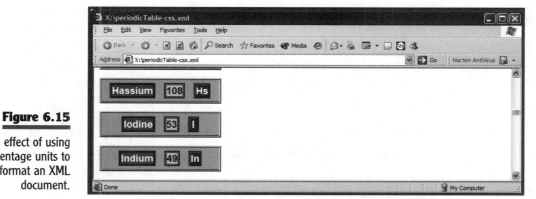

Figure 6.15

The effect of using percentage units to format an XML document.

Using Color

CSS supports a variety of ways to express colors. The most basic method is to just use the name of a color for the value of a property that represents that color (like `color` and `background-color`). While most new computers are capable of displaying millions of colors, the computers that may access your XML documents can range from high-end desktop systems to handheld devices with limited color-display capabilities.

Colors are sometimes arranged into a group, called a *palette*. There's a color palette that most browsers are capable of rendering, referred to as the *named color palette* or just *named colors*. The great thing about named colors is that you can refer to them by name so that you don't have to remember any special codes or numeric values.

Here are the 16 named colors:

- aqua
- gray
- navy
- silver
- black
- green
- olive
- teal
- blue
- lime
- purple
- white
- fuchsia
- maroon
- red
- yellow

Some browsers support additional named colors. However, there's no guarantee that users on other browsers will see the colors the way you designed them to be displayed, because other browsers' vendors may not be able to recognize colors beyond the named color palette.

At the most fundamental level, all colors you see on your computer's monitor and on a printed page are derived from a combination of three colors: red, green, and blue. You can mix colors based on a percentage value for each. For example, setting red at 50%, green at 50%, and blue at 50% yields gray, while setting them all to 100% yields white. CSS provides a shorthand notation for mixing colors based on their percentage of red, green, and blue:

```
rgb(percentRed, percentGreen, percentBlue)
```

Set the `color` property as shown to change the background color of the `name` element in the periodic table XML document to green:

```
name {
  background-color: rgb(0%,50%,0%);
}
```

Percentage values are a little difficult to get used to at first, especially if you haven't worked with them. However, their key benefit is that they allow a high degree of flexibility. Table 6.3 lists the 16 basic colors that all Web browsers support, along with their equivalent RGB color percentages, to help you understand how RGB values transform into colors. One thing you should watch out for is creating RGB values that may be difficult for other browsers to display. If you create a color combination that's not directly supported by the browser on a particular system, the browser will determine the closest color match and use it instead. The colors may end up looking a little different than you intended.

Another way of creating colors using RGB values is to use numbers. RGB values range between 0 and 255. For example, `rgb( 0, 0, 0 )` represents black, and `rgb( 0, 128, 0 )` represents green. Table 6.4 lists the 16 named colors and their equivalent RGB numeric values.

TABLE 6.3 NAMED COLORS AND THEIR RGB PERCENTAGE EQUIVALENTS

Color	RGB Values
aqua	rgb (0%, 100%, 100%)
black	rgb (0%, 0%, 0%)
blue	rgb (0%, 0%, 100%)
fuchsia	rgb (100%, 0%, 100%)
gray	rgb (50%, 50%, 50%)
green	rgb (0%, 50%, 0%)
lime	rgb (0%, 100%, 0%)
maroon	rgb (50%, 0%, 0%)
navy	rgb (0%, 0%, 50%)
olive	rgb (50%, 50%, 0%)
purple	rgb (50%, 0%, 50%)
red	rgb (100%, 0%, 0%)
silver	rgb (80%, 80%, 80%)
teal	rgb (0%, 50%, 50%)
white	rgb (100%, 100%, 100%)
yellow	rgb (100%, 100%, 0%)

TABLE 6.4 NAMED COLORS AND THEIR EQUIVALENT RGB NUMERIC VALUES

Color	RGB Values
aqua	rgb (0, 255, 255)
black	rgb (0, 0, 0)
blue	rgb (0, 0, 255)
fuchsia	rgb (255, 0, 255)
gray	rgb (128, 128, 128)
green	rgb (0, 128, 0)
lime	rgb (0, 255, 0)
maroon	rgb (128, 0, 0)
navy	rgb (0, 0, 128)
olive	rgb (128, 128, 0)
purple	rgb (128, 0, 128)
red	rgb (255, 0, 0)
silver	rgb (192, 192, 192)
teal	rgb (0, 128, 128)
white	rgb (255, 255, 255)
yellow	rgb (255, 255, 0)

If you look closely at the RGB values in Table 6.4, you'll notice that the values are equivalent to the values in Table 6.3. For example, the RGB value for silver is 192,192,192. This corresponds to the percentage values of silver in Table 6.3, where the percentages are 80%, 80%, and 80%. If you want to convert percentage values into their numeric values, simply multiply the percentage value by 255. Numeric values are useful when you use a graphics editor, because they tend to express colors using numeric RGB values as opposed to their equivalent percentages.

The final way of expressing colors is to use another, more compact numeric notation that also uses individual numbers for RGB values. However, this notation expresses RGB values using a single long number, as opposed to three different numbers. The long number that you use to define an RGB value is expressed using hexadecimal notation, which is based on the number 16. This is a number that's important to both computers and programmers.

The numbers you use every day are based around the number 10, referred to as base-10, so that valid digits range between 0 and 9. In hexadecimal numbering, referred to as base-16, valid digits range between 0 and 9 and the letters A to F. Table 6.5 shows the relationship between base-10 and base-16 numbering systems.

At first glance, the relationship between the two numbering systems looks a little strange. However, it's a very efficient way of representing large numbers using a compact notation that computers and developers can easily understand. When you use hexadecimal numbers, prefix the number using the pound sign, #, which is also referred to as a *hash mark* or simply the *number sign*.

One of the advantages of using hexadecimal numbers for RGB color values is that you don't have to put the number into an rgb (...) declaration, as you've done so far. The following CSS declaration sets the background color of the atom element to silver:

```
atom {
  background-color: #C0C0C0;
}
```

TABLE 6.5 SELECTED BASE-10 AND BASE-16 NUMBERS	
Base-10 Number	**Equivalent Base-16 Number**
0	0
1	1
9	9
10	A
11	B
15	F
16	10
20	14
32	20
41	29
42	2A
128	80
192	C0
255	FF
256	100

The hexadecimal notation is much more compact than the percentage and numeric representations, because it provides all three values for red, green, and blue using a single number. The format of the number is #rrGGbb, where rr represents two digits for the red component, GG represents two digits for the green component, and bb represents two digits for the blue component.

The case of the letters in the hexadecimal number isn't important. However, developers usually stick to using uppercase or lowercase throughout a single CSS document to make it easier to read.

Table 6.6 lists the named colors and their equivalent RGB hexadecimal colors.

TABLE 6.6 NAMED COLORS AND EQUIVALENT RGB HEXADECIMAL VALUES	
Color	**RGB Values**
aqua	#00FFFF
black	#000000
blue	#0000FF
fuchsia	#FF00FF
gray	#808080
green	#008000
lime	#00FF00
maroon	#800000
navy	#000080
olive	#808000
purple	#800080
red	#FF0000
silver	#C0C0C0
teal	#008080
white	#FFFFFF
yellow	#FFFF00

If you decide to start using hexadecimal numeric notation, you'll be able to save a few keystrokes when you type certain color values. You can use a special shorthand notation that uses only three hexadecimal numbers, as opposed to six, for certain colors. Here's how you can create some colors using the shorthand notation:

```
atom { color: #0FF }   /* Aqua */
name { color: #FFF }   /* White */
symbol { color: #F00 } /* Red */
```

The shorthand notation works in the same way that the longhand notation does. You still provide RGB values, but CSS doubles up each digit for you. For example, the value #0FF expands to #00FFFF, and #F00 expands to #FF0000. You can impress your friends and coworkers with your in-depth knowledge of CSS!

Background Images

Adding color to your XML documents using CSS makes them look more interesting and more appealing to a lot of readers. You can go a little further by adding images to your documents. For example, Figure 6.16 shows the periodic table XML document with a background image of an atom on the right side.

You can add a background image to any element in an XML document using the background-image property, as shown in the following listing:

```
periodicTable {
   background-image: url(x:\atom-background.jpg);
}
```

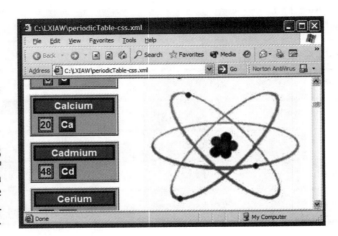

Figure 6.16

Adding a background image to an XML document.

The background-image property takes a single value, which is the name and location of the file that contains the image you want to use for your document's background. The url(...) in this listing can contain the name and location of the file on your local system's hard drive or somewhere out on the Internet. In this example, the file's name is atom-background.jpg and its location is x:\. If you use the CSS statements as shown, you won't be able to see the background image because you need to add a couple of properties:

```
periodicTable {
  width:100%;
  background-image: url(x:\atom-background.jpg);
}


atom { ...
/* rest of CSS follows */
```

The width property in this listing sets the width of the element that the property appears in. In this case, the width of the periodicTable element is equal to the width of the browser window because the width is 100 percent. As previously discussed, you can use various units of measurement to express the value for a property like width. However, using a percentage value ensures that the periodicTable element uses the full width of the browser window regardless of how large or small the user makes it. The CSS statements in the preceding listing produce the document shown Figure 6.17.

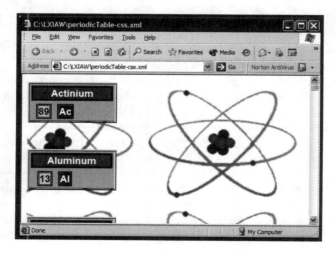

Figure 6.17

Using the background-image **property.**

If you look closely at Figure 6.17, you'll notice that the image of the atom appears to be tiled. That is, it repeats throughout the document. (I increased the space between each element on the left side of the document to make the image of the atom more visible.)

There are several more properties that you can use to control the layout of the background image. One of these properties, background-position, controls the location of the background image with respect to its containing element. Another property, background-repeat, controls how the browser tiles the background image. The following listing uses both properties to make the background image appear only along the right side of the browser's window:

```
periodicTable {
    width:100%;
    background-image: url(x:\atom-background.jpg);
    background-repeat: repeat-y;
    background-position: 100% 0%;
}
```

The background-repeat property can have one of several values, as shown in Table 6.7.

TABLE 6.7 VALID VALUES FOR THE BACKGROUND-REPEAT PROPERTY

Value	Description
repeat	Repeats the background image throughout the document. The background image first appears at the top-left corner of the document and tiles to the right until it reaches the right side of the document. The background image continues to repeat this way to the end of the document.
no-repeat	The image appears once, at the top-left corner of the document, and doesn't repeat.
repeat-x	The image repeats horizontally, in rows, to the end of the document.
repeat-y	The image repeats vertically, in columns, to the end of the document.

The background-position property allows you to specify exactly where you want the background image to appear within a given element. The format of the property's value is

```
background-position: verticalPosition horizontalPosition;
```

The verticalPosition value indicates how high or low you want the background image to appear within its enclosing element, and the horizontalPosition value indicates how far to the left or right you want it to appear. You can specify the position using a number of approaches, including numeric values that use absolute (cm, in, px) or relative (%, em, ex) units of measure, or predefined named values.

Figure 6.18 summarizes some of the values you can use for the background-position property. The figure shows predefined named property values along with their equivalent percentage values. For example, if you want to position an image in the top-left corner, you can specify the values of the background-position property using either top left or 0% 0%.

The browser positions the image by setting the coordinates of its top-left corner, as shown in the small gray box in Figure 6.18. When you want an image

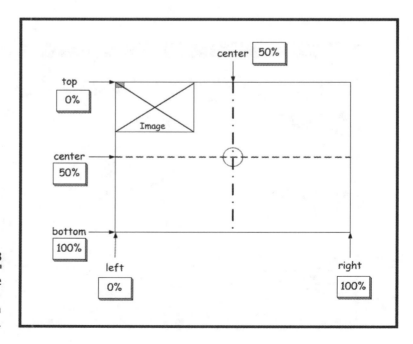

Figure 6.18

A summary of the background-position property's values.

to appear at the bottom-right corner of a document and use a `background-position` value of `bottom right`, the browser calculates the width and height of the image and positions it so that the image's bottom-left corner is at the bottom-right corner of the document.

Because specifying a background image and setting its position is common, CSS provides a shorthand syntax that allows you to specify both properties using a single property, as shown in the following listing:

```
periodicTable {
    background: url(x:\atom-background.jpg) 100% 0%;
    background-repeat: repeat-y;
    width:100%;
}
```

This listing demonstrates how you can use the `background` property to provide the name and location of the background image, along with its position. The preceding listing positions the background image as shown in Figure 6.19.

You can use negative values to specify an image's position. A negative value positions the top-left corner of an image outside of the browser's window, as shown in Figure 6.20. I've added a dotted border around the `periodicTable`

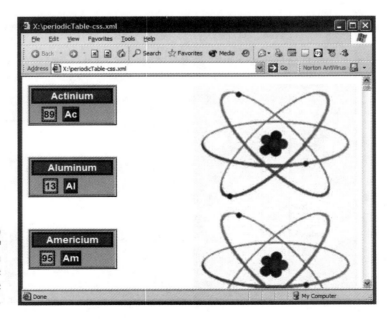

Figure 6.19

Positioning a background image along the right side of a document.

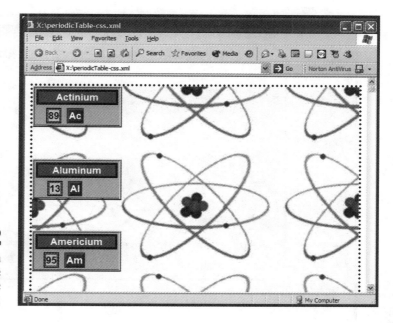

Figure 6.20

Positioning a
background image
using negative
values.

element to demonstrate that the background image begins and ends with half of the image missing.

Figure 6.21 is similar, except that it outlines the dimensions of the background image to give you an idea of how Internet Explorer positions the image so that it starts outside of the browser's window.

Manipulating Text and Fonts

You can improve the presentation of your XML documents by manipulating text and varying some fonts. Figure 6.22 shows a small sample of the effects you can achieve with CSS.

All of the formatted text in the figure is underlined, in addition to having some additional formatting applied to it. The first text manipulation, applied to the text "document's content", is subscript, so the text appears slightly below the surrounding text. The second effect, applied to the text "CSS formatting", is a transformation into uppercase. The next manipulation, applied to the text "rendering engine", expands the space between letters. You can change the font and its relative size, as in the "and applies" text.

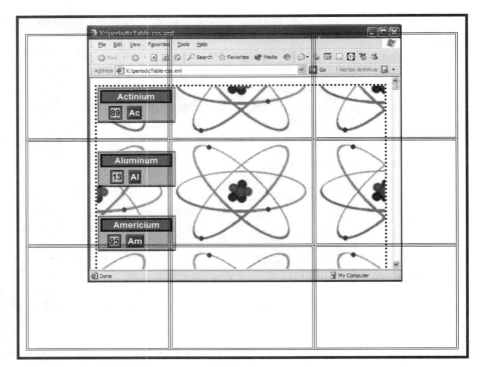

Figure 6.21

The same
background image
with its dimensions
outlined.

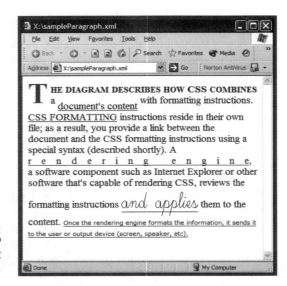

Figure 6.22

Manipulating text
and fonts.

The last manipulation, applied to the last sentence in the paragraph, makes the font about 60% of the size of the surrounding text.

The following listing is the XML document that contains the sample paragraph in the figure:

```
<?xml version="1.0" encoding="UTF-8"?>
<?xml-stylesheet type="text/css" href="sampleCSS.css"?>
<paragraphs>
  <paragraph>
    The diagram describes how CSS combines a <A>document's content</A>
    with formatting instructions. <B>CSS formatting</B> instructions
    reside in their own file; as a result, you provide a link between
    the document and the CSS formatting instructions using a special
    syntax (described shortly). A <C>rendering engine</C>, a software
    component such as Internet Explorer or other software that's
    capable of rendering CSS, reviews the formatting instructions
    <D>and applies</D> them to the content. <E>Once the rendering
    engine formats the information, it sends it to the user or output
    device (screen, speaker, etc).</E>
  </paragraph>
</paragraphs>
```

The sample paragraph has some additional tags (A, B, C, D, and E) to facilitate CSS formatting. The following listing shows the CSS used to format the document shown in Figure 6.22:

```
paragraph  {
  width: 100%;
  font-family: Serif;
  font-size: 14pt;
}
paragraph:first-letter {
  font-size: 300%;
  color: Red;
  font-weight: bold;
  float: left ;
  padding-right: 5px;
}
paragraph:first-line {
```

```
    font-variant: small-caps;
    font-weight: bold;
}
A {
    vertical-align: sub;
    text-decoration: underline;
}
B {
    text-transform: uppercase;
    text-decoration: underline;
}
C {
    letter-spacing: 1em;
    text-decoration: underline;
}
D {
    font-size: 250%;
    font-family: script;
    text-decoration: underline;
}
E {
    font-size: 60%;
    font-family: verdana,arial;
    text-decoration: underline;
}
```

This listing introduces a number of new CSS statements:

➤ `float`
➤ `padding`
➤ `vertical-align`
➤ `text-decoration`
➤ `text-transform`
➤ `letter-spacing`

Floating elements should be familiar to you, although you're probably not familiar with their name. One example of a floating element appears in a typical newspaper, where an article flows, or wraps around, a photograph or a quote from the article. The sample paragraph document has one floating element, the large letter T in Figure 6.22. You can float any element (table, text, images, etc.) using the `float` property, which has three valid values: `none` (the default value), `left`, and `right`.

An element's `padding` property adds some space within its borders. Whereas a margin indicates content boundaries, padding inserts space between the margin and the content, and around individual elements. Like most other CSS properties, you can use absolute or relative values. The sample uses an absolute value of `5px` in addition to using just the `padding-right` property.

The `vertical-align` property can have several values. However, the only values suitable for text are `sub` and `super`. You can use the `vertical-align` property with text, images, or other types of elements to add some interesting visual effects.

You can underline, strikethrough, and overline text using the `text-decoration` property. Specify what effect you want to apply to text using one of four values: `underline`, `overline`, `line-through`, and `blink`. Note that although `blink` is available, browsers aren't required to implement it and most do not. You can use this value, but it's not likely that you'll actually see blinking text.

The `text-transform` property is useful when you want to capitalize a portion of text without manipulating the source document. There are four valid values: `none` (the default value), `uppercase`, `lowercase`, and `capitalize`. The `capitalize` value causes each word affected by the property to have its first letter transformed into uppercase. The `font-variant` property allows you to change the casing of a font to small caps. You can see this effect in the first line of Figure 6.22.

You can change the spacing of letters using the `letter-spacing` property. You can use a value of `normal` (the default value) to allow the browser to determine an appropriate value, or you can provide a length using absolute or relative units of measure. A related property is `word-spacing`, which sets the amount of space that appears between individual words.

Figure 6.23 shows a floating text box that has some interesting effects, based on what we've seen so far, to create a quote from the sample paragraph to get a reader's attention.

The text in the floating text box comes from the sample paragraph and is designed to stand out from the surrounding text. The font is 85% of the size

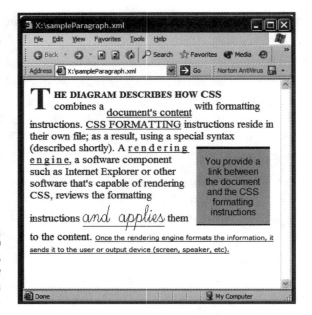

Figure 6.23

Getting a reader's
attention by
quoting text from a
paragraph.

of the rest of the document's font and uses a sans-serif style. The box that the
text appears in is offset from the surrounding text using a margin of 2% and
(internal) padding of 10% to make it easier to see the quoted text. The box
takes up 30% of the available space and has two borders, top and bottom.
The text in the quote box comes directly from the sample paragraph, so the
first letter is in lowercase. The quote's style uses the `first-letter` pseudo-
element to ensure that the first letter of the quote is always in uppercase.

The CSS that's used to create this effect appears in the following listing:

```
QUOTE:first-letter {
  text-transform:capitalize;
}

QUOTE {
  width: 30%;
  float: right;
  font-size:85%;
  font-family: sans-serif;
  text-align: center;
  margin: 2%;
```

```
    padding: 10%;
    border-top: medium black solid;
    border-bottom: thin black solid;
    background: silver;
}
```

CSS provides great facilities for adding interesting effects to your XML documents, making them more appealing both in print and onscreen. However, CSS has some limitations that can present problems when you want to access an element's attributes, for example. While efforts are under way to address these limitations, there's already a widely accepted standard called XSL that provides a lot of flexibility and is designed specifically for XML documents.

Good job—time for a break! Take a few minutes to look back and see what you've learned so far and congratulate yourself. The next section looks at more advanced formatting using XSL.

Understanding and Using XSL

The XSL processing model uses three documents:

➤ A source document that represents the document you want to transform.

➤ An instruction document that contains directions for transforming the source document.

➤ A result document that represents the transformed source document.

An XSL processor uses the instruction document to construct the result document based on the source document, as shown in Figure 1.1 on Friday evening's lesson, "Introducing XML." You can add more information to the result document based on instructions in the instruction document. In other words, the result document's size is *not* dependent on the source document's size. You make the XSL processor add information to the result document or ignore information in the source document.

Understanding XPath

Many of the benefits that XSL provides are based on its capability to easily identify and manipulate information in the source document using a notation called the XML Path Language, or XPath. This allows you to refer to parts of an XML document using absolute and relative expressions, making it possible to address parts of an XML document without actually knowing its underlying structure. Consider the following fragment of an XML document that contains a listing of systems, subsystems, components, and parts of a car:

```
<car>
  <!-- other systems omitted for brevity -->
  <system name="Fuel System">
    <subsystem name="Cruise Control">
      <components>
        <component name="Actuator Assy"/>
        <component name="Actuator Switch"/>
        <component name="Control Switch"/>
        <component name="Release Switch"/>
        <component name="Servo"/>
        <component name="Speed Sensor "/>
      </components>
    </subsystem>
    <subsystem name="Fuel Induction">
      <components>
        <component name="Fuel Injection">
          <parts>
            <part>Fuel Pressure Regulator</part>
            <part>Idle Speed Control</part>
            <part>Injector</part>
            <part>Injector Wiring </part>
          </parts>
        </component>
        <component name="Intake">
          <parts>
            <part>Intake Manifold</part>
            <part>Manifold Gasket </part>
          </parts>
        </component>
        <component name="Throttle Body "/>
      </components>
    </subsystem>
    <subsystem name="Fuel Supply">
      <components>
```

```
            <component name="Fuel Pump"/>
            <component name="Fuel Tank"/>
            <component name="Throttle Cable "/>
        </components>
      </subsystem>
    </system>
    <!-- other systems omitted for brevity -->
</car>
```

When you work with XPath, it's helpful to think of an XML document as a tree structure, as shown in Figure 6.24.

The tree begins at the car element, the document's root element. An element is referred to as a *node*, because it's part of a larger structure (the rest of the XML document) that's made up of a set of nodes. The root node contains a set of system nodes, each of which has a name (defined by the node's name attribute). Each system node can contain other nodes, including the subsystem, components, component, parts, and part nodes. The figure shows that the Electrical system node is the currently selected node, known as the *context node*.

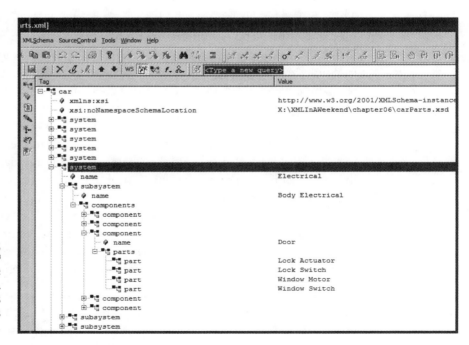

Figure 6.24

The tree structure of an XML document as viewed in Stylus Studio.

While visualizing an XML document as a tree structure is a key concept to understanding XPath, the concept of *context* is critical to understanding the XPath *expressions* that identify nodes within an XML document. Think of context as a pointer to the node that an XSLT processor is currently reviewing. You saw an example of context in a listing earlier in this lesson, although I didn't introduce it as a context at the time. Here's the listing again:

```
<xsl:template match="atom">              -->     <atom>
  <tr>
    <td>
      <xsl:value-of select="name"/>      -->       <name>Carbon</name>
    </td>
    <td>
      <xsl:value-of select="number"/>    -->       <number>6</number>
    </td>
    <td>
      <xsl:value-of select="symbol"/>    -->       <symbol>C</symbol>
    </td>
  </tr>
</xsl:template>                          -->     </atom>
```

This listing is divided into two sides, left and right. The left side of the listing shows XSL instructions, and the right side shows the XSL processor's context. When the XSL processor encounters the <xsl:template...> instruction, it sets its pointer to refer to the atom element in the source document and proceeds to read subsequent instructions. The two tags that follow (<tr> and <td>) are HTML tags, which the XSL processor simply passes on to the result document because they aren't XSL PIs. The <xsl:value-of...> instruction causes the XSL processor to move its context ahead by one node in the source document to refer to the name element, and then extract the value associated with that element (Carbon). The process continues until the context reaches the end of the atom element at the closing atom tag (</atom>), at which point the XSL processor resumes processing the rest of the document. If the first <xsl:value-of...> instruction's select attribute is set to "description" instead of "name", the XSL processor won't be able to find that element in the current context because it only knows about the atom, name, number, and symbol elements.

An XPath expression allows you to set or manipulate the context. For example, the XPath expression /car/system[6] refers to the Electrical system node of the document in Figure 6.24. When the XSL processor encounters an

XPath expression, it evaluates the expression, which yields one of four types of results:

➤ Node-set (a collection of nodes)

➤ Boolean value (a value that represents true or false)

➤ Number (a numeric value that can have a decimal)

➤ String (a sequence of characters)

For example, the expression /car/system[6] yields a node-set that describes the sixth system node, which is a sub-node (child node) of the car node (which represents the document's root node) in the source XML document (the Electrical system node).

I have introduced several new terms and concepts as part of the XPath discussion so far:

➤ Absolute and relative expressions

➤ Tree structure

➤ Node

➤ Context and context node

➤ XPath expressions

It's time to learn about these terms through some examples. I'll use XML Spy and Stylus Studio for these demonstrations. Don't worry if you can't or don't want to follow along at this point, because the discussion includes several figures to help you along the way. If you intend to follow along, start XML Spy, open the carParts.xml file (located in the XMLInAWeekend\chapter06 folder), and select XML, Evaluate XPath from the menu.

The XML Spy XPath Expression evaluator allows you to interactively experiment with XPath expressions and see immediate results. The evaluator window has three parts: a box where you can type an XPath expression, a series of options, and a large results box that displays the result of evaluating the XPath expression. Type **car/system** into the XPath field. (You don't have to press Enter, but make sure that you use the correct slash character.) The result is shown in Figure 6.25.

The evaluator displays several system nodes in the large results box. The expression begins at the car node and selects all system nodes. The cursor should still be at the end of the expression you just typed in. Continue by adding /[@name] to the end of the expression so that the whole expression

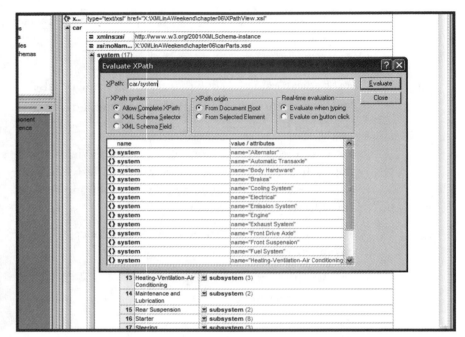

Figure 6.25

The result of evaluating a simple XPath expression using XML Spy.

becomes car/system/[@name] (note the square brackets). The evaluator changes the contents of the result window to only display the values of all the system nodes' name attributes. The XPath expression you just typed selects all car nodes (there's only one because it's the root node) and all system nodes that appear within the car node, and selects all system nodes' name attributes.

The XPath expression is rather general right now because it just selects any nodes that match the expression. XPath expressions can identify particular nodes, though. Edit the XPath expression to read as follows:

```
/ car / system [ @name= "Electrical" ]/ *
```

The expression includes some additional spaces to make it easier to read. You can exclude these spaces if you prefer. It doesn't make any difference in the final result. Also, please note the following points about the expression:

➤ You can use single quotes (') or double quotes (") around the word Electrical.

➤ The word Electrical must appear as shown, with an uppercase letter E followed by the remaining letters in lowercase.

➤ The last character in the expression is an asterisk (*).

This time the expression yields a list of six subsystem nodes that are children of the Electrical system node, along with the value of each node's name attribute.

The expressions you've seen so far are referred to as *absolute expressions* because they explicitly identify which nodes will be part of the resulting node-set. The preceding expression begins with the slash character (which represents the root node), selects the car node and then all system nodes, and filters out all nodes except for the system node that has an attribute called name with the value "Electrical". While absolute paths are great when you have a clear understanding of the context node's position (because the expression modifies the context node), they're inefficient when you want to traverse from the context node to some other part of the document. It doesn't make sense to refer to the Emission System system node (the seventh system node in the document) using an absolute expression when the context node refers to the Electrical system node (the sixth system node in the document).

One effective means of traversing a document from the context node to another node is based on the idea of a relative path. Relative paths are easy to understand when you see them in action.

Close the Evaluate XPath window in XML Spy and select View, Enhanced Grid View from the menu to ensure that XML Spy is in the appropriate display mode. (Don't worry if the display doesn't change, because chances are XML Spy is already displaying the document in Enhanced Grid View.) The XML Spy window should look similar to the one in Figure 6.26.

Figure 6.26

Viewing an XML document using XML Spy's Enhanced Grid View.

XML Spy allows you to set the context node so you can test XPath expressions from another point in the XML document. The following directions describe how to make /car/system[3]/subsystem[1] (the "Body Hardware" "Door" subsystem) the current node:

1. Click on the small arrow to the left of the word "car," as shown in Figure 6.27. This expands the car node, revealing two namespaces and one system node.

2. Click on the small arrow to the left of the system node, at the bottom of the box in the main window. This expands the system node to reveal a number of subsystem nodes.

3. Locate the third system node and click on the small arrow to the left. This reveals a number of subsystem nodes.

4. Click on the word "Door" to make that node the context node, as shown in Figure 6.27. Make sure that you click on the word "Door," not on the number 1 to its left or the word "components" to its right.

Before you continue, ensure that the XML Spy window looks similar to the one in Figure 6.27.

Time to try a few experiments! Select XML, Evaluate XPath from the menu to invoke the XPath evaluator as you did before. You can select from three groups of options in the middle of the evaluator's window. The group in the middle

Figure 6.27

Selecting the context node in XML Spy's Enhanced Grid View.

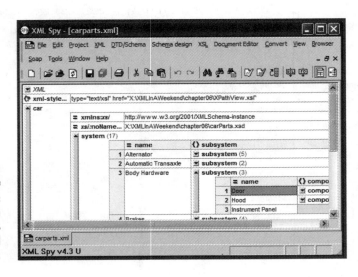

is labeled XPath Origin. Click on the circle to the left of the phrase "From Selected Element," or simply press Alt+L if you prefer to use the keyboard.

XPath supports a number of axes, which allow you to refer to part of a document without referring to it by name. For example, when you refer to yourself, you usually use a word like "I," "myself," or "me," because you're the speaker and it's understood that you're referring to yourself. XPath axes work in the same way. For example, you can refer to the context node (the current node in the XML document) using the `self` axis that always refers to the context node. Type the following expression into the XPath field:

```
self::*
```

Note that the word `self` is followed by two colons (::) and an asterisk (*). The evaluator's results box (the large box at the bottom of the evaluator's window) should show a reference to the "Door" subsystem using two columns. The column on the left contains the string `()` `subsystem`, and the column on the right contains the string `name="Door"`. This confirms that the context (current) node is indeed the `/car/system[3]/subsystem[1]` node. You can get an idea of how far you are from the document's root node by adding `/ancestor::*` to the expression in the XPath field so that the complete expression is as follows:

```
self::*/ancestor::*
```

As before, the word `ancestor` is followed by two colons and an asterisk. The evaluator's results box should now show two nodes: a `system` node with a `name` attribute equal to `"Body Hardware"`, and a `car` node with a namespace declaration. This indicates that the context node is two nodes from the document's root node. Looking around some more, you can get an idea of which other elements are at the same level as the current node by changing the XPath expression to the following:

```
self::*/following-sibling::*
```

The `following-sibling` axis refers to all nodes that have the same parent node as the context node. The previous example revealed that the context node's parent node is the third `system` node (the `"Body Hardware"` node). The evaluator's results box shows that there are two additional `subsystem` nodes that follow the context node in the XML document (the `"Hood"` and `"Instrument Panel"` nodes). You can confirm that the parent node is indeed the "Body Hardware" system node by modifying the XPath expression so that it looks like this one:

```
self::*/parent::*
```

You can get an idea of how far the context node is from the end of the document by getting a reference to all nodes that descend from the context node. Modify the XPath expression so that it appears as follows:

```
self::*/descendant::*
```

The evaluator's results box shows a node-set that lists the components node followed by four component nodes.

These demonstrations are interesting so far, but they just explore the nodes that surround the context node. What if you want to analyze a document to understand how many nodes are in the document without directly referring to the names of the nodes? Try the following XPath expression:

```
count(/child::*/descendant::*)
```

The evaluator's results box should have the number 348 in it. This number represents how many nodes are in the document! Want proof? Remove the count(string from the beginning of the expression and the closing bracket from the end of the expression to get a complete list.

How about a listing of system nodes that start with the letter E? This type of expression is a bit of a challenge. The expression needs to evaluate each system node it encounters to determine if it starts with a capital letter E, and then it must generate a node-set that includes only the nodes that qualify. You can make this challenge a little more interesting by using only XPath axes. Don't use any names that appear in the XML document.

Give it some consideration before you look at the answer. Perhaps refer to the XPath Reference section in Appendix A.

Here's the answer:

```
/child::*/child::*/attribute::*[starts-with(@*,"E")]
```

Try it in the XPath Expression evaluator and you'll see the listing of nodes shown in Figure 6.28.

That's neat! So how does the expression work? It cheats a little with some knowledge of the structure of the XML document, because it begins by

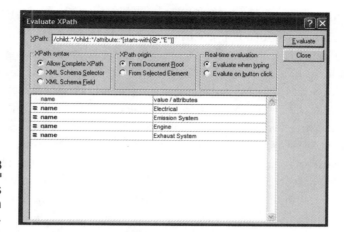

Figure 6.28

A listing of nodes whose names begin with the letter E.

referring to the child axis' children (the /car/system node-set). The next part of the expression, attribute::*, limits the expression to referring to a node-set that contains only attributes. The last part of the expression is a predicate that uses the XPath starts-with string function to evaluate the value of each node (@*) to determine if it starts with the capital letter E.

If you're not interested in knowing the names of the matching nodes and just want to know how many there are, modify the expression as shown:

```
count(/child::*/child::*/attribute::*[starts-with(@*,"E")])
```

Now that you're a master of XPath, it's time to put your newfound knowledge to work by transforming the carParts.xml document into an HTML page. If you're not familiar with HTML, refer to Appendix A. There you'll also find an XPath reference, in case you need a refresher.

Transforming an XML Document into HTML

Let's skip the theoretical discussion and get right into working with XSL. First, let's look at how to transform the listing of car parts you've been working with into an HTML page that you can view using Internet Explorer. Although XSL is great at transforming XML into other formats, using it to transform a document into HTML makes it easy to visualize the transformation process and work with the results.

Although you've been working with the carParts.xml file, you haven't been formally introduced. The carParts system element describes a major system in a car, such as the brake, cooling, and electrical systems. Each system is made up of a number of subsystems, such as fuel induction and fuel supply. Going into further detail, subsystem elements can act as a container for components, although that's not always the case. The components element acts as a container for component elements that represents elements that make up the subsystem. The parts element represents the lowest level of detail, because it acts as a container for the list of part elements representing individual parts that make up a particular component. The only required element in the document is the system element. All other elements are optional.

At this point, you should be able to read either a DTD or an XSD to gain a quick and thorough understanding of the document's structure. The following listing is for your reference. It represents the XSD for the carParts XML document:

```xml
<?xml version="1.0" encoding="UTF-8"?>
<xs:schema xmlns:xs="http://www.w3.org/2001/XMLSchema"
  elementFormDefault="qualified">

  <xs:element name="car">
    <xs:complexType>
      <xs:sequence>
        <xs:element name="system"
          type="systemType"
          maxOccurs="unbounded"/>
      </xs:sequence>
    </xs:complexType>
  </xs:element>

  <xs:complexType name="systemType">
    <xs:sequence>
      <xs:element name="subsystem"
        type="subsystemType"
        minOccurs="0"
        maxOccurs="unbounded"/>
    </xs:sequence>
    <xs:attribute
```

```
        name="name" type="xs:string"
        use="required"/>
</xs:complexType>

<xs:complexType name="subsystemType">
  <xs:sequence>
    <xs:element name="components"
      type="componentsType"
      minOccurs="0"/>
  </xs:sequence>
  <xs:attribute name="name"
    type="xs:string"
    use="required"/>
</xs:complexType>

<xs:complexType name="componentsType">
  <xs:sequence>
    <xs:element name="component"
      type="componentType"
      maxOccurs="unbounded"/>
  </xs:sequence>
</xs:complexType>
<xs:element name="part" type="xs:string"/>

<xs:complexType name="componentType">
  <xs:sequence>
    <xs:element name="component"
      type="componentType"
      minOccurs="0"
      maxOccurs="unbounded"/>
    <xs:element name="parts"
      type="partsType"
      minOccurs="0"/>
  </xs:sequence>
  <xs:attribute name="name"
    type="xs:string"
    use="required"/>
</xs:complexType>
```

```
<xs:complexType name="partsType">
  <xs:sequence>
    <xs:element ref="part"
      maxOccurs="unbounded"/>
  </xs:sequence>
</xs:complexType>
```

```
</xs:schema>
```

The carParts XML document provides a lot of interesting information, but it can be difficult to read when you use Internet Explorer to view the document because it applies a default format. This is especially true if you're not familiar with XML. Figure 6.29 shows what the XML document will look like after transforming it using XSL.

The formatting looks simple at first glance, but the document has some features that make it easier to figure out which subsystems, components, and parts make up individual systems. For example, subsystems are *sometimes* made up of components, which in turn *may* contain parts. Figure 6.30 shows a segment of the parts listing that shows all optional elements using a sublist, or a list within a list.

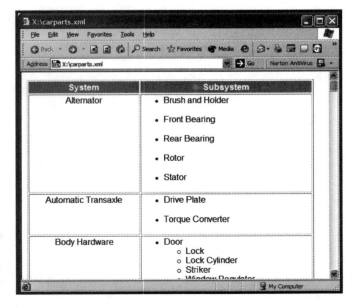

Figure 6.29

The final transformed car parts listing.

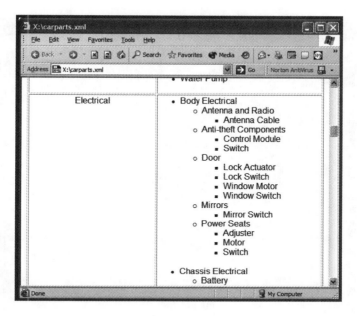

Figure 6.30

Details of the transformed car parts listing.

You'll work with XML Spy and Stylus Studio from this point on. If you plan to follow along, start both of those applications now. If not, read this section anyway to get an idea of how these tools work.

The XSL that transforms the XML document is a little too complicated to completely generate using XML Spy. However, you can use it to generate the base XSL and then use the XML Spy IDE to add additional features.

The first thing that you need to ensure is that you have a schema, a DTD or XSD document, for the carParts XML document because XML Spy's XSLT Designer relies on it. You can use the XML Spy IDE to create the schema for you, because you already have a complete copy of the XML document. Use the XML Spy IDE to open the carParts.xml file in the chapter06 directory of the XMLInAWeekend folder, and select DTD/Schema from the menu. Then select Generate DTD/Schema, as shown in Figure 6.31.

The Generate DTD/Schema dialog box offers some options for generating the schema. XML Spy can generate five types of schemas, but DTD and W3C Schema are the only options relevant for most XML documents. You should already be familiar with DTDs and some of their limitations, so using XSD makes sense because it has gained broad acceptance. XML Spy uses the

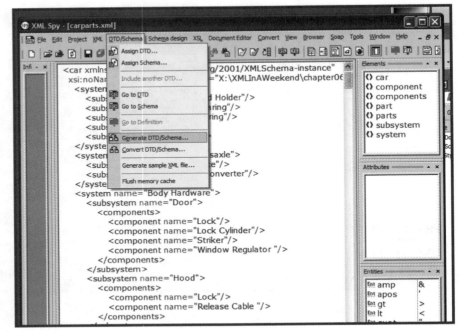

Figure 6.31

Generating a schema using XML Spy.

term *W3C Schema* to represent what you've come to know as XSD. The List of Values options allow you to limit possible values that an element or attribute can have. That option isn't useful in this case, so configure it as shown in Figure 6.32. Because XSD is data type-aware, you can configure XML Spy to generate a schema for all data types or numeric data types only, or simply to not generate any data type information through the Attribute/Element type detection options. The last two options affect how XML Spy declares complex types and global definitions. Configure the options as shown in Figure 6.32 to generate a schema that's similar in structure to the ones you've been working with throughout this book.

When XML Spy generates the schema for you, a message box pops up, offering you the opportunity to assign the schema to the XML document. Select Yes. XML Spy needs to save the schema before it can assign it to the carParts document, so it asks you to provide a name and location for the new schema. You can save it in the XMLInAWeekend\chapter06 folder and assign the schema a name that's easy to remember. Select File, Close All to close any open files, and then start the XSLT Designer.

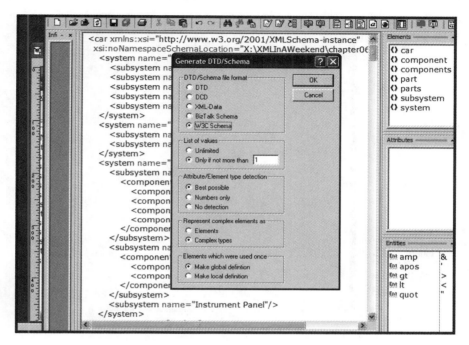

Figure 6.32

Configuring schema generation options.

The XML Spy XSLT Designer is capable of creating a lot of interesting effects, as you saw earlier in Sunday morning's lesson, "Understanding XML Editors." However, because the transformation in this example is complex, you'll use the XSLT Designer to create the basic XSL and then add additional transformation directives manually.

The XSLT Designer actually works with the schema file you just created, and uses the XML document to generate sample output whenever you want to check your progress. Begin by opening the schema you just generated using the File, Open menu options. When the designer opens the schema file, it displays the structure of the document on the left and the design surface on the right, as shown in Figure 6.33.

Expand the schema as shown in Figure 6.33 by clicking on the plus sign that appears beside each element in the schema. The XSLT Designer uses the drag and drop approach to editing a style sheet, where you drag each element from the schema view onto the design surface and drop it where you want it to appear in the final document. Click on the `system` element, press and hold the left mouse button, and drag to the right side of the screen, as shown in

Figure 6.33

The XSLT Designer
schema view and
design surface.

Figure 6.34. The pointer changes to a circle with a line through it when you move it over a location that you cannot drop the element on. Keep moving the pointer until it's at the spot between the word (contents) and the ending mark. Release the mouse button when the pointer appears as shown in Figure 6.34.

When you release the mouse button, the designer presents you with a pop-up menu that asks how you would like to create contents in the final document. You can choose from several options, but select the Create Table option for now. Then the designer asks you which columns you want to have in the table. Accept the default options and click OK. The designer generates the table, as shown in Figure 6.35.

You can get an idea of your progress so far by having the designer generate a preview of the final document. Because the designer actually works with the schema, it doesn't have any data to generate the preview document for you. It has the specification to generate the preview, but it doesn't know what data to display when it performs the transformation. You can assign what the designer refers to as a *working XML document*, which contains the data you

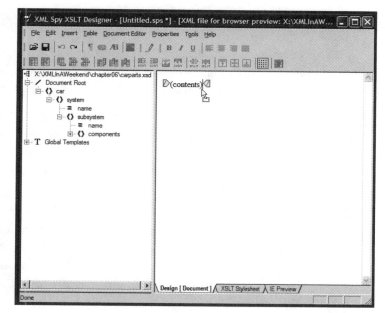

Figure 6.34

Dragging an element onto the XSLT Designer design surface.

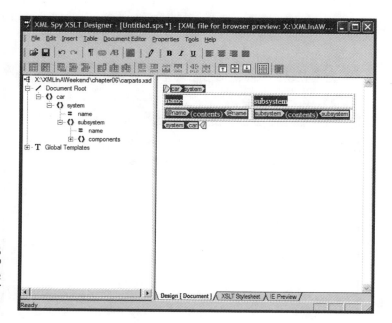

Figure 6.35

Creating a table using the XSLT Designer.

use to generate the preview document. You can assign a working XML document by clicking on File, Assign Working XML File, selecting the carParts.xml file, and clicking the Open button. Click on the IE Preview tab at the bottom of the design surface's window. You can see that the final document is starting to take shape, although the data isn't quite right.

Click on the Design Document tab at the bottom of the designer window to display the designer view again. You can correct the data in the final document by dragging the subsystem element's name attribute onto the design surface and dropping it within the subsystem element, as shown in Figure 6.36.

You drag the subsystem element's name attribute onto the design surface by clicking on the =name symbol, just below the subsystem element in the schema view on the left side of the screen. Drag the attribute to the location shown in Figure 6.36. As before, the designer will ask you how you want the element to appear in the final document. Select Create Contents for now. If you did everything correctly, you should end up with the design surface shown in Figure 6.37.

Click on the IE Preview tab at the bottom of the designer window to see the results of what you just did. Notice that the data is correct this time, but it

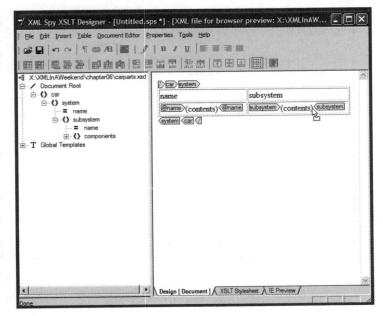

Figure 6.36

Dragging an attribute onto the design surface.

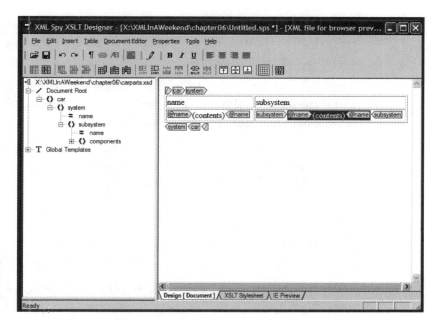

Figure 6.37

Adding an attribute
to an existing
document.

still needs some formatting to make it easier to read. Click on the @name marker to the left of the word (contents), right-click, and select Change to List from the pop-up menu. When you click on the IE preview tab again, you'll see that the information in the document is correct.

This is as far as we can go using the XSLT Designer, so save your work by clicking on the File, Save Generated XSLT File. Name the file carParts.xsl and save it in the same folder as the schema file. You won't work with the XSLT Designer, so close it and switch back to XML Spy (or open it again if you closed it) and open the carParts.xsl file. Despite the document's seemingly simple appearance, the XSLT Designer generated a lot of code for you. Fortunately, it's fairly easy to read and understand, as you'll see shortly.

You might be asking why you need to understand XSL in the first place if applications like the XSLT Designer generate the XSL code for you. While you can do some amazing things with the XSLT Designer and tools like it, you'll find that once you reach a certain level of complexity, the tool either cannot implement the functionality or becomes too cumbersome to describe what you want to do using the tool. I personally use the XSLT Designer to create the base document that I want to transform an XML document into, and then manually edit the code to add the final details. It boosts productivity because the designer makes it easy to generate the base XSL code using a drag and drop approach.

The XSL that the XSLT Designer generated is fairly long (about two pages) and includes XSL elements along with HTML elements. It's easier to understand what's happening if you break the XSL into smaller parts.

This exercise will show you how to add the final details to produce the result shown back in Figure 6.29. The following listing shows the first three lines of the XSL code that the XSLT Designer generated:

```
<?xml version="1.0" encoding="UTF-8"?>
<xsl:stylesheet version="1.0"
xmlns:xsl="http://www.w3.org/1999/XSL/Transform"
xmlns:xsi="http://www.w3.org/2001/XMLSchema-instance">
```

This listing begins with an XML declaration, because XSL is an XML vocabulary. No surprises here. The next line declares the `stylesheet` element and defines two namespaces: `xsl` and `xsi`. The `xsl` namespace contains all XSL elements, so all XSL elements will have an `xsl:` prefix. The `xsi` namespace was discussed earlier on Saturday evening under the heading, "Associating an XSD with an XML Document."

As described earlier in the lesson, XSL uses a declarative approach to describe how to transform an XML document. The next three lines of the XSL declare the template that the XSL processor uses to transform the document:

```
<xsl:template match="/">
  <html>
    <head/>
    <body>
```

The template matches all root elements in an XML document. Recall that there's only one root element per XML document, so the template acts as the starting point for the transformation. Because the final document is an HTML page, the first few tags that the template produces are the HTML declaration, the `head` element, and the `body` element that contains the page's content. Refer to Appendix A for the HTML reference.

One thing that will help you learn XSL is to read through XSL documents that others have created. The XSL document in this section uses a single template to transform the whole document, the beginning of which is in the preceding listing. Other XSL documents that you'll come across don't use this approach, as you saw earlier in the overview. It's common for XSL documents to have several templates that interact with one another to transform an XML document. The carParts.xsl document takes another approach, declaring a single template that contains all transformation instructions using structures like loops and decision statements to transform the XML document. This approach makes it easier to understand XSL.

The following two lines establish the first of several loop structures you'll encounter in the document:

```
<xsl:for-each select="car">
  <xsl:for-each select="system">
```

A loop structure works by executing a series of instructions repeatedly until a certain condition is met. In this case, the for-each loop carries out the enclosed instructions once for each member of the node-set identified by the for-each element's select attribute. The xsl:for-each loop's select attribute contains an XPath expression that refers to a node-set. The for-each structure carries out the commands that the element encloses once for each node in the node-set.

When a for-each element contains another for-each element, the elements are said to *nest*, with the *inner* element nesting within the *outer* element. The two loops work sequentially; that is, the outer for-each invokes the inner for-each. The outer for-each cannot carry out any more instructions until the inner for-each finishes carrying out its enclosed instructions for each of the nodes in its node-set.

Processing continues with some <xsl:if...> elements, as shown in the following listing:

```
<xsl:if test="position()=1">
  <xsl:text disable-output-escaping="yes">&lt;table
border="1"&gt;</xsl:text>
</xsl:if>
<xsl:if test="position()=1">
  <thead>
    <tr>
      <td>name</td>
```

```
      <td>subsystem</td>
    </tr>
  </thead>
</xsl:if>
<xsl:if test="position()=1">
  <xsl:text disable-output-escaping="yes">&lt;tbody&gt;</xsl:text>
</xsl:if>
```

This listing generates the beginning of the HTML table shown in Figure 6.29. The XSL code uses an if element to determine when to generate the HTML table, thead, tr, and td elements by checking the value the XPath position function returns.

An if element's role is to make a decision based on the result of a test, which returns a Boolean value (true or false). The instructions enclosed within the if element are carried out when the test returns Boolean true. Otherwise, the enclosed instructions aren't carried out and processing continues at the closing if tag (the end of the <xsl:if...> element). You provide the condition to test for in the if element's test attribute, which contains an XPath expression. The preceding listing uses the XPath position node-set function, which refers to the position of the context node relative to an enclosing node-set. In this example, the position function refers to the context node's position within the node-set specified by the second for-each element in the previous listing (<xsl:for-each select="system">). In other words, the position function determines the position of the context node relative to all of the system nodes in the document.

You'll notice that the preceding listing uses XML entity references, or special characters, on lines 2 and 13. Recall that XSL is an XML vocabulary, so it must follow the same strict rules that all other XML documents must follow. One of XML's rules requires that all elements have both a starting tag and an ending tag. The code on line 2 uses an HTML tag whose closing tag appears on line 13, long after the closing if tag on line 3. The entity references allow you to generate HTML tags that are closed after the current XML element closes. In effect, you're tricking the XML processor into thinking that you're generating text that requires you to use entity references, when in fact you're generating an HTML tag.

So far you've learned how to generate HTML elements by including them within an XSL document. When the XSL processor encounters non-XSL elements, it simply appends them to what ultimately becomes the resulting document. The following listing goes a step further and demonstrates how to extract information from the source XML document using a value-of element (the relevant line appears in bold):

```
<tr>
  <td>
    <xsl:for-each select="@name">
      <xsl:value-of select="."/>
    </xsl:for-each>
  </td>
</td>
```

The value-of element's select attribute contains an XPath expression that refers to some information in the source document that you want to copy to the resulting document. The XPath expression can refer directly to the name of an element or attribute, call an XPath function, or simply refer to the context node as in this case. The context node in this example refers to the name attribute of the system node. In other words, it generates a cell in an HTML table that contains the name of a system. The XSLT Designer generates a for-each element that refers to all name attributes of a system node. Because there's only one name attribute, you can rewrite the three XSL instructions in the preceding listing as one instruction: <xsl:value-of select="@name"/>. Don't actually change the code here, but be aware that there's usually more than one way to do something in XSL.

Processing continues with the following listing:

```
  <td>
    <xsl:for-each select="subsystem">
      <xsl:for-each select="@name">
        <xsl:if test="position()=1">
          <xsl:text disable-output-
escaping="yes">&lt;ul&gt;</xsl:text>
        </xsl:if>
        <li>
          <xsl:value-of select="."/>
        </li>
        <xsl:if test="position()=last()">
          <xsl:text disable-output-
escaping="yes">&lt;/ul&gt;</xsl:text>
```

```
            </xsl:if>
          </xsl:for-each>
        </xsl:for-each>
      </td>
  </tr>
```

The XSL in this block generates a listing of a system's subsystem nodes enclosed within an HTML unordered list (the HTML <ul> element). The listing generates the beginning HTML ul tag when the XSL processor encounters the first subsystem node, adds each subsystem node's name attribute's value to the list using an HTML li element, and closes the HTML ul tag when the XSL processor encounters the last subsystem node. The listing uses entity references to work around XML's strict syntactical rules and generate the opening and closing HTML ul tags.

The last part of the automatically generated XSL closes the HTML tbody and table elements when all system nodes have been processed. The XSL instructions also close the for-each elements you saw earlier, the HTML body and html elements, and the XSL template and stylesheet elements, as shown in the following listing:

```
            <xsl:if test="position()=last()">
              <xsl:text disable-output-
escaping="yes">&lt;/tbody&gt;</xsl:text>
            </xsl:if>
            <xsl:if test="position()=last()">
              <xsl:text disable-output-
escaping="yes">&lt;/table&gt;</xsl:text>
            </xsl:if>
          </xsl:for-each>
        </xsl:for-each>
      </body>
    </html>
  </xsl:template>
</xsl:stylesheet>
```

You can now add some new instructions to the XSL document to complete the transformation into the document you saw earlier in Figure 6.29, now that the basic XSL is in place. The sample code that accompanies this book, which you can get from the book's Web site (see the Preface), has the complete XSL document that you can use to generate the result document in Figure 6.29. I won't review every part of the XSL, but I will show you the relevant parts of the document that make the most noticeable difference, when compared to the XSL that the XSLT Designer generated.

The first major change is right at the beginning of the XSL document, as shown in the following listing (the new code appears in bold):

```
<?xml version="1.0" encoding="UTF-8"?>
<xsl:stylesheet
  version="1.0"
  xmlns:xsl="http://www.w3.org/1999/XSL/Transform"
  xmlns:xs="http://www.w3.org/2001/XMLSchema">

  <xsl:template match="/">
    <html>
      <head>
        <style type="text/css">

          td.header {
            text-align:center;
            font-weight:bold;
            background-color:silver;
            color:white;
          }

          body {
            font-family: sans-serif;
          }

        </style>
      </head>
```

The XSL document includes an HTML CSS declaration to provide a consistent look to the resulting document without adding a lot of HTML tags. The CSS defines a class for the HTML td element that creates the bold white text on a silver background in the first row of the table. The CSS also modifies the HTML body element's style to use a sans serif font, which is usually easier to read when you view it onscreen. The new CSS class is used a little later in the XSL when it generates the table's first row, as shown in the following listing:

```
<xsl:if test="position()=1">
  <thead>
    <tr>
      <td class="header">System</td>
      <td class="header">Subsystem</td>
    </tr>
  </thead>
</xsl:if>
```

Essentially, the bold HTML code associates the td elements with the td.header CSS formatting declaration.

The next change handles a special case where a system node doesn't have any subsystem nodes. There's only one occurrence of this case in the whole carParts.xml document. However, letting the subsystem's cell in the table remain blank looks a little different from the rest of the document. The following listing demonstrates how to determine if a system node has any subsystem nodes:

```
<xsl:if test="count(subsystem)=0">
  No Subsystems
</xsl:if>
```

This listing's instructions generate the message "No Subsystems" if there aren't any subsystem nodes within the current system node.

The final change occurs within the for-each element that generates the unordered HTML list of subsystem nodes, as shown in the following listing:

```
<xsl:if test="../child::*">
    <ul>
    <xsl:for-each select="../components/component">
        <li>
        <xsl:value-of select="@name"/>
        <xsl:if test="parts">
            <ul>
            <xsl:for-each select="parts/part">
                <li>
                <xsl:value-of select="."/>
```

```
            </li>
          </xsl:for-each>
          </ul>
        </xsl:if>
        </li>
    </xsl:for-each>
    </ul>
</xsl:if>
```

The first XSL instruction, in the if element, determines if a subsystem node has any components using the XPath child axis. The XPath expression (../child::*) begins with a reference to the parent axis using the double dot (..) shorthand notation. This is because when the context node reaches this point during XSL processing, it resides at the subsystem node's name attribute (as a result of the last instruction, which was a for-each element). The double dot notation (..) repositions the context node at the subsystem node, and the child:* notation references a node-set made up of the children of the subsystem node (the components node). The instructions within the if element are carried out when the XPath expression of the if element's test attribute results in a non-empty node-set. The instructions within the if element generate a contained HTML unordered list of components. The instructions within the if element also include a test for any parts nodes, which the instructions render as an enclosed unordered listing of part nodes.

You can review the results of the changes using Internet Explorer. Start Windows Explorer and locate the \XMLInAWeekend\chapter06 folder. Double-click on the carPartsTable.xml file to open it in Internet Explorer, or right-click on the file and select Open With, Internet Explorer.

Not only can XSL transform XML into HTML, but it can transform one XML document into another. That's the topic of the next section.

Repurposing XML Documents with XSL

In the majority of cases, presenting data on the Web involves presenting information directly to end users. However, often you could end up presenting XML to another system. Other applications, computers, other devices, and software usually have a specific purpose for using an XML document. If you or the consuming system change an XML document's content or schema before it's consumed, it's said to be *repurposed*. In the previous section, you transformed an XML document into a specific format (HTML) that ended up being used by Internet Explorer. Essentially, you repurposed the XML document for display by another application using XSL.

Another aspect of repurposing is producing another XML document based on a source XML document. In this section, you'll use Excelon Stylus Studio to create the basic transformation and do some manual editing to achieve the final result. The manual editing is necessary because this transformation is rather complex, and it can be a little difficult to describe the transformation using the editor. However, the editor is fully capable of representing the transformation using its built-in graphical editor.

You'll also get a sense for one of the product's very unique features, the built-in XSL debugger. When you're developing XSL, things don't always work out smoothly. It's often necessary to figure out what the XSL processor "sees" to determine why a transformation isn't producing the desired results. The Stylus Studio XSL Debugger allows you to interactively inspect the intermediate results of an XSL transformation as it takes place, which helps you quickly and easily locate problems in your XSL code. While you can buy a separate XSL debugger, Stylus Studio is the only general-purpose XML editor that includes its own XSL debugger.

This exercise uses the carParts XML document because you're probably familiar with its structure and content. You'll create an XSL document that dramatically changes the structure of the original document so that it looks like the following XML document:

```
<partsInventory>
  <item name="Fuel Pressure Regulator"
    component="Fuel Injection"
    onHand="4"
  >
    Install in Fuel System System in/on/near the Fuel Injection
  </item>
  <item name="Idle Speed Control"
    component="Fuel Injection"
    onHand="4"
  >
```

```
     Install in Fuel System System in/on/near the Fuel Injection
   </item>

   <item name="Injector"
     component="Fuel Injection"
     onHand="4"
   >
     Install in Fuel System System in/on/near the Fuel Injection
   </item>
   <item name="Injector Wiring"
     component="Fuel Injection"
     onHand="4"
   >
     Install in Fuel System System in/on/near the Fuel Injection
   </item>
</partsInventory>
```

This listing represents a service station's inventory parts. The document is enclosed within a partsInventory element, which describes all item elements. Each item has three attributes:

➤ name is the name of the part. This value comes from the part element in the original document.

➤ component is the component the part comes from. This value comes from the component element in the original document.

➤ onHand is the number of parts on hand. This is a new value that's introduced during the transformation.

Each item also has a value that describes what system and subsystem the part resides in. The description is based on the same static (unchanging) text, in addition to the values of the name attributes of the system and subsystem elements in the original document.

The transformation considers the subsystem's components that have parts and excludes any that don't have any parts. The transformation also needs to ensure that parts match with their respective components so that the description of where to install the part is accurate. Clearly, the new document has a different purpose than the original document. Your role is to create the XSL that repurposes the document.

The process you're about to follow introduces some flaws into the XSL to facilitate debugging. The final, correct version of the XSL document that correctly performs the transformation appears at the *end* of the discussion. I'll warn you ahead of time that you're about to introduce an error into the XSL. If you're not interested in debugging an XSL document, you can jump ahead to another subsection to continue the process of accurately creating the XSL. Whether you skip the debugging section or not, you'll end up with a correct XSL document.

Stylus Studio refers to an XSL document that repurposes an XML document as an XML-to-XML Mapping Stylesheet. The process is based on mapping the structure of an existing XML document onto the structure of a new XML document using the drag and drop editing of the XML Mapper. Stylus Studio works with XML schemas, because the mapping process relies on the structure of XML documents. So, you need to create a new schema of the new XML document before you can create the Mapping Stylesheet. (There's already a copy of the original carParts schema in the sample code, ready for you to work with.)

Creating a New Schema

You'll use the Stylus Studio tree editor to create the new schema that models the new XML document. Start Stylus Studio and select File, New, XML Schema. This brings up an almost-empty document window. The document itself isn't that interesting yet, but look at the window in which it resides. There are two tabs at the bottom of the schema document's window marked Text and Tree. The Text tab is already active and allows you to manually edit the document. Click on the Tree tab to view the XML schema document using the tree-based editor. Several elements on the screen change. The most obvious change is that you'll no longer see the simple text document in the main window. Stylus Studio now displays a graphical view of the document. There's a vertical toolbar on left side of the window that helps you add new content to the XML schema. You may also see a Properties window on the left side of Stylus Studio's main window. Here you can edit the properties of the currently selected item that resides in the document's window.

The vertical toolbar on the left of the document has a number of icons that you can use to add new XSL content to the document. Each icon has a specific purpose and becomes active only if it's applicable to the item that's currently selected in the schema document. Figure 6.38 describes most of the icons on the toolbar. You'll see these descriptions in this section.

Start by creating two new global element declarations. Click on the New Element Definition icon on the upper-left corner of the toolbar, type **partsInventory**, and press Enter. As soon as you press the Enter key, Stylus Studio moves the cursor to a new field and offers you a number of options. The list contains the available data types you can assign to the new element. Simply press Enter to leave the field blank. Take a look at the toolbar on the left. Only some of the icons are available. The rest of them are grayed-out, because they're not applicable to the partsInventory node. Notice that the New Element Definition icon isn't applicable because you cannot add an element to an existing element.

Add another element to the schema by clicking on the Schema node. Then click on the New Element Definition icon, type **item**, and press Enter twice.

So far, the schema contains global declarations for two elements. Based on the previous listing, item elements have three attributes. Recall from Saturday evening's lesson, "Document Modeling," that only complex types can

Figure 6.38

Icons in the Schema tree view toolbar.

Icon	Name
	New Element Definition
	New Attribute Definition
	New Group
	New Attribute Group
	New Model Group
	New Simple Type
	New Complex Type
	New Restriction
	New Extension
	New Content
	New Aggregator
	New Facet
	New Notation
	New Identity Constraint
	New Selector/Key
	New Reference To Element
	New Reference To Attribute
	New Reference To Group
	New Reference To Attribute Group
	New Annotation
	New Documentation
	New Text
	New Comment
Text Tree	Text and Tree Tabs

have attributes, so the first thing you need to do is make the item element a complex type. You can do that by clicking on the item element and clicking on the New Complex Type icon in the toolbar. Then press the Enter key when Stylus Studio puts the cursor into a new text box. (Stylus Studio is asking for the name of the new complex element. You don't need one in this example.) Add attributes to the element by clicking on the New Attribute Definition icon and entering the name of the attribute, along with its optional data type. Keep the process simple by creating three attributes without a data type: name, component, and onHand. Remember to click on the item element after you add each new attribute.

Now that the item element is complete, it's time to reference it from the partsInventory element. Select the partsInventory element and click on New Complex Type icon. (Leave the name blank, as before.) You need to define what compositor you'll base the complex type on. (Refer to Saturday evening's lesson under the heading "Composing Elements Using Compositors.") Click on the New Model Group icon and select Sequence from the pop-up group of choices, as shown in Figure 6.39.

Create a reference to the item element by clicking on the New Reference To Element icon, and select item from the pop-up listing of available options. If you're more comfortable reviewing the schema's text, click on the Text tab at

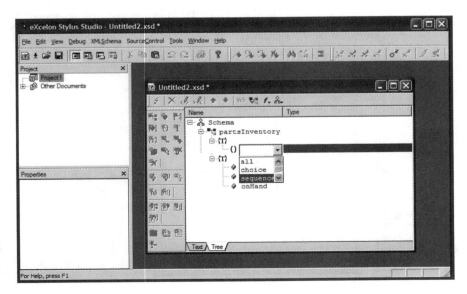

Figure 6.39

Creating a sequence.

the bottom of the window, and then select Edit, Indent XML Tags from the menu to format the schema. You should recognize all of the elements, and the format of the document is similar to the ones you've worked with so far.

Save the new schema in the chapter06 folder using the file name carPartsInventory.xsd. Close the document by selecting File, Close from the menu.

Mapping from One Schema to Another

As mentioned previously, Stylus Studio refers to XSL documents that repurpose an XML document as an *XML-to-XML Mapping Stylesheet*. There are two parts to mapping an XML document into a new layout:

➤ Designing the transformation.

➤ Executing the transformation.

The following discussion covers both aspects, as well as debugging XSL.

The editor you're going to work with uses drag and drop editing. The directions assume that you're familiar with the how to drag and drop.

From Stylus Studio's menu, select File, New, XML To XML Mapping Stylesheet. This causes the Choose Source and Destination Schema selection box to pop up, as shown in Figure 6.40.

The Choose Source and Destination Schema selection box requires you to fill in all fields, although Stylus Studio makes an educated guess at the value of the Root Element field and fills it in for you automatically. Click on the

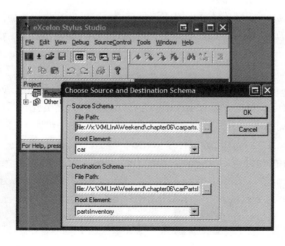

Figure 6.40

Selecting a source and destination schema.

button with three dots to the right of the File Path field under the Source Schema to bring up the Open dialog box. Navigate to the \XMLInAWeekend\chapter06 folder and open the carParts.xsd file. Double-click on the file, or click once and then click the Open button. As soon as you open the file, Stylus Studio reviews the contents and fills in the Root Element field for you. Generally Stylus Studio selects the correct element, but sometimes it makes a mistake. Always make sure that the value in the field is correct.

Click on the button beside the Destination Schema's File Path field and open the carPartsInventory.xsd file. Stylus Studio may select the item element as the root element for the document, which is incorrect. Set the value of the Root Element field to partsInventory by clicking on the small down arrow on the right side of the field and selecting the partsInventory option.

Stylus Studio opens a window that has two documents in it. The source document is on the left side of the window, and the destination document is on the right side of the window. Both documents are shown using a tree view.

The documents start out in collapsed view. That is, all of the elements are present, but they're not visible because they haven't been expanded yet. You can expand a branch of the tree either by clicking on the plus sign beside each item or by double-clicking on the name of the element. I prefer the second approach because it's easier to double-click on a word than to position the mouse pointer over a little plus sign!

The documents' root elements appear at the top of their corresponding tree view. You can map the root car element from the source document to the root partsInventory element by dragging the car element to the partsInventory element. Stylus Studio draws a line that follows the pointer as you drag, and it highlights elements in the destination document as the pointer approaches. Stylus Studio completes the line between the source and destination elements when you release the mouse button. There should be a dotted line between the car element and the partsInventory element. In this case, the dotted line represents an xsl:for-each element. You can review the XSL that Stylus Studio has generated by clicking on the XSLT Source tab at the bottom of the document's window. By dragging the car element to the partsInventory element, you indicate that you want to create one partsInventory element for each car element. In other words, you want to create one root element in the destination document for each root element in the source document.

Switch back to the tree view by clicking on the XML Mapper tab, and expand the item element in the destination document on the right side of the screen. You'll notice that all three attributes (name, component, and onHand) are now visible. The goal is to map the value of the source part element to the value of an item element's name attribute. (Refer to "Repurposing XML Documents with XSL" earlier in the lesson to get an idea of what the final document should look like.) Expand the source document's tree view by clicking on the plus sign (or double-clicking on the name) of the system, subsystem, components, component, and parts elements. When you expand the component element, you may notice that there's another component element within it. Please ignore the second component element.

Define the mapping by dragging the part element to the name attribute, and dragging the name attribute that appears just below the component element to the component attribute in the destination document. Stylus Studio's display should look like the one shown in Figure 6.41.

The problem is that you'll end up with only one element in the resulting document, because you're mapping from the single source car element to the single destination partsInventory element. Although it seems reasonable to

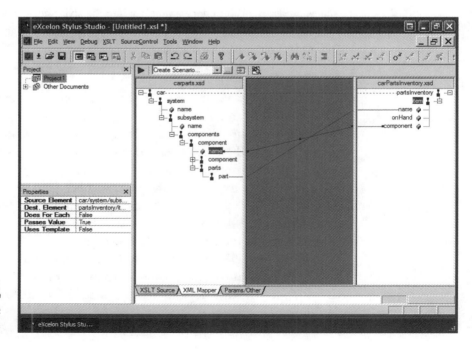

Figure 6.41

Mapping from one schema to another.

expect that mapping a root element in a source document to the destination document will cause the child nodes to map as well, that's simply not how XSL works. Remember that you're creating an XSL document that relies on XPath expressions, which require you to explicitly describe exactly how to transform an element. The description you have in place right now is flawed, because there's only one root element in each document. So, the xsl:for-each loop you created by dragging the car element to the partsInventory element executes only once.

You can correct the problem by deleting the mapping of car to partsInventory and defining a new mapping of system to item elements. Use the following directions to define the mapping:

1. Delete the car to partsInventory mapping. Move the mouse pointer over the dotted line in the gray area between the two documents. Right-click on the dotted line and select Delete from the menu that pops up.
2. Define a new mapping for the system to item element. Drag the system element to the item element.

NOTE The following directions introduce a problem into the style sheet, so you'll have to work with the Stylus Studio debugging feature. If you're not interested in doing this, please skip ahead to "Completing the Mapping."

You're ready to carry out the mapping to see if you're on the right track. Stylus Studio refers to an instance of a mapping as a *scenario*. Essentially, a scenario defines the source XML document for which you want to carry out the mapping, along with some other parameters. When you select XSLT, Preview XSLT Result from the menu, Stylus Studio asks you to create a scenario for the mapping. You can reuse the scenario once you create it and save the project, so you'll likely do this only once for each project. Stylus Studio displays the Scenario Properties window, which asks for the name of the scenario (you can use the default name or assign your own), the source XML URL, and the base URL for HTML links resolution. To carry out the mapping, click on the button with three dots to the right of the Source XML URL field, open the carParts.xml file, and click OK at the bottom of the Scenario Properties window.

When Stylus Studio finishes the mapping, it draws a new window in the bottom third of the screen that contains a preview of the mapping. The XSLT Preview begins using a tree view, but it offers two other views: browser preview and text preview. The tree view can make it difficult to figure out if the mapping was successful, because you have to click on a lot of item elements to see all of the results. Click on the Browser Preview icon, the second one from the top. The screen should look like the one in Figure 6.42.

You'll notice that the preview document is missing a number of values in the item element's name and component attributes. Some elements have only one attribute filled in and there are too few item elements. In short, the transformation is incorrect. You can try to figure out where the problem is by reading through the XSL code that Stylus Studio has generated for you, but that can be difficult when you're just learning XSL. A better option is to use the integrated XSL debugger.

The goal now is to start a debugging session and interactively track down where the transformation is going wrong so that you can generate the desired

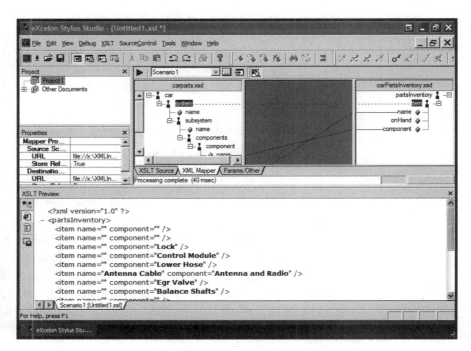

Figure 6.42

Previewing the results of a mapping using the Browser Preview.

document. Invoke the debugger by selecting Debug, Start Debugging from the menu. The problem with this approach is that it appears not to work!

The debugger works by carrying out the instructions in the XSL document until one of two things happens: the instructions in the document are carried out, or the debugger encounters a breakpoint. A *breakpoint* is an arbitrary location in a document where you want the debugger to temporarily suspend processing so you can inspect certain aspects of the transformation, such as intermediate (incomplete) output and the position of the context node. When you invoked the debugger, it didn't find any breakpoints in the document, so it just carried out all of the instructions in the XSL document and showed the preview window again (which contains the same result as last time).

Let's add a breakpoint to the document. First, close the XSLT Preview window, which occupies the bottom third of the Stylus Studio window, by clicking on the small X symbol in the upper-right corner. Click on the XSLT Source tab at the bottom of the editor's screen to view the XSL code, and click anywhere on the third line of code to place the cursor on it. The third line is

```
<xsl:template match="/">
```

To create a new breakpoint, select Debug, Toggle Breakpoint from the menu. Stylus Studio adds a large red dot to the left of the document's margin to indicate the breakpoint. Start the debugging session by selecting Debug, Start Debugging from the menu.

This time, processing stops at the breakpoint. Stylus Studio indicates which line it's about to execute by putting a yellow arrow in the margin. This arrow appears to be on top of the large red dot because Stylus Studio has encountered the breakpoint that you just created. The window to the right of the XSL code displays the value of the XSL processor's context node, which refers to the root node (/) at this point. (If you don't see a window called Variables to the right, select Debug, Variable Window from the menu.) Open the preview window, which allows you to inspect the XSL processor's intermediate results, by selecting XSLT, Display Preview Window from the menu. Ensure that the preview window is showing the text preview by clicking on the text preview icon on the left side of the preview window (the third icon from the top).

You can get the debugger to execute each instruction, step by step, so you can see the result of each one. Step through the transformation by slowly pressing the F11 key 11 times. Note how the contents of the preview window and the value of the context node change after each time you press F11. The output in the preview window is clearly incorrect, but the value of the context node is correct. Expand the context node to view its details, and confirm that it does indeed correctly point to the first system node.

Press F11 four more times to carry out the first three instructions of the `xsl:for-element`, and expand all the members of the context node. Scroll the contents of the XSL code window to the right to review the value of the `select` attribute of the `xsl:value-of` element. The context node is currently pointing to the second `system` node, and the `select` attribute of the `xsl:value-of` element refers to the `subsystem/components/component/parts/part` XPath expression. You can see that the XPath expression doesn't exist in the current context, so the values of the `item` element's `name` and `component` are empty. You can confirm this by pressing F11 six more times and reviewing the output in the XSLT Preview window. Because the output will be exactly as you saw before, cancel the session by selecting Debug, Stop and selecting Yes from the pop-up window.

Based on the results of this debugging session, it appears that at least one XPath expression in the generated XSL is incorrect. Take a another look at the document that you want to create (it's located in the "Repurposing XML Documents with XSL" section). The goal is to repurpose the `part` element into an `item` element. That's what the result document is: a listing of repurposed `part` elements, not `system` elements. The next section describes how to correct the problem.

Completing the Mapping

If you skipped the debugging section, the mapping is incomplete, and if you've been following along, the mapping is incorrect. Here's how to complete or correct the mapping.

Delete the `system` to `item` mapping by moving the mouse pointer over the dotted line in the gray space between the `system` and `item` elements, right-clicking, and selecting Delete from the menu that pops up. The `part` to `name` mapping is correct, but it's incomplete because the result document has one item element for each part element in the source document. You can express the one-to-one relationship between part and item elements by dragging the part element to the item element.

You can map an element to more than one element in the destination document. The dotted line indicates that Stylus Studio created an xsl:for-each element that executes once for each part element, which is what you want. You can confirm that you're on the right track by selecting XSLT, Preview XSLT Result from the menu. Switch to the browser view by clicking on the second icon from the top on the left side of the preview window (see Figure 6.43).

Almost done. Referring back to the resulting document, there's one more attribute and one value to add, and you haven't written a single line of code yet!

Things get interesting now, because you have to use an XPath function to generate the value of the item element's onHand attribute and the value that appears within the item element. Stylus Studio allows you to use XPath

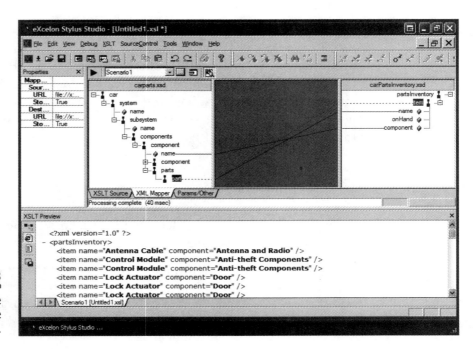

Figure 6.43

Previewing the mostly complete mapping.

functions directly within the mapper. You'll do that, and then edit the XSL code manually to add some finishing touches. The first function you'll add is the XPath concat function, which is used to generate the string that appears in the item element's value.

Right-click anywhere in the gray area between the source and destination documents. Make sure that you don't right-click on one of the lines that runs between elements. Move the mouse pointer to the XSLT Function item in the menu that pops up, and click on concat (the third item in the long menu). Stylus Studio places a green box on the gray area between the two documents. The XPath concat function appends two or more strings to create one long string. You'll use concat to append the values of the system element's name attribute, and you'll use the value of the component element's name attribute to generate the item element's value.

Drag the system element's name attribute to the green box that Stylus Studio created (which represents the concat XPath function), and drop it onto the word "AnyType?" in the pop-up menu just below the green box. If you perform the action correctly, you'll see the word "name" just below the bold word "concat" near the green box. Repeat the process for the component element's name attribute. Drop it onto the next instance of the word "AnyType?" Move the mouse pointer to the bold word "concat" and drag it to the item element on the right side of the screen. (If a pop-up menu appears, select the first option.) Select XSLT, Preview XSLT Result to confirm that you're still on the right track. You'll notice that the item element now has a value made up of two strings. In a few moments, you'll format the string and add some additional text to it.

The next XPath function you'll use is the count function, which generates the value for the item element's onHand attribute. Right-click anywhere in the gray area except on a line or the green box, move the mouse pointer to the XSLT Function menu option, and click on count. Drag the parts element to the purple box that Stylus Studio created and drop it onto the word "Nodeset?" Move the mouse pointer to the bold word "count", and drag it to the onHand attribute on the right side of the screen. Try the mapping again to confirm that everything is working correctly (see Figure 6.44).

The last thing you'll have to do to get the final result is some manual editing. You'll need to close the XSLT Preview window to clear up some space on the screen. Select XSLT, Display Preview Window from the menu, or

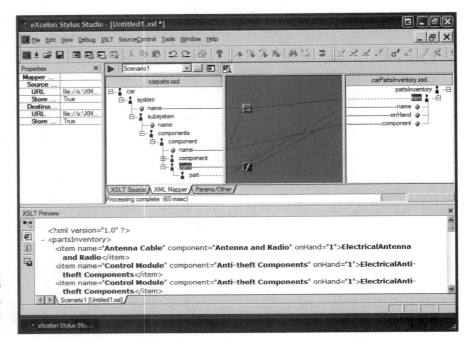

Figure 6.44

XPath functions
and previewing the
mapping.

click on the small X in the upper-right corner of the preview window. Then
click on the XSLT Source tab to display the code that Stylus Studio generated for you, and locate the three lines that look like this:

```
<xsl:attribute name="onHand">
  <xsl:value-of select="count(..)"/>
</xsl:attribute>
```

Edit the xsl:value-of element so that it looks like this (add the /* characters after the two dots in the count function):

```
<xsl:value-of select="count(../*)"/>
```

Locate the line that looks like this:

```
<xsl:value-of select="concat(../../../../../@name,../../@name)"/>
```

Modify the line so that it appears as follows (the additions appear in bold,
and you can add line breaks as shown to make the XSL easier to read):

```
<xsl:value-of select="concat('Install in ',
  ../../../../../@name,
```

```
' System in/on/near the ',
../../@name)"/>
```

Carry out the mapping by selecting XSLT, Preview XSLT Result from the main menu. You should now see the complete `partsInventory` document! Save the document by selecting File, Save from the menu and assigning a name to the file. Stylus Studio saves the file as an XSL file, so you don't need to export or otherwise save the XSL code. You can save the resulting XML file by clicking on the Export Preview icon on the left side of the preview window (the fourth icon from the top) and assigning a name and location to the file.

What's Next

Well done. You've just learned the essence of XML and XML Tools, and you deserve a well-earned break! Sunday evening's lesson is called "Programming with XML" because you'll use XML with Active Server Pages, ADO (Microsoft ActiveX Data Objects), and the Microsoft .NET Framework. You should browse through the lesson even if you're not familiar with these technologies, because it will give you a sense of how XML integrates with existing and newer technologies.

Programming with XML

- ➤ XML Data Binding with Internet Explorer
- ➤ Exploring an XML Document Using the XML DOM
- ➤ XML and the .NET Framework

You've come a long way in a very short time. Congratulations! With the essential aspects of XML behind you, you're now ready to get into working with XML.

This lesson is made up of three major parts:

➤ XML data binding with Internet Explorer.

➤ Working with the XML DOM in Internet Explorer.

➤ Using the Microsoft .NET Framework to work with XML.

The first part requires next to no programming experience at all, but the last two parts get into a fair amount of programming. You don't necessarily have to be a professional programmer to be able to understand the material in this lesson. A lot of people know just enough programming to write applications for themselves, while others are interested in programming to a degree but haven't had the opportunity to explore it on their own. If the latter describes your situation, this section will be of interest to you. Even if you're not at all experienced in programming, you should at least skim through this section to see XML from another perspective.

The samples in the last three major sections use the following programming languages: C# (pronounced "see-sharp"), JavaScript, and VBScript. You don't necessarily need to know any of those programming languages, but some programming experience will help you understand the samples more easily. The discussion of the .NET Framework explains what it is and how it uses XML.

XML Data Binding with Internet Explorer

Data binding is a general term for connecting a data source with a control that's capable of displaying data. *Data source* describes anything that acts as a source of data, such as a database or an XML document. *Control* is another general term for a visual element that's used to lay out information on the screen, like a table.

Internet Explorer can bind an HTML table to an XML data source, without programming, so you can easily display formatted XML data within a table on an HTML page. This is made possible by something called a *Data Source Object (DSO)*. The DSO doesn't require any programming and is very easy to work with. It often satisfies most people's requirements. The only drawback to using the DSO is that it's available only with Internet Explorer version 4.0 and later.

You're limited to working with an HTML table to display data that you acquire through the DSO, and the DSO is capable of working with relatively simple data structures. The first example, shown in Figure 7.1, demonstrates how to use the DSO to generate a table that contains a listing of books, authors, and each book's Library of Congress (LOC) classification.

NOTE

• •
The Library of Congress (LOC) Classification System's class and subclass information is shown in the last two columns of the table. For more information on the Library of Congress Classification System, visit http://www.loc.gov/.
• •

The listing is based on information in the books.xml document, located in the \XMLInAWeekend\chapter07 folder. The page itself is called dso1.htm.

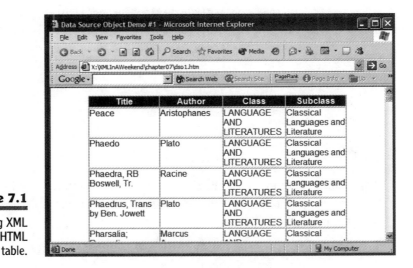

Figure 7.1

Displaying XML data in an HTML table.

It's made up of HTML code, and also includes tags that describe where the data in the table comes from and which cells of the table contain the data. The following listing presents most of the page, with the relevant sections shown in bold:

```
<html>
  <head>
    <title>Data Source Object Demo #1</title>
  </head>
  <body>
    <XML ID="xmldata" src="books.xml"></XML>
    <table datasrc="#xmldata" id="ListOfBooks"
      width="80%" align="center" cellpadding="0"
      cellspacing="0" border="1">
      <tr>
        <thead>
          <tr>
            <th>Title</th>
            <th>Author</th>
            <th>Class</th>
            <th>Subclass</th>
        </thead>
        <td valign="top"><div datafld="title"></div></td>
        <td valign="top"><div datafld="author"></div></td>
        <td valign="top"><div datafld="loc_class"></div></td>
        <td valign="top"><div datafld="loc_subclass"></div></td>
      </tr>
    </table>
    <br>
    <hr>
  </body>
</html>
```

Appendix A contains an HTML reference that describes all of the elements that make up a table and demonstrates how to create a table, so I won't repeat how to do that here.

The first bold part of the listing is the xml element. This xml element is very different from the xml element you've seen in XML document declarations.

This one delimits what's referred to as an *XML data island*, which allows you to have an XML document either reside directly within an HTML document or refer to an XML document. The ID attribute is required because it's used to assign a name of the data island. Later you'll use the name of the data island to bind an HTML table to it. Instead of having the XML document appear inline with the rest of the HTML, this example refers to the XML document that resides in a separate file, as the src attribute indicates. Note that the xml element must have a closing tag.

An HTML table appears immediately following the XML data island declaration. Most of the table uses common attributes, except for the datasrc and ID attributes. The datasrc attribute associates the table with the XML data island by name. Note that the name is prefixed with the pound (#) sign. The table's ID attribute assigns a name to the table. This is optional, but it's a good practice to provide a name because you may wish to take advantage of the additional features that are demonstrated in the next example.

The names of the XML elements that you want to have in certain cells appear later in the table's declaration. Each field you want to have in the table must reside in an HTML div element, as shown in the preceding listing. The value of the datafld attribute must exactly match the name of the XML element's value you want to have in the cell. You can also specify the names of attributes in the datafld attribute. The DSO is capable of matching XML attribute names and generally can handle rather complex XML documents. However, the DSO doesn't seem to like attributes in the root element's declaration.

You can open the page directly in Internet Explorer to see the final result. Depending on how fast your system is, you may be able to see the table being formatted as Internet Explorer reads through the XML document and populates the table with data. The DSO reads XML data asynchronously, meaning that Internet Explorer picks up new data from the DSO whenever it's ready, while the DSO continues to read the data as quickly as it can. This feature boosts overall performance and makes users feel that Internet Explorer remains responsive, even when it loads larger data sets.

While the results are interesting, they can be better. There's a lot of information on the screen, and scrolling up and down can become tedious. The DSO provides a means of paging through a data set using a few buttons and a tiny bit of coding.

Paging Through Long Data Sets

The DSO provides paging support for longer data sets. This is the primary benefit for users because they can easily navigate through a data set on a page-by-page basis (see Figure 7.2).

The sample file is called `dso2.htm` and is also located in the \XMLInAWeekend\chapter07 folder. Open it directly in Internet Explorer and try the navigation buttons.

Another advantage a paged data set provides is responsiveness. I mentioned earlier that the DSO and Internet Explorer work asynchronously to acquire and present data. When you first load `dso2.htm`, the table appears to be populated as soon as you open the page in Internet Explorer. As you play with the navigational controls or just look at the information on the screen, the DSO and Internet Explorer are hard at work, continuing to populate the table with information from the XML document. As a result, Internet Explorer continues to feel responsive even though it's working to keep the table completely populated.

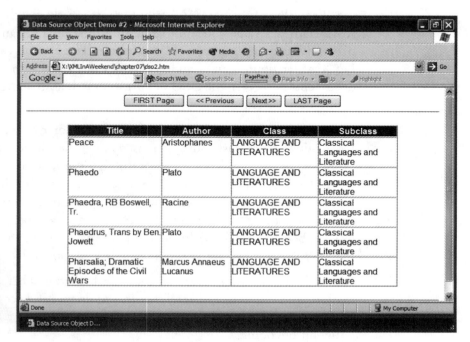

Figure 7.2

Navigational controls for paging through a long data set.

The dso2.htm file is almost identical to dso1.htm, with a few minor changes, so I'll just focus on the new parts of the document. The following listing begins just after the opening HTML body tag and ends just after the first HTML tr tag of the table:

```
<body>
  <XML ID="xmldata" src="books.xml"></XML>
  <center>

    <input type="button" value="FIRST Page"
      onclick="ListOfBooks.firstPage();">

    <input type="button" value="&lt;&lt; Previous"
      onclick="ListOfBooks.previousPage();">

    <input type="button" value="Next &gt;&gt;"
      onclick="ListOfBooks.nextPage();">

    <input type="button" value="LAST Page"
      onclick="ListOfBooks.lastPage();">

  </center>
  <hr>
  <br>

  <table datasrc="#xmldata" datapagesize="5" id="ListOfBooks"
      border="1" width="80%" align="center"
      cellpadding="0" cellspacing="0" >

    <tr>
```

The listing begins just after the HTML body element with the now familiar XML element, which is identical to the one you saw before. Immediately following that declaration is an HTML center element, which centers everything that resides within the beginning and ending tags.

There are four buttons on the page, as described by the HTML input elements. All of the input elements' type attributes cause them to be rendered as buttons, while the value attribute declares the caption that appears in the button. The `value` attribute uses predefined HTML entity references for the less-than symbol (< - <) and greater-than symbol (> - >) to avoid confusion with an HTML tag, because there are a lot of HTML tags close by.

The values of the `onclick` attributes are the key factors in providing navigational support to the user. Each `onclick` attribute's name comes from the event that the attribute captures. Internet Explorer evaluates the value of the `onclick` attribute when the user clicks one of the buttons. The value of the attribute uses the name of the table that displays the data, as shown in the table's `ID` attribute (`ListOfBooks`). This is followed by a dot, followed by the named page you want to navigate to. There are four named pages that you can navigate to: `firstPage()`, `lastPage()`, `nextPage()`, and `previousPage()`. The spelling, case, and parentheses that follow the name of each page are important and must appear *exactly* as shown.

The `table` element has one new attribute, `datapagesize`, which describes how many rows you want the table to display on a given page. Specify the number of items per page using a numeric value, optionally in quotes, as shown in the preceding listing.

While paging support is helpful, you can go a step further by allowing users to define how many items they want to show per page.

Dynamically Changing the Number of Items Per Page

Allowing your users to change how many items appear per page increases the usability of the solution, because it helps to accommodate users with smaller or lower-resolution screens that can't fit as much information. This option also makes the solution more interactive by allowing users to customize the display to suit their preference.

This solution builds on the last one by adding two more HTML `input` elements and some simple JavaScript code. The `input` elements capture the user's requested number of items per page, and the JavaScript code dynamically reconfigures the DSO and resets the display after each change. The overall effect is shown in Figure 7.3.

To get a feel for how this feature works, use Internet Explorer to open the dso3.htm file, located in the \XMLInAWeekend\chapter07 folder. Navigate

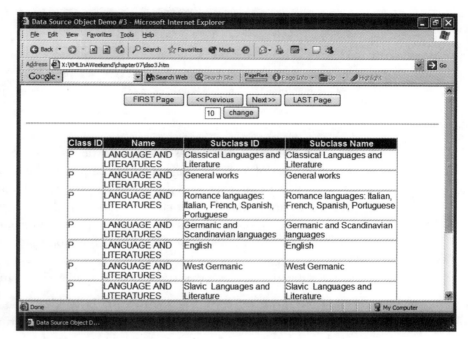

Figure 7.3

Allowing users to change the number of items per page.

to another page in the data set and then change the number of pages. The number of items changes and the page resets to the first page of the data set. Changing the number of items per page can make it difficult to figure out where you are in the data set, but resetting the display to the first page will minimize that effect.

The first change to the page occurs with the introduction of two more HTML input elements, as shown by the bold lines in the following listing:

```
<center>

  <input type="button" value="FIRST Page"
    onclick="ListOfBooks.firstPage();">

  <input type="button" value="&lt;&lt; Previous"
    onclick="ListOfBooks.previousPage();">

  <input type="button" value="Next &gt;&gt;"
    onclick="ListOfBooks.nextPage();">
```

```
<input type="button" value="LAST Page"
  onclick="ListOfBooks.lastPage();">

<input type="text" maxlength="2" size="2" id="itemsPerPage">
<input type="button" value="change" onclick="changePageSize();">
```

```
</center>
```

The first new `input` element is a text input field that captures the user's preferred number of items per page. The critical part of the declaration is the `ID` attribute that assigns a name to the field (`itemsPerPage`). The second `input` element is a button that the user clicks to carry out the requested change. Like other buttons on the page, this button has an `onclick` attribute. This time, the attribute refers to the name of a JavaScript function that applies the change. You can use any name you like when you create your own pages, but be sure to use a descriptive name that suggests what the JavaScript function does.

The page is not yet complete, because the JavaScript code that handles the new button's click event is not part of the page. JavaScript code typically resides within a `script` element, which in turn resides between the HTML page's `head` starting and ending tags (which appear just after the `html` element, but before the `body` element), as shown in the following listing:

```
<html>
  <head>
    <title>Data Source Object Demo #3</title>

    <script language="JavaScript">

    function Initialize()
    {
      itemsPerPage.value = ListOfBooks.dataPageSize;
    }

    function changePageSize()
    {
      ListOfBooks.dataPageSize = itemsPerPage.value;
      ListOfBooks.firstPage();
    }
```

```
    </script>

  </head>

  <body onload="Initialize();">

    <XML ID="xmldata" src="loc_classes.xml"></XML>
    <!-- rest of page... -->
```

There's a lot going on in this listing, so let's start in somewhat familiar territory with the body tag, near the end of the listing. The body tag has an attribute called onload, which you saw in Saturday morning's lesson. Internet Explorer evaluates the value of the onload attribute when it has finished loading the document but hasn't displayed it yet. As a result, the onload attribute usually refers to the name of a function that carries out initialization tasks, which get the page ready for display.

JavaScript is a popular programming language that most Web developers are at least familiar with. It's so popular because it's easy to use and is supported by major browsers, including Internet Explorer. JavaScript code on an HTML page must appear within a script element whose declaration includes the name of the programming language used by the code within it. Internet Explorer is adept at figuring out which programming language appears within a script element, making the value of the language attribute optional. However, it's good practice to specify the name of the programming language you're using. For Internet Explorer, valid settings for the script element's language attribute are JavaScript, JScript, and VBScript.

The body element's onload attribute refers to a function called Initialize() that appears immediately after the script element's starting tag. You can place this function wherever you want, as long as it appears within the script element. Generally, it's good practice to put a function like this immediately after the starting script tag, or just before the ending script tag.

The Initialize() function sets the value that appears in the itemsPerPage input field so it's equal to the number of items per page that the table (ListOfBooks) displays, to let the user know how many items per page the table starts with. The single line of code in the function refers to the name of the input field, itemsPerPage, followed by the field's property that holds the value you see on the screen (value), followed by an equals sign. So far, the statement says, "Assign a value to the itemsPerPage field." The code that follows the equals sign describes what to assign to the input field: the value of the number of pages that the table displays.

The next function, changePageSize(), handles the onclick event for the button that's next to the input field. The first line of the function assigns the value in the itemsPerPage input field to the ListOfBooks dataPageSize attribute. The line that follows resets the table's page back to the first page of the data set.

Keep the following in mind as you design your own pages that use the DSO:

➤ Root XML elements cannot have attributes.

➤ XML documents can be reasonably complex.

➤ The DSO is capable of working with attributes. Simply refer to them by name.

➤ Assign names to all buttons, tables, and text input fields using the ID attribute.

➤ When creating a paged data set, assign a value to the dataPageSize attribute of the table that displays the data set for best performance.

The next example uses VBScript and the XML DOM to explore the structure of an XML document and write its contents to the screen.

Exploring an XML Document Using the XML DOM

The XML DOM (Document Object Model) provides a means of programmatically creating and manipulating XML documents. The DOM exposes (presents) an XML document by reading it into the computer's memory and then representing each aspect of it as a distinct object. An *object* is a logical element (meaning that it doesn't really exist) that represents something like a part of an XML document, a string, or even a file. An object not only refers to something, it also offers a means of manipulating it by exposing functionality that's appropriate for the object. For example, an object that represents a string of characters (simply referred to as a string) exposes functionality that allows programmers to compare, add, and manipulate strings. An object that represents part of an XML document may expose functionality that allows you to navigate to another part of the document, transform it using XSL, or add new information to it.

While an XML document essentially conveys information about the structure and content of the document using elements, an XML DOM represents an XML document as a collection of *node* objects. XML documents have several types of elements, so the XML DOM has several types of nodes, as shown in Table 7.1.

TABLE 7.1 TYPES OF XML NODES

Type	Description
document	Represents the document starting at the XML declaration. The document has only one child node (an element) that represents the document's root element.
documentFragment	Represents a fragment of an XML document.
element	Represents an XML element.
text	Represents the (text) content of an element and an attribute.
attribute	Represents an element's attribute.
cdatasection	Represents an element's CDATA data.
processinginstruction	Represents a processing instruction.
comment	Represents a comment.
entity	Represents an entity, as described by the document's DTD.
entityreference	Represents an entity reference, as described by the document's DTD.
documenttype	Represents the document's DTD.
notation	Represents a node notation in the document's DTD.

Each node in the XML DOM exposes a property called nodeType that describes what type of node it is, enabling you to process nodes based on their type. The example in this section processes attributes and elements based on the value in an XML document's nodeType property, as you'll see shortly.

One of the interesting features of the XML DOM is that it allows you to traverse an entire document without actually referring to nodes by name, very much like you saw in the previous lesson using XPath expressions. The example for this lesson is an HTML page containing VBScript code that explores the structure of an XML document using the XML DOM, and then writes out the structure and data onto the screen. Figure 7.4 shows what the output of the page looks like.

The sample is in the XML-DOM.htm file located in the \XMLInAWeekend\ chapter07 folder. If you extracted the contents of the book's accompanying ZIP file, as described in the Preface, you're set to go. Otherwise, you'll have to edit the page to change the location of the XML document the sample relies on. The sample uses the carparts.xml document from the previous

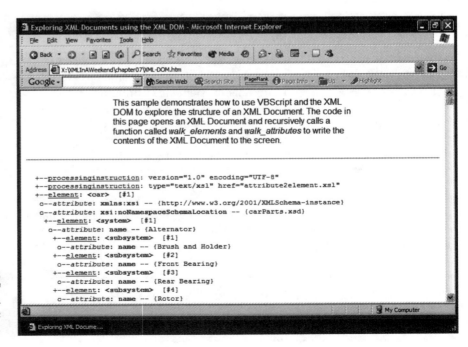

Figure 7.4

Exploring an XML document using the XML DOM.

lesson, because you're probably familiar with its structure and content by now. Open the document to view its results. There's a chance that Internet Explorer will ask if you want to continue to let the page run. Answer Yes to allow the code in the page to continue processing the complete document.

The page is made up of about 95% VBScript code, with the remaining 5% representing supporting HTML code, so I won't describe the HTML code here.

The code is made up of three functions, all written in VBScript. The Initialize function acts as the starting point and gets called when you first load the page. Its role is to load the XML document into the DOM and start the processing by calling the walk_elements function. The walk_elements function traverses elements in the XML DOM by recursively calling itself to display the contents of each element. When walk_elements encounters an element with attributes, it calls the walk_attributes function, which displays the contents of all attributes for an element. The code isn't too complex, except for the part where walk_elements calls itself. When a function calls itself, it's said to be *recursive*. Recursive programming is an efficient means of processing many types of logical structures. Rather than present all 95 lines that make up the code on the page in one chunk, I'll walk you through the code as it executes when it processes an XML document.

The very first thing that happens when the page loads is that the following line executes:

```
indent = 0
```

This line creates a numeric, global variable that all code on the page can access, and sets its initial value to 0. This variable controls a key factor in the page's layout: the indentation of each line. Next, the now-familiar Initialize function is called as a result of the HTML document's body element onload attribute setting. The following listing presents most of the Initialize function:

```
Function Initialize()
   Dim root
   Dim xmlDoc
   Dim child
   Dim indent
```

```
indent=0
Set xmlDoc = CreateObject("Msxml.DOMDocument")
xmlDoc.async = False
xmlDoc.validateOnParse=False

xmlDoc.load("\XMLInAWeekend\chapter06\carparts.xml")

If xmlDoc.parseError.errorCode = 0 Then
   Document.Write("<pre>")
   walk_elements(xmlDoc)
   Document.Write("</pre>")
Else
   ' code omitted for brevity...
End If
End Function
```

After the initial Dim statements that declare some local variables, the function begins by creating an instance of the XML DOM object using the VBScript CreateObject function. The XML DOM exposes some properties that control its behavior when working with XML documents. The two lines that follow set the DOM object's async and validateOnParse properties to False, essentially disabling those two options (loading the document asynchronously and validating the document as it loads). The If statement determines if there were any errors loading the document by evaluating the value of the DOM object's errorCode property. If there weren't any errors, the function calls walk_elements to begin processing the document.

The walk_elements function takes a single parameter: a node. When Initialize calls walk_elements the first time, it passes the function the instance of the XML DOM, which is essentially a special type of node that represents the entire XML document. (See Table 7.1 for the types of nodes.) The function begins by initializing a For loop that executes once for each child node, as shown in the following listing:

```
function walk_elements(node)
   dim nodeName
   dim count
   count = 1
   indent=indent+2
```

```
For Each child In node.childNodes
  For i = 1 To indent
      Document.Write(" ")
  Next
```

The next thing it does is indent the line it's about to write out by writing out several non-breaking space characters using the   predefined HTML entity reference. The next block of code writes out the node's type and its name, as shown in the following listing:

```
Document.Write("+--")
Document.Write("<u>" & child.nodeTypeString & "</u>: ")
If child.nodeType < 3 Then
  Document.Write "<b>&lt;" & child.nodeName _
    & "&gt;</b>  [#" & count & "]<br>")
  count = count + 1
End If
```

The `child.nodeTypeString` represents the node's type as a string value, as shown in the Type column in Table 7.1. The `child.nodeType` property represents the node type as a numeric value. An element's `nodeType` value is 1, and an attribute's `nodeType` value is 2. As a result, the `If` statement ensures that only elements and attributes are shown on the screen.

The next block of code checks the current node to determine if it's an element, and then checks it for any attributes:

```
If (child.nodeType = 1) Then
  If (child.attributes.length > 0) Then
    indent=indent+1
    walk_attributes(child)
    indent=indent-1
  End If
End If
```

If the node has any attributes, as determined by the value of the `attributes.length` property, the function calls the `walk_attributes` function, passing it the current node to generate a list of attributes. The `walk_attributes` function is discussed shortly. The last actions that the walk_elements function takes are to call itself to process any child nodes and manage the value of the indent variable by decreasing its value:

```
    If (child.hasChildNodes) Then
      walk_elements(child)
    Else
      Document.Write  child.text & "<br>"
    End If
  Next
  indent=indent-2
End Function
```

The walk_attributes function is a lot simpler than the walk_elements function because it uses a simple structure made up of a name-value pair, as described in Saturday afternoon's lesson. The walk_attributes function is shown in the following listing:

```
Function walk_attributes(node)
  For Each attrib In node.attributes
    For i=1 to indent
      Document.Write(" ")
    next
    Document.Write("o--<i>" & attrib.nodeTypeString & "</i>")
    Document.Write(": <b>" & attrib.name & "</b> -- {" _
      & attrib.nodeValue & "}<BR>")
  Next
End Function
```

This function behaves in a similar way to the walk_elements function. It indents each line by the number of spaces described by the value of the indent variable, writes out the string representation of the nodeType property, and writes out the attribute's value. The function's code resides within a For loop that executes once for each attribute.

You can try this sample with other, relatively short XML documents by changing the value in the parameter to the xmlDoc.load call in the Initialize function.

The Microsoft .NET Framework is a set of technologies that provide a unified programming model for traditional Windows-based and Web-based applications, based on a comprehensive class library that exposes system functionality. The .NET Framework uses XML in many ways, including transferring information between systems. The next section provides a brief introduction to the .NET Framework and demonstrates an application that uses the C# programming language.

XML and the .NET Framework

The .NET Framework is made up of three key elements:

➤ Common Language Runtime
➤ .NET Class Library
➤ Unifying Components

The Common Language Runtime is a logical layer that separates an application from the platform it executes on, providing execution services such as memory management, error handling, and thread management. It abstracts the details of the operating system, processor architecture, and interface between it and a specific programming language. This makes it easier for developers to create applications, and for applications to work with one another. One of the key benefits of the Common Language Runtime is that it supports a variety of programming languages, including Visual C++ .NET, Visual Basic .NET, JScript .NET, and Visual C# .NET.

The .NET Class Library provides a consistent programming model because its functionality is accessible through all programming languages supported by the .NET Framework. It allows developers to easily access system functionality such as file and database access, advanced drawing support, input and output operations, and interoperability features, such as data interchange between networked systems.

The .NET Framework's functionality is exposed through a set of unifying components that include ASP.NET, Windows Forms, and Visual Studio .NET. ASP.NET is the next generation of Microsoft's Active Server Pages (ASP), with support for a programming model that's familiar to developers who create traditional Windows-based applications. ASP.NET also supports Web Services, a new way of exposing services that are designed to be used by people through applications and Web sites. Windows Forms is a unified means of creating traditional Windows applications that have a graphical user interface across all supported programming languages. Visual Studio

.NET is a development environment that's tightly integrated with the .NET Framework, making it a great tool for developing and deploying network-centric and network-aware applications and services.

The .NET Framework uses XML throughout, for everything from configuration files to native support for XML in ADO.NET (a data access technology) to interchanging information with other systems. The .NET Class Library provides many classes that work with XML, making it easier to create applications that are XML-aware.

The example for this discussion is a traditional Windows-based application, written in Visual C# .NET, that reads an XML document and displays it in a Windows Forms TreeView control, as shown in Figure 7.5.

Your system must have the .NET Framework installed on it to compile and work with this application. The .NET Framework is available for free from Microsoft's MSDN Web site at http://msdn.microsoft.com. The system requirements are posted there as well. Please review them before you download the .NET Framework, because it's a large download. If you already have the .NET Framework installed but don't have Visual Studio .NET, I've provided a compiled version of the sample code along with the book's source code distribution. You should be able to just start the application to try it out. The name of the application is xmlTreeView, and it's located in the \XMLInAWeekend\chapter07\dotNET folder. The name of the application's executable is xmlTreeView.exe.

The application's controls are straightforward. Click on the button to open a file selection dialog box and initiate reading the XML document you want

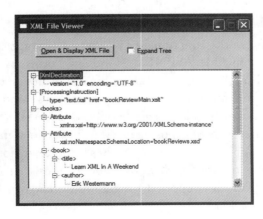

Figure 7.5

A Windows Forms application showing the contents of an XML document.

to view. Use the Expand Tree check box *before* you select a file to have its contents expanded in the tree view automatically when the file is loaded. Expanding all elements automatically can take a long time if the document is large or has a complex structure, so use this feature with caution. One feature of the application that's not readily apparent is that you can drag the left and bottom borders of the window, which drags the left and bottom edges of the tree view control along with it. This makes it possible to view longer or wider XML documents in the tree view control without having to scroll sideways or up and down.

Unlike the pervious example, which uses the XML DOM to explore the structure and content of an XML document, this example uses a forward-only, read-only stream of data to quickly read through the XML document. (If you're familiar with XML processor programming models, this programming model is similar to the one offered by SAX, the Simple API for XML. The difference is that the parser doesn't raise events as it reads the XML document. Instead, the application informs the parser when to read the next block of information from the XML document.) The application displays the document in a `System.Windows.Forms.TreeView` control, which makes it easy for users to inspect the document using a familiar interface while using relatively little space on the screen.

The code that manages the display is rather involved and is beyond the scope of this book, so I won't cover it here. I'll describe most of the code as it would execute when you run the application. The code is a lot simpler than the previous example, because its focus is on reading the XML document and adding information to the tree view control. The .NET Class Library handles the rest of the details.

The application begins by presenting what's referred to as a *file dialog box* that allows the user to select which file to view. The following listing shows how the application creates an instance of the dialog and works with it:

```
OpenFileDialog oFileDlg = new OpenFileDialog();
oFileDlg.Filter = "XML files (*.xml;*.xsl)|*.xml;*.xsl|All files
(*.*)|*.*";
oFileDlg.FilterIndex = 1;
oFileDlg.RestoreDirectory = true;
populateTreeView(oFileDlg.FileName);
```

Visual C# .NET is similar to C++, making it very easy to learn. The code in the preceding listing simply captures the name of the file that the user wants to view and passes it onto another function called `populateTreeView`, which is where the core functionality of the application resides.

The role of the `populateTreeView` function is to read XML data from the XML document and transfer that information to the `TreeView` control for display. The function uses a `System.Xml.XmlTextReader` object that provides fast, forward-only access to an XML document without validating it as it reads the document. The first thing the function does is open the XML document based on a `System.IO.FileStream` object, as shown in the following listing:

```
FileStream fileStreamObject;
XmlTextReader xmlReader;
// strFile contains the name of the file the user wants to open
fileStreamObject = new FileStream(strFile, FileMode.Open,
FileAccess.Read);
xmlReader = new XmlTextReader(fileStreamObject);
```

The code reads through the XML document using a loop that continues as long as `XmlTextReader` is able to successfully read information from the XML document. The application uses a `switch` statement to determine what type of node it's working with, because some nodes, like comments, CDATA sections, and processing instructions, are displayed a little differently than element nodes. The following listing presents the part of the application that handles element nodes:

```
switch(xmlReader.NodeType)
{
  // code omitted for brevity...
  case XmlNodeType.Element:

    xmlNode = new TreeNode("<" + xmlReader.Name + ">");
    emptyElement = xmlReader.IsEmptyElement;

    while(xmlReader.MoveToNextAttribute())
    {
      TreeNode attNode = new TreeNode("Attribute");
      attNode.Nodes.Add(xmlReader.Name + "='" + xmlReader.Value +
```

```
"'");
      xmlNode.Nodes.Add(attNode);
    }
  continue;
  // code omitted for brevity...
}
xmlTree.Nodes.Add(xmlNode);
```

This application creates an instance of a `TreeNode` object that contains the name of the element, along with its attributes. Attributes are added as children of the element's node to take advantage of the `TreeView` control's display capabilities. Just before moving on to the next node, the code adds the `TreeNode` object it created earlier to the `TreeView` control (the last line of the listing).

This concludes the brief tour of the .NET Framework and Windows Forms applications. If you're interested in learning more about the .NET Framework or the various programming languages used in this lesson, visit my Web site (http://www.designs2solutions.com). I have the same resources, but I keep the links up to date in case they change.

Wrapping Up

You've come a long way this weekend, and now you're ready to use your newly acquired understanding of XML and its related technologies. XML technologies are rapidly changing to meet the changing needs of industry. You should try to keep up with the latest developments by regularly checking the World Wide Web Consortium's Web site (http://www.w3c.org) and perhaps subscribing to some of the excellent newsletters that are available from the major XML portal sites. XML is a great technology that's working its way into all facets of the computing industry, and it reflects the industry's drive to address some of its long-standing problems using an open, publicly available standard.

HTML and XPath Reference

- ➤ HTML Reference
- ➤ XPath Reference

his appendix contains an HTML quick reference and an XPath reference. In addition to reference material, both references include examples (and the HTML reference includes figures) that demonstrate how HTML elements look when viewed with Internet Explorer. The core reference material resides mainly in tables, except for a part of the XPath reference. Supplemental information appears throughout the appendix to supplement the information in the tables, or to guide you through some of the notations and conventions the tables use.

HTML Reference

HTML is a broad subject, and there are entire books that discuss it in detail. Use this as an essential reference. It contains enough information to help you understand most HTML documents and create basic HTML documents on your own.

Table Conventions

The tables in this appendix contain a lot of information. The following notations make the tables easier to read:

➤ All elements require a starting and an ending tag, unless otherwise noted.

➤ "color" indicates that you can use a named color, RGB color using the rgb(...) notation with percentage or numeric values, or hexadecimal RGB values.

➤ "class name" describes the name of a class that CSS uses to format an element.

➤ For style="CSS statements", replace "CSS statements" with the actual CSS statements separated by semicolons.

➤ Replace "value and units" with a numeric value immediately followed by the units the value is measured in (%, cm, in, and so on).

➤ Values that contain slash marks (/) define the values you can select. The first value is the initial (default) value.

Table A.1 lists the elements that structure an HTML document. Structure elements organize the overall document into important sections. As a result, structure elements usually don't have a direct visual result, but they can make it easier to apply visual effects to a document's content.

TABLE A.1   HTML STRUCTURE ELEMENTS

Element	Attributes	Description
Comment	None	A comment begins with <!-- and ends with -->. Comments can appear anywhere within an HTML document.
<html>	None	HTML file declaration—encloses the entire document.
<head>	None	File header; contains information about the HTML file but is not part of the HTML document. The most common elements that appear within a <head> are <title>, <script>, and <meta>.
<title>	None	Configures the title of the document. The title usually appears along the top of the browser's window.
<body>	bgcolor="color" text="color" style="CSS statements"	Encloses the HTML document's content that appears on the screen.
<div>	class="class name" style="CSS statements"	Creates a logical boundary around a block of text that you want to manipulate using programming or CSS.
<span>	class="class name" style="CSS statements"	Creates an inline, logical boundary around text that appears within another element. This element is similar to <div>, except that it's used to create a logical boundary around text that's part of some other content, instead of enclosing an entire paragraph, table, or other large parts of a document.

The following listing demonstrates how to use each of the elements in Table A.1, and Figure A.1 shows what the document looks like when you use Internet Explorer to view it.

```html
<html>
  <head>
    <title>Sample HTML Page</title>
    <meta name="author" content="Essam Ahmed">
  </head>
  <body bgcolor="white">
    <div style="border:solid;padding:2%">
      <p>This is a basic HTML page with paragraph (&lt;p&gt;) element,
        <span style="background-color:yellow;">a span (&lt;span&gt;)
        element</span>, and a div (&lt;divp&gt;) element</p>
    </div>
  </body>
</html>
```

HTML text elements change the appearance of the text they enclose. They don't organize it in any way. So, you can use them freely within an HTML body element.

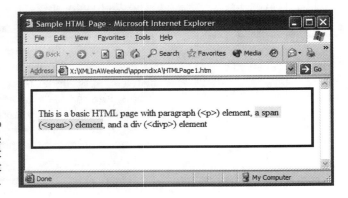

Figure A.1

Displaying a simple HTML document using Internet Explorer.

TABLE A.2 HTML TEXT ELEMENTS

Element	Attributes	Description
` `	None	Line break—creates a blank line. This element does not have a closing tag.
`<p>`	`align="left/right/center/justify" class="class name"`	Paragraph element—encloses a paragraph or line.
`<b>`	None	Makes the enclosed text bold.
`<i>`	None	Makes enclosed text italic.
`<font>`	`face="font name" size=+/-value color="color" class="class name" style="CSS statements"`	Changes the font or appearance of the enclosed text.
`<hr>`	`width="value and units"`	Creates a horizontal rule that usually spans the width of the document. *This element does not have a closing tag.*
`<u>`	None	Underlines the enclosed text.
`<h1>`	`class="class name" style="CSS statements"`	Formats the enclosed text as a level one heading.
`<h2>`	`class="class name" style="CSS statements"`	Formats the enclosed text as a level two heading.
`<h3>`	`class="class name" style="CSS statements"`	Formats the enclosed text as a level three heading.
`<h4>`	`class="class name" style="CSS statements"`	Formats the enclosed text as a level four heading.
`<h5>`	`class="class name" style="CSS statements"`	Formats the enclosed text as a level five heading.
`<h6>`	`class="class name" style="CSS statements"`	Formats the enclosed text as a level six heading.

The following listing demonstrates how to use each of the elements in Table A.2, and Figure A.2 shows what the document looks like when you use Internet Explorer to view it.

```
<h1>Level One Heading</h1>
<h2>Level Two Heading</h2>
<h3>Level Three Heading</h3>
<h4>Level Four Heading</h4>
<h5>Level Five Heading</h5>
<h6>Level Six Heading</h6>
<p>A horizontal rule (&lt;hr&gt; element) follows...</p>
<hr>
<p>This is <b>bold text</b>, and this is <i>italic text</i>.</p>
<p class="sample">This paragraph uses the
<font face="courier">class attribute</font>
and a font element</p>
```

HTML list elements make it easy to create visually appealing bulleted or numbered lists. A list appears within an enclosing element for that type of list, while individual list items use a common list item element.

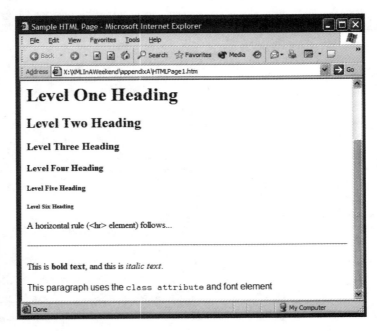

Figure A.2

Using Internet Explorer to view headings, fonts, and paragraphs.

TABLE A.3 HTML LIST ELEMENTS

Element	Attributes	Description
`<ul>`	`type="circle/disc/square"` `class="class name"` `style="CSS statements"`	Encloses an unordered list with bullets instead of numbers beside each item.
`<ol>`	`type="1/A/a/I/i"` `start="initial counter"` `value" class="class name"` `style="CSS statements"`	Encloses an ordered list with a number or letter beside each item.
`<li>`	None	Contains an individual list item. You can use this for ordered and unordered lists. *This element's closing tag is optional.*

The following listing demonstrates how to use each of the elements in Table A.3, and Figure A.3 shows what the document looks like when you use Internet Explorer to view it.

```
<p>This is a simple ordered list (&lt;ol&gt; element)</p>
<ol>
   <li>This is item one</li>
   <li>This is item two</li>
</ol>
<p>Another numbered list follows, using a different numbering style
and starting number...</p>
<ol type="a" start="3">
   <li>This is item three</li>
   <li>This is item four</li>
</ol>
<p>This is an un-ordered list (&lt;ul&gt; element)</p>
<ul>
   <li>This is item one</li>
   <li>This is item two</li>
</ul>
```

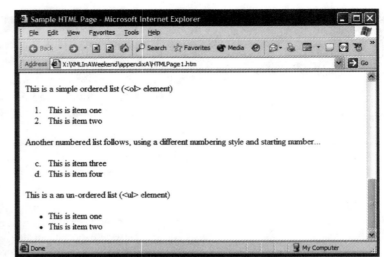

HTML table elements organize information and make it easy to view a lot of it. They're also used to organize the layout of a page. For example, a large table can enclose a document to make it appear in several columns that span a page horizontally (similar to a typical newspaper), instead of a single, wide column (similar to a page in a typical book).

The following listing demonstrates how to use each of the elements in Table A.4, and Figure A.4 shows what the document looks like when you use Internet Explorer to view it.

```
<table width="50%" border="1" cellpadding="5">
  <thead>
    <tr bgcolor="silver">
      <td class="heading">Element</td>
      <td class="heading">Description</td>
    </tr>
  </thead>
  <tbody>
    <tr>
      <td class="markup">&lt;table&gt;</td>
      <td>Encloses a table</td>
    </tr>
    <tr>
```

```
      <td class="markup">&lt;tr&gt;</td>
      <td>Encloses a table row</td>
    </tr>
    <tr>
      <td class="markup">&lt;tr&gt;</td>
      <td>Encloses an individual cell within a row (table data)</td>
    </tr>
   </tbody>
  </table>
```

TABLE A.4 HTML TABLE ELEMENTS

Element	Attributes	Description
`<table>`	`border=value width="value and units"` `cellspacing=value cellpadding=value` `bgcolor=color class="class name"` `style="CSS statements"`	Encloses a table.
`<thead>`	`class="class name"` `style="CSS statements"`	Encloses a table's header row—typically used to show the name of each of the table's columns.
`<tbody>`	`class="class name"` `style="CSS statements"`	Encloses the table's body—the area where the table's data resides.
`<tr>`	`valign="middle/top/bottom"` `bgcolor="color"`	Encloses a table row.
`<td>`	`align="left/center/right"` `valign="middle/top/bottom"` `nowrap width="value and units"` `colspan=value rowspan=value` `bgcolor=color class="class name"` `style="CSS statements"`	Encloses an individual cell within a row (table data).

HTML link elements have two roles: providing a link to another document, and providing a link *within* a document (sometimes referred to as a *bookmark*). Links help you create a logical structure, or thread, within a group of related documents, and bookmarks make it easy for readers to locate important parts of a document.

The following listing demonstrates how to use each of the elements in Table A.5, and Figure A.5 shows what the document looks like when you use Internet Explorer to view it.

```
<p>The following demonstrates two links:
  one to my Web site, the other to another
  part of this document...</p>
<ul type="circle">
  <li> <a href="http://www.designs2solutions.com"
    target="_blank">This is a link to my Web site</a> </li>
  <li> <a href="#headings">This link points back to
    the <i>Headings</i> section of this document</a> </li>
</ul>
```

TABLE A.5 HTML LINK ELEMENTS

Element	Attributes	Description
`<a>`	`href="address of file or #nameOfBookmark" class="class name" style="CSS statements"`	Creates a link to another document or bookmark within the same document.
`<a>`	`name="nameOfBookmark" class="class name" style="CSS statements"`	Creates a bookmark within a document.

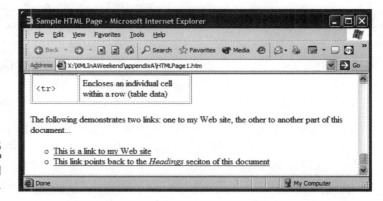

Figure A.5

HTML links and bookmarks.

HTML meta elements contain information about an HTML document. This information is used by the browser, Web server, or other software. Meta elements don't usually have any effect on the document's display (with the exception of the `http-equiv` meta element). Table A.6 describes two meta elements. The first uses the `name` and `content` attributes, and the second describes the `http-equiv` attribute.

The following listing demonstrates how to use each of the elements in Table A.6. Because `meta` elements don't change the document's content, they don't affect the document's display.

```
<meta name="author" content="Erik Westermann">
<meta name="generator" content="notepad">
<meta http-equiv="refresh" content="15,HTMLpage1.htm">
```

TABLE A.6 HTML META ELEMENTS

Element	Attributes	Description

`<meta>`	`name="author/description/`
	`keywords/expiration/generator"`
	`content="values"`
		Adds information about the document that Web servers and browsers use. *This element does not have a closing tag.*

`<meta>`	`http-equiv="refresh"`
	`content="seconds,`
	`nameOfFileToLoad"`
		Causes a page to automatically refresh (reload) after a number of seconds. You can reload the current page or provide the name and address of another page. *This element does not have a closing tag.*

HTML pages often contain characters like greater-than, less-than, and the copyright symbol. HTML provides a number of named, special characters and allows you to refer to other special characters using a numeric notation.

The following listing demonstrates how to use each of the elements in Table A.7, and Figure A.6 shows what the document looks like when you use Internet Explorer to view it.

```
<p>This page is <u>&copy;</u> 200x. This is what a
trademark <u>&#153;</u> symbol looks like, and this
is a registered <u>&#174;</u> mark.  Did you ever
want to add your 2<u>&cent;</u> to a conversation,
end up getting all heated up (100<u>&deg;</u>+),
and end up debating for hours?!</p>
```

Figure A.6

Using special characters in an HTML document.

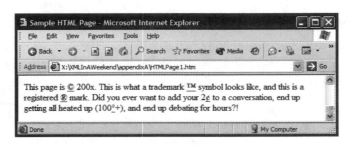

TABLE A.7 SPECIAL CHARACTERS		
Name	**Symbol**	**HTML Entity**
Ampersand	&	`&amp;`
Copyright symbol	©	`&copy; or &#169;`
Greater-than symbol	>	`&gt;`
Less-than symbol	<	`&lt;`
Non-breaking space	None	` `
Cent symbol	¢	`&cent;`
Degree symbol	°	`&deg;`
Registered trademark	®	`&#174;`
Trademark	™	`&#153;`

XPath Reference

XPath allows you to address part of an XML document using a special notation. It usually works in conjunction with XSL; in fact, a lot of functionality that XSL exposes is directly related to XPath. This reference covers the most common aspects of XPath that you're likely to come across.

XPath is a W3C recommendation, which means that it's well-documented by the W3C, on the Internet, and in many books. You can find the W3C specification, which describes XPath in complete detail, at the http://www.w3.org/TR/xpath. (Note: You must type the address exactly as shown because everything that appears after ".org" is case-sensitive.)

The following sections use some terms that you may not be familiar with:

➤ **argument:** This is sometimes referred to as a *parameter*. An argument represents a value on which a function or operator operates. For example, the arguments in the expression 1+2 are 1 and 2, and the operator is +.

➤ **node-set:** A node represents a particular point or references a specific element; a node-set is a collection of nodes.

➤ **object**: A general term that represents a logical structure. For example, a node, a node-set, and a number are all objects.

➤ **Boolean**: Represents an object with two possible values: true and false. Boolean values are elementary values that are often used to represent the result of a test. For example, the result of testing the validity of the expression 1+2=5 is false, but the expression 10-5=5 is true.

➤ **operator**: A symbol that usually appears between two arguments and operates on both arguments to produce a single result. Examples of operators include +, >, and, and or.

➤ **operand**: A formal term for the argument of an operator. When there are two operands, they are referred to based on their position relative to the operator. For example, the expression 1+2 has two operands. The number 1 is the left operand and the number 2 is the right operand. The operator is +.

XPath Functions

XPath supports three types of functions:

➤ Node-set functions operate on or use a node-set (a group of nodes).

➤ String functions operate on or manipulate a string of characters.

➤ Numeric functions operate on or manipulate numbers.

Table A.8 describes selected node-set functions that you'll commonly find in XPath expressions in XSL documents.

TABLE A.8 NODE-SET FUNCTIONS		
Function	**Return Value**	**Description**
position()	Number	Returns a number representing the context's position.
count(node-set)	Number	Returns the number of nodes in the argument node-set.
namespace-uri(node-set)	String	Returns the namespace of the argument's node-set.

String functions make it possible to manipulate, acquire information about, and format strings of characters. These functions usually return string values, but some return a Boolean (true/false) value.

Function	Return Value	Description
TABLE A.9 STRING FUNCTIONS		
Function	Return Value	Description
string(object)	String	Converts the argument object into a string.
concat(string,...., string)	String	Appends the string arguments to one another to create a single string.
starts-with(string1, string2)	Boolean	Returns true when the string1 argument begins with the string2 argument.
contains(string1, string2)	Boolean	Returns true when string1 contains the string2 argument.
substring-before (string1,string2)	String	Returns part of a string1 that appears before the string2 argument. For example, substring-before("baseball football","ball") returns "base".
substring-after (string1,string2)	String	Returns the part of string1 that appears after the string2 argument. For example, substring-after("baseball football","ball") returns " football".
substring(string1, number1, number2)	String	Returns the part of the string1 argument that begins at the number1 position and is number2 characters long.
string-length (string1,	Number	Returns the number of characters in the string1 argument.
normalize-space (string1,	String	Removes leading, trailing, and extra whitespace characters in string1 argument, and returns the new string.
translate(string1, string2,string3)	String	Replaces characters in string1 with characters in string3 based on string2. Think of this function as "replace" or "transform". This function is usually used to convert a string into uppercase. For example, translate("abcd","abc","ABC") returns "ABCd". (Note that the last character is still in lowercase because "d" does not appear in the string2 argument.)

Numeric functions allow you to convert objects into numbers and work with them. When a numeric function is unable to covert its argument into a number, it returns NaN—a special value that represents "Not a Number".

TABLE A.10 NUMERIC FUNCTIONS		
Function	**Return Value**	**Description**
number(object)	Number	Converts the argument object into a number.
sum(node-set)	Number	Adds the values in a node-set and returns their sum. Strings that contain numbers are first converted into numbers.
round(number)	Number	Rounds its argument to the closest integer.

XPath Axes

XPath supports 13 axes. An *axis* allows you to select (or address) parts of an XML document with partial or no knowledge of the document's underlying structure. It's a lot like when you're telling someone where your home is located (as opposed to describing how to get there). You could start with a description of the area in terms of nearby streets, major landmarks, and adjacent homes or buildings, without actually providing the address of your home. Think of the terms "nearby streets," "landmarks," and "adjacent homes or buildings" as general identifiers. They describe something in general terms without directly referring to that thing. If I had to describe the location of Toronto's CN Tower to you, the description would be something like this: "The closest major streets are the intersection of Yonge and Front Street, which is very close to Lake Ontario. It's between the Metro Convention Center and the SkyDome (a stadium), and you have to walk across a short bridge that goes over railway tracks to get to it." This description is vague, but if you're ever in Toronto and forget the name "CN Tower," these directions will help you find it. XPath axes work the same way.

XPath expressions often refer to a node-set, which is a collection of nodes. You can refer to a node-set using the node() or * notation. The node() notation selects all nodes, regardless of type, while the * notation selects nodes that match the type that precedes the asterisk. See Table A.11 for more information on the asterisk notation.

Some XPath expressions contain predicates, which are numbers that appear in square brackets following the name of an axis. An example of a predicate is /car/system[1], where the [1] predicate refers to the first system node-set that's a child of the car node.

The following list contains all 13 XPath axes, a brief description of each one, and examples to make the descriptions clearer. All example expressions are based on and work with the carParts.xml file, which is located in the XMLInAWeekend\appendixA folder.

(You can use XML Spy or Stylus Studio to test the examples for a clearer idea of how each expression works. Excelon Stylus Studio refers to an XPath expression as a query. You can test the expressions by starting Stylus Studio, opening the carparts.xml file, and typing the sample expressions into a document window toolbar, where Stylus Studio prompts you to enter a new query. XML Spy also supports XPath expressions. Start XML Spy, open the carparts.xml file, select XML, Evaluate XPath from the menu, and type the expression into the XPath field.)

child axis

Refers to the nodes contained within the current (context) node. This is called *child axis* because nodes contained within the context node are considered to be children of the current node. A node that contains child nodes (children) is known as a *parent node*. The child axis does not include attributes or namespaces because they're not considered to be children of the context node. The following XPath expression gets a listing of subsystem nodes that are children of the system node:

```
child::system/child::subsystem
```

parent axis

Refers to the parent node of the context (current) node. XPath expressions that include the double dot notation (..) also refer to the parent axis, so the two notations are equivalent. If the context node is the root node of the document, a reference to the parent node results in a reference to an empty nodeset. The following expression refers to the parent node of all subsystem nodes:

```
/car/system/subsystem/parent::node()
```

self axis

Refers to the context node. XPath expressions that include the single dot notation (.) also refer to the self axis. The following expression refers to the context node:

```
self::node()
```

attribute axis

Refers to the attributes of the context node. You can get a listing of all attributes of the context node, along with their values, by using the following expression:

```
/car/system/attribute::*
```

ancestor axis

Contains a node-set made up of the parent node and all parent nodes up to the root node. This axis always contains the root node. For example, the following expression represents a node-set containing the document root, system, and car elements:

```
/car/system[1]/subsystem/ancestor::node()
```

ancestor-or-self axis

Includes the same information as the ancestor axis, in addition to the context node. The following expression demonstrates how to use this axis:

```
/car/system[1]/subsystem/ancestor-or-self::node()
```

descendant axis

Represents a node-set that includes all children of the context node, up to and including any leaf nodes (nodes at the end of a branch). The node-set includes all nodes except for attribute and namespace nodes. The following expression refers to a node-set that contains all descendants of the system node:

```
/car/system/descendant::node()
```

descendant-or-self axis

Includes the same information as the descendant axis, in addition to the context node. The following expression demonstrates how to use this axis:

```
/car/system[1]/descendant-or-self::node()
```

preceding-sibling axis

Refers to all nodes that have the same parent as the context node and appear before the context node. For example, the following expression refers to a node-set containing all subsystem nodes except for subsystem[6], which represents the context node:

```
/car/system[6]/subsystem[6]/preceding-sibling::node()
```

following-sibling axis

Refers to all nodes that have the same parent as the context node and appear after the context node. For example, the following expression refers to a node-set containing all subsystem nodes except for subsystem[1], which represents the context node:

```
/car/system[6]/subsystem[1]/following-sibling::node()
```

preceding axis

Refers to all nodes that appear before the context node and excludes the ancestor axis (ancestor nodes), attribute nodes, and namespace nodes. The following expression refers to a node-set that includes all nodes that appear before the context node:

```
/car/system[6]/subsystem[1]/preceding::node()
```

following axis

Similar to the preceding axis, except that it refers to all nodes after the context node. The following expression refers to a node-set that includes all nodes that appear after the context node:

```
/car/system[1]/subsystem[1]/following::node()
```

namespace axis

Represents the namespace nodes of the context node, if it refers to an element node. The axis is empty when the context node refers to a non-element node. The following expression refers to a node-set that contains the namespace of the car node:

```
/car/namespace::node()
```

XPath Operators

XPath supports three types of operators:

➤ Expression operators

➤ Boolean operators

➤ Mathematical operators

XPath expression operators allow you to construct expressions that represent a set of nodes in an XML document. Table A.11 presents each operator, along with a brief description.

TABLE A.11 XPATH EXPRESSION OPERATORS	
Operator	**Description**
/	The slash acts as a node path separator. A slash mark at the beginning of an XPath expression refers to the root node.
//	This operator is the shorthand notation for the descendant-or-self axis.
.	The dot operator is the shorthand notation for the self axis.
..	The double-dot operator is the shorthand notation for the parent axis.
@	The at symbol facilitates access to a node's attribute(s). You can follow the at symbol with the name of an attribute, or use the * operator for a reference to all attributes.
*	Represents any node that matches the type that precedes the asterisk. For example, the @* expression refers to all attributes, while the //* expression refers to all elements.
[]	An expression within square brackets is referred to as a predicate. This allows you to address a node by position, using a numeric value or filter nodes based on an expression. The /car/system[@name="Alternator"]/* expression refers to all system nodes whose name attribute is "Alternator".
$	Indicates that the symbol that follows the dollar sign is a variable.

XPath Boolean operators use two operands and return the result of evaluating them as a single Boolean (true/false) value. Usually, Boolean operators are used to make decisions while transforming an XML document into another format.

TABLE A.12 XPATH BOOLEAN OPERATORS	
Operator	**Description**
=	True if the left side of the operator is equal to the right side.
!=	True if the left side of the operator is not equal to the right side.
>	True if the left side of the operator is greater than the right side.
<	True if the left side of the operator is less than the right side.
>=	True if the left side of the operator is greater than or equal to the right side.
<=	True if the left side of the operator is less than or equal to the right side.
and	Tests the left and right side of the operator and yields the results shown in Table A.13.
or	Tests the left and right side of the operator and yields the results shown in Table A.14.

Table A.12 includes the and operator, which is a little different than the other operators. The and operator works by evaluating its operands and converting the results into Boolean (true/false) values. It then evaluates the Boolean values to yield the results shown in Table A.13. Essentially, the and operator converts two input values (which are the result of evaluating each of its operands and converting each result into a boolean [true/false] value) into one Boolean output value. The output is false at all times, except when both operands are true.

TABLE A.13 AND OPERATOR		
Input One	**Input Two**	**Result**
False	False	False
False	True	False
True	False	False
True	True	True

Much like the and operator, the or operator is a little different from the other operators. It works by first evaluating its operands and converting the results into Boolean (true/false) values. It operator then evaluates the Boolean values to yield the results shown in Table A.14. Essentially, the or operator converts two input values (which are the result of evaluating each of its operands and converting each result into a boolean [true/false] value) into one Boolean output value. The output is true when at least one of the operands is true.

TABLE A.14 OR OPERATOR		
Input One	**Input Two**	**Result**
False	False	False
False	True	True
True	False	True
True	True	True

XPath mathematical operators allow you to perform calculations. These operators are self-explanatory, except for the `mod` operator. This operator divides its operands and only returns the remainder of the division. For example, 4 `div` 2 equals 2 with 0 remainder. Therefore, 4 `mod` 2 results in 0.

TABLE A.15 XPATH MATHEMATICAL OPERATORS

Operator	Description
+	Adds two numbers.
-	Subtracts the number on the right side of the operator from the number on the left side.
*	Multiplies the operands.
div	Divides the number on the left side of the operator by the number on the right side.
mod	Yields the remainder of the result of dividing the number on the left side of the operator by the number on the right side.

Summary of XML Productions

- ➤ XML Productions
- ➤ Character Table

This appendix describes how you can write parts of XML, which are referred to as *productions*. The information is useful when you cannot remember how to add a CDATA section to your XML document, for example. The XML specification describes in detail how to do this. However, searching through pages and pages of detailed specifications can be time-consuming. Using the CDATA section as an example, you could refer to this appendix and quickly look up the specification for how to create a CDATA section, which is defined as CDStart CData CDEnd. The production describes a CDATA section as being made up of a CDStart, a CData, and a CDEnd production, all of which you can also easily look up since related productions appear in groups.

XML Productions

Table B.1 describes symbols you'll find in XML productions and uses the following columns:

➤ **Symbol:** The symbol used in the notation

➤ **Name:** The name of the symbol

➤ **Meaning:** What the symbol means

XML productions use a special notation called Extended Backus-Naur Form (EBNF) notation. When you want to implement a production (type it), you'll find that productions refer to each other. For example, the xml-6 production (Names) is defined as

```
Name (Space Name)*
```

The production defines Names as being made up of a Name, optionally followed by any number of Name productions separated by a space (S). To find out what each symbol means (Name and S), look them up in the table. The definitions of Space and Name follow:

```
Space (#x20 | #x9 | #xD | #xA)+
Name (Letter | '_' | ':' ) (NameChar)*
```

TABLE B.1 XML PRODUCTION SYMBOLS

Symbol	Name	Meaning
*	Asterisk	Indicates that the production is optional and can appear 0 or more times.
|	Pipe	Read as "or," this symbol appears in a list of possible choices. You can select only one item from the list.
?	Question mark	Indicates that the production is optional. If you do decide to use the production, you can use it only once.
( )	Parentheses	Encloses choices or sequences.
,	Comma	List separator.
'	Quote	Encloses literals. Add items appearing in quotes exactly as they appear in the production's specification.
+	Plus sign	The production appears one or more times.
-	Minus sign	The production is not allowed.
^	Caret	Indicates a sequence of characters that you may not use.

The definition for Space describes a *whitespace* character having the hexadecimal values 20, 9, D, or A. A Name is defined as starting with a Letter production, or an underscore, or a colon, followed by any number of NameChar productions. As a result, you need to look up the Letter and NameChar productions to find out what each of those mean. Once you have the complete definition, you'll be able to write out a Name. For example, the following is a valid Name:

```
Hello-XML
```

The following listing presents XML productions based on the Extensible Markup Language version 1.0 and Namespaces in XML, along with examples and discussions where applicable. Please keep in mind that this information is only a summary, and some information may change if the XML specification changes. Please consult the XML Specification for complete details. The complete specification is available online at http://www.w3.org/TR/REC-xml. (The last two parts of the address are case-sensitive. Please type the address into your browser's address bar exactly as shown.)

Document Declaration

```
document ::= prolog element Misc*
```

Example

```
<?xml version="1.0"?>
<rootElement>
...
</rootEelement>
```

Character

```
Character ::= #x9 | #xA | #xD | [#x-20-#Xd7ff] | #Xe0000-#XFFFD] |
[#X10000-#X10FFFF]
```

Example

```
X [tab character] [newline character]
```

Whitespace

```
Space ::= (#x20 | #x9 | #xD | #xA)+
```

Example

This production defines what characters can be used as whitespaces: space, tab, carriage return, and the line feed (new line) character

Element and Attribute Names

```
NameChar ::= Letter | Digit | '.' | '-' | '_' | ':' | CombiningChar |
Extender
Name ::= (Letter | '_' | ':') (NameChar)*
```

Example

```
_1-23
rootElement
root.element
```

Discussion

This production states that element and attribute names can begin with a letter, underscore character, or colon, which can be followed by one or more letters, digits, periods, and other characters as defined in the `NameChar` production. Although you can use a colon as part of the `Name` production, you should only use it when using namespaces.

Group of Names

```
Names ::= Name (Space Name)*
```

Example

```
inventory system component part
```

Tokens and Groups of Tokens

```
Nmtoken ::= (NameChar)+
Nmtokens ::= Nmtoken (Space Nmtoken)*
```

Example

```
loc_class
book title author
```

Literal Values

```
EntityValue ::= ' " ' ([^&"]Reference* ' " '
AttValue ::= ' " ' ([^<&"] | Reference* ' " '
SystemLiteral ::= (' " ' [^"]* ' " ')
PubidLiteral ::= ' " ' PubidChar* ' " '  | " ' " (PubidChar- " ' ")* "
' "
PubidChar ::= #x20 | #xD | #xA | [a-zA-Z0-9] | [-'()+,./:=?;!*!*#@$_]
CharData ::= [^<&]* - ([^<&]* ']]>' [^<&]*)
```

Example

```
EntityValue ::= "entity value"
AttValue ::= "attribute value"
SystemLiteral ::= "personSchema.dtd."
PubidLiteral (includes PubidChar) ::= " "-//IETF//DTD HTML//EN"
CharData ::= see discussion
```

Discussion

The definition of CharData describes character data as any character (or any number of characters) that does *not* include the <, &, and]]> characters and sequences.

Comment

```
Comment ::= '<!-' ((Character - '-') | ('-' (Character - '-')))* '->'
```

Example

```
<!- Learn XML In A Weekend ->
```

Processing Instruction

```
PI ::= '<?' PTarget (Space (Character* - (Character* '?>' Charac-
ter*)))? '?>'
PITarget ::= Name - (('X' | 'x') ('M' | 'm') ('L' | 'l'))
```

Example

```
<?printer type=color?>
```

CDATA Section

```
CDATASection ::= CDStart CData CDEnd
CDStart ::= '<![CDATA['
CData ::= (Character* - (Character* ']]>' Character*))
CDEnd ::= ']]>'
```

Example

```
<![CDATA[
  This text can contain characters
  like <, &, and >. It can also contain the
  character sequence: <![CDATA[
]]>
```

Prolog

```
prolog ::= XMLDecl? Misc* (docTypeDeclaration Misc*)?
XMLDecl ::= '<?xml' VersionInfo EncodingDecl? SDDecl? Space? '?>'
VersionInfo ::= Space 'version' EqCharacter (' VersionNum ' | " Ver-
sionNum ")
VersionNum ::= ([a-zA-Z0-9_.:] | '-')+
EqCharacter ::= Space? '=' Space?
Misc ::= Comment | PI | Space
```

```
docTypeDeclaration ::= '<!DOCTYPE'Space  Space Name (Space ExternalID)?
Space? ('[' (markupDeclaration | PEReference | Space)* ']' Space?)?
'>'
markupDeclaration ::= elementdecl | AttlistDecl | EntityDecl | Nota-
tionDecl | PI | Comment
extSubset ::= TextDecl? extSubsetDecl
extSubsetDecl ::= (markupDeclaration | conditionalsect | PEReference |
Space)*
SDDecl ::= Space 'standalone' EqCharacter (' " ' ('yes' | 'no') ' " ')
LanguageID ::= Langcode ('-' Subcode)*
Langcode ::= ISO639Code | IanaCode | userCode
ISO639Code ::= ([a-z] | [A-Z]) ([a-z] | [A-Z])
IanaCode ::= ('i' | 'I') '-' ([a-z] | [A-Z])+
userCode ::= ('x' | 'X') '-' ([a-z] | [A-Z])+
Subcode ::= ([a-z] | [A-Z])+
```

Example

```
<?xml version ="1.0" standalone="no" encoding="UTF-8"?>
<!DOCTYPE books SYSTEM "schema.dtd">
<!-- The DTD resides in the same folder -->
```

Discussion

The specification for this section is rather long because the Prolog is made up of a number of features, including the XML declaration and the document type declaration. The XML declaration, the first line of the example, contains the version number, optionally followed by the document's encoding and standalone declarations. The document type declaration is made up of either a reference to a DTD, as shown in the example, or an inline DTD. The final feature of the prolog is an optional comment, processing instruction, or blank line. The example includes a comment.

Elements and Attributes

```
element ::= EmptyElemTag STag content ETag
STag ::= '<' Name (Space Attribute)* Space? '>'
Attribute ::= Name EqCharacter AttValue
ETag ::= '</' Name Space? '>'
content ::= (element | CharData | Reference | CDATASection | Pi |
Comment)*
EmptyElemTag ::= '<' Name (Space Attribute)* Space? '/>'
```

Example

```
<atom /> <!-- Empty Element -->
<atom weight="1" /> <!-- Empty Element and an Attribute-->
<atom> <!-- Element with content -->
  <name>Carbon</name>
  <number>6</number>
  <symbol>C</symbol>
</atom>
```

Element Declaration (DTD)

```
elementdecl ::= '<!ELEMENT' Space Name Space contentspec Space? '>'
contentspec ::= 'EMPTY' | 'ANY' | Mixed | children
```

Example

```
<!ELEMENT atom ANY>
```

Discussion

The element declaration is part of an XML document's DTD. It describes an element in terms of its name and content model.

Content Models (DTD)

```
children ::= (choice | seq) ('?' | '*' | '+')?
cp ::= (Name | choice | sequence) ('?' | '*' | '+')?
choice ::= '(' Space? cp (Space? '|' Space? cp)* Space? ')'   seq
<![CDATA['(' Space? cp (Space? ',' Space? cp)* Space? ')'
seq ::= '(' Space? cp (Space? ',' Space? cp)* Space? ')'
Mixed ::= '(' Space? '#PCDATA' (Space? '|' Space? Name)* Space? ')*' |
'(' Space? '#PCDATA' Space? ')'
```

Example

```
<!ELEMENT periodicTable (atom+)>
<!ELEMENT atom (name, number, symbol)>
<!ELEMENT name (#PCDATA)>
<!ELEMENT number (#PCDATA)>
<!ELEMENT symbol (#PCDATA)>
```

Discussion

The content model is part of an XML document's DTD and describes what an element may contain in terms of a choice, sequence, or mixture of both models. The content model usually includes details of how many parts of the model can be included using the ?, *, and + characters.

Attribute List Declaration (DTD)

```
AttlistDecl ::= '<!ATTLIST' Space Name Attdef* Space? '>'
```

Example

```
<!ATTLIST name NMTOKEN>
```

Attribute Definition (DTD)

```
AttDef ::= Space Name Space AttType Space DefaultDecl
```

Example

```
<!ATTLIST location NMTOKEN>
```

Attribute Type (DTD)

```
AttType ::= StringType | TokenizedType | EnumeratedType
StringType ::= 'CDATA'
TokenizedType ::= 'ID' | 'IDREF' | 'IDREFS' | 'ENTITY' | 'ENTITIES' |
'NMTOKEN' | 'NMTOKENS'
EnumeratedType ::= NotationType | Enumeration
NotationType ::= 'NOTATION' Space '(' Space? Name (Space? '|' Space?
Name)* Space? ')'
Enumeration ::= '(' Space? Nmtoken (Space? '|' Space? Nmtoken )*
Space? ')'
```

Example

```
<!ATTRIBUTE location (inside | outside)>
```

Default Attribute Value (DTD)

```
DefaultDecl ::= '#REQUIRED' | '#IMPLIED' | (('#FIXED' S)? AttValue)
```

Example

```
<!ATTRIBUTE location (inside | outside) "outside">
```

Conditional Section (DTD)

```
conditionalSect ::= includeSect | ignoreSect
includeSect ::= '<![' Space? 'INCLUDE' Space? '[' extSubsetDecl ']]>'
ignoreSect ::= '<![' Space? 'IGNORE' Space? '[' ignoreSectContents*
']]>'
ignoreSectContents ::= Ignore ('<![' ignoreSectContents ']]>' Ignore)*
Ignore ::= Character* - (Character* ('<![' | ']]>') Character*)
```

Example

```
<!INCLUDE [
  <!ELEMENT atom (weight?, name)>
]]>
```

References (DTD)

```
Reference ::= EntityRef | CharRef
CharRef ::= '&#' [0-9]+ ';' | '&#x' [0-9a-fA-F]+ ';'
EntityRef ::= '&' Name ';'
PEReference ::= ' ' Name ';'
EntityDecl ::= GEDecl | PEDecl
GEDecl ::= '<!ENTITY' Space Name Space EntityDef Space? '>'
PEDecl ::= '<!ENTITY' Space ' ' Space Name Space PEDef Space? '>'
EntityDef ::= EntityValue | (ExternalID NDataDecl?)
PEDef ::= EntityValue | ExternalID
```

Example

```
<!ENTITY % pt 'INCLUDE' >
<![%pt;[
<!ELEMENT atom (weight?, name)>
]]>
```

XML Text Declaration (DTD)

```
TextDecl ::= '<?xml' VersionInfo? EncodingDecl Space? '?>'
EncodingDecl ::= Space 'encoding' EqCharacter ( ' " ' EncName ' " ' )
EncName ::= [A-Za-z] ([A-Za-z0-9._] | '-' )*
```

Example

```
<?xml version="1.0" encoding="UTF-8"?>
```

Notation Declaration (DTD)

```
NotationDecl ::= '<!NOTATION' Space Name Space (ExternalID | PublicID)
Space? '>'
PublicID ::= 'PUBLIC' Space PubidLiteral
```

Example

```
<!NOTATION JPG SYSTEM "image/jpg">
```

Characters

```
Letter ::= BaseChar | Ideographic
BaseChar ::= see character table (Table B.2)
Ideographic ::= see character table (Table B.2)
CombiningChar ::= see character table (Table B.2)
Digit  ::= see character table (Table B.2)
Extender  ::= see character table (Table B.2)
```

Example

```
a-bc 1,2&3;
```

Character Table

Table B.2 describes the XML Character Table. Use this table to look up the definition of a character that's described where the production reads "see character table."

The table's columns are defined as follows:

➤ Name: The name of the production.

➤ Production: The specification for creating the production.

The productions in Table B.2 represent the character codes that the productions use. The character codes represent Unicode character points (codes) and are specified using hexadecimal notation. (The "#x" notation in front of each character code identifies the code as a hexadecimal number.)

When character codes appear within square brackets ([]), they represent a range that starts with the number on the left and ends with the number on the right. For example, the range [#x0041-#x005A] begins at #x0041 and ends at #x005A. When a character code appears without square brackets, just that one character applies. The vertical lines represent the word "or" to indicate that the definition is based on a choice of characters. For example, the BaseChar production begins with

```
[#x0041-#x005A] | [#x0061-#x007A]...
```

The production specifies that a BaseChar is one of the range [#x0041-#x005A] or [#x0061-#x007A] or the ranges that appear in the rest of the production. Because BaseChar includes ranges and choices, you can select only one character value from all ranges and choices.

Visit http://www.unicode.org for more information on Unicode.

TABLE B.2 XML CHARACTER TABLE

Name	Production	
BaseChar	[#x0041-#x005A] | [#x0061-#x007A] | [#x00C0-#x00D6] | [#x00D8-#x00F6] | [#x00F8-#x00FF] | [#x0100-#x0131] | [#x0134-#x013E] | [#x0141-#x0148] | [#x014A-#x017E] | [#x0180-#x01C3] | [#x01CD-#x01F0] | [#x01F4-#x01F5] | [#x01FA-#x0217] | [#x0250-#x02A8] | [#x02BB-#x02C1] | #x0386 | [#x0388-#x038A] | #x038C | [#x038E-#x03A1] | [#x03A3-#x03CE] | [#x03D0-#x03D6] | #x03DA | #x03DC | #x03DE | #x03E0 | [#x03E2-#x03F3] | [#x0401-#x040C] | [#x040E-#x044F] | [#x0451-#x045C] | [#x045E-#x0481] | [#x0490-#x04C4] | [#x04C7-#x04C8] | [#x04CB-#x04CC] | [#x04D0-#x04EB] | [#x04EE-#x04F5] | [#x04F8-#x04F9] | [#x0531-#x0556] | #x0559 | [#x0561-#x0586] | [#x05D0-#x05EA] | [#x05F0-#x05F2] | [#x0621-#x063A] | [#x0641-#x064A] | [#x0671-#x06B7] | [#x06BA-#x06BE] | [#x06C0-#x06CE] | [#x06D0-#x06D3] | #x06D5 | [#x06E5-#x06E6] | [#x0905-#x0939] | #x093D | [#x0958-#x0961] | [#x0985-#x098C] | [#x098F-#x0990] | [#x0993-#x09A8] | [#x09AA-#x09B0] | #x09B2 | [#x09B6-#x09B9] | [#x09DC-#x09DD] | [#x09DF-#x09E1] | [#x09F0-#x09F1] | [#x0A05-#x0A0A] | [#x0A0F-#x0A10] | [#x0A13-#x0A28] | [#x0A2A-	

TABLE B.2   XML CHARACTER TABLE (CONTINUED)

Name	Production
BaseChar (cont.)	#x0A30] | [#x0A32-#x0A33] | [#x0A35-#x0A36] | [#x0A38-#x0A39] | [#x0A59-#x0A5C] | #x0A5E | [#x0A72-#x0A74] | [#x0A85-#x0A8B] | #x0A8D | [#x0A8F-#x0A91] | [#x0A93-#x0AA8] | [#x0AAA-#x0AB0] | [#x0AB2-#x0AB3] | [#x0AB5-#x0AB9] | #x0ABD | #x0AE0 | [#x0B05-#x0B0C] | [#x0B0F-#x0B10] | [#x0B13-#x0B28] | [#x0B2A-#x0B30] | [#x0B32-#x0B33] | [#x0B36-#x0B39] | #x0B3D | [#x0B5C-#x0B5D] | [#x0B5F-#x0B61] | [#x0B85-#x0B8A] | [#x0B8E-#x0B90] | [#x0B92-#x0B95] | [#x0B99-#x0B9A] | #x0B9C | [#x0B9E-#x0B9F] | [#x0BA3-#x0BA4] | [#x0BA8-#x0BAA] | [#x0BAE-#x0BB5] | [#x0BB7-#x0BB9] | [#x0C05-#x0C0C] | [#x0C0E-#x0C10] | [#x0C12-#x0C28] | [#x0C2A-#x0C33] | [#x0C35-#x0C39] | [#x0C60-#x0C61] | [#x0C85-#x0C8C] | [#x0C8E-#x0C90] | [#x0C92-#x0CA8] | [#x0CAA-#x0CB3] | [#x0CB5-#x0CB9] | #x0CDE | [#x0CE0-#x0CE1] | [#x0D05-#x0D0C] | [#x0D0E-#x0D10] | [#x0D12-#x0D28] | [#x0D2A-#x0D39] | [#x0D60-#x0D61] | [#x0E01-#x0E2E] | #x0E30 | [#x0E32-#x0E33] | [#x0E40-#x0E45] | [#x0E81-#x0E82] | #x0E84 | [#x0E87-#x0E88] | #x0E8A | #x0E8D | [#x0E94-#x0E97] | [#x0E99-#x0E9F] | [#x0EA1-#x0EA3] | #x0EA5 | #x0EA7 | [#x0EAA-#x0EAB] | [#x0EAD-#x0EAE] | #x0EB0 | [#x0EB2-#x0EB3] | #x0EBD | [#x0EC0-#x0EC4] | [#x0F40-#x0F47] | [#x0F49-#x0F69] | [#x10A0-#x10C5] | [#x10D0-#x10F6] | #x1100 | [#x1102-#x1103] | [#x1105-#x1107] | #x1109 | [#x110B-#x110C] | [#x110E-#x1112] | #x113C | #x113E | #x1140 | #x114C | #x114E | #x1150 | [#x1154-#x1155] | #x1159 | [#x115F-#x1161] | #x1163 | #x1165 | #x1167 | #x1169 | [#x116D-#x116E] | [#x1172-#x1173] | #x1175 | #x119E | #x11A8 | #x11AB | [#x11AE-#x11AF] | [#x11B7-#x11B8] | #x11BA | [#x11BC-#x11C2] | #x11EB | #x11F0 | #x11F9 | [#x1E00-#x1E9B] | [#x1EA0-#x1EF9] | [#x1F00-#x1F15] | [#x1F18-#x1F1D] | [#x1F20-#x1F45] | [#x1F48-#x1F4D] | [#x1F50-#x1F57] | #x1F59 | #x1F5B | #x1F5D | [#x1F5F-#x1F7D] | [#x1F80-#x1FB4] | [#x1FB6-#x1FBC] | #x1FBE | [#x1FC2-#x1FC4] | [#x1FC6-#x1FCC] | [#x1FD0-#x1FD3] | [#x1FD6-#x1FDB] | [#x1FE0-#x1FEC] | [#x1FF2-#x1FF4] | [#x1FF6-#x1FFC] | #x2126 | [#x212A-#x212B] | #x212E | [#x2180-#x2182] | [#x3041-#x3094] | [#x30A1-#x30FA] | [#x3105-#x312C] | [#xAC00-#xD7A3]
Ideographic	[#x4E00-#x9FA5] | #x3007 | [#x3021-#x3029]

TABLE B.2 XML CHARACTER TABLE (CONTINUED)

Name	Production
CombiningChar	[#x0300-#x0345] | [#x0360-#x0361] | [#x0483-#x0486] | [#x0591-#x05A1] | [#x05A3-#x05B9] | [#x05BB-#x05BD] | #x05BF | [#x05C1-#x05C2] | #x05C4 | [#x064B-#x0652] | #x0670 | [#x06D6-#x06DC] | [#x06DD-#x06DF] | [#x06E0-#x06E4] | [#x06E7-#x06E8] | [#x06EA-#x06ED] | [#x0901-#x0903] | #x093C | [#x093E-#x094C] | #x094D | [#x0951-#x0954] | [#x0962-#x0963] | [#x0981-#x0983] | #x09BC | #x09BE | #x09BF | [#x09C0-#x09C4] | [#x09C7-#x09C8] | [#x09CB-#x09CD] | #x09D7 | [#x09E2-#x09E3] | #x0A02 | #x0A3C | #x0A3E | #x0A3F | [#x0A40-#x0A42] | [#x0A47-#x0A48] | [#x0A4B-#x0A4D] | [#x0A70-#x0A71] | [#x0A81-#x0A83] | #x0ABC | [#x0ABE-#x0AC5] | [#x0AC7-#x0AC9] | [#x0ACB-#x0ACD] | [#x0B01-#x0B03] | #x0B3C | [#x0B3E-#x0B43] | [#x0B47-#x0B48] | [#x0B4B-#x0B4D] | [#x0B56-#x0B57] | [#x0B82-#x0B83] | [#x0BBE-#x0BC2] | [#x0BC6-#x0BC8] | [#x0BCA-#x0BCD] | #x0BD7 | [#x0C01-#x0C03] | [#x0C3E-#x0C44] | [#x0C46-#x0C48] | [#x0C4A-#x0C4D] | [#x0C55-#x0C56] | [#x0C82-#x0C83] | [#x0CBE-#x0CC4] | [#x0CC6-#x0CC8] | [#x0CCA-#x0CCD] | [#x0CD5-#x0CD6] | [#x0D02-#x0D03] | [#x0D3E-#x0D43] | [#x0D46-#x0D48] | [#x0D4A-#x0D4D] | #x0D57 | #x0E31 | [#x0E34-#x0E3A] | [#x0E47-#x0E4E] | #x0EB1 | [#x0EB4-#x0EB9] | [#x0EBB-#x0EBC] | [#x0EC8-#x0ECD] | [#x0F18-#x0F19] | #x0F35 | #x0F37 | #x0F39 | #x0F3E | #x0F3F | [#x0F71-#x0F84] | [#x0F86-#x0F8B] | [#x0F90-#x0F95] | #x0F97 | [#x0F99-#x0FAD] | [#x0FB1-#x0FB7] | #x0FB9 | [#x20D0-#x20DC] | #x20E1 | [#x302A-#x302F] | #x3099 | #x309A
Digit	[#x0030-#x0039] | [#x0660-#x0669] | [#x06F0-#x06F9] | [#x0966-#x096F] | [#x09E6-#x09EF] | [#x0A66-#x0A6F] | [#x0AE6-#x0AEF] | [#x0B66-#x0B6F] | [#x0BE7-#x0BEF] | [#x0C66-#x0C6F] | [#x0CE6-#x0CEF] | [#x0D66-#x0D6F] | [#x0E50-#x0E59] | [#x0ED0-#x0ED9] | [#x0F20-#x0F29]
Extender	#x00B7 | #x02D0 | #x02D1 | #x0387 | #x0640 | #x0E46 | #x0EC6 | #x3005 | [#x3031-#x3035] | [#x309D-#x309E] | [#x30FC-#x30FE]

Web Resources

The following is a list of Web resources that will help you keep up-to-date on XML and its related technologies. The W3C (World Wide Web Consortium) maintains and updates many standards, including those for XML. Although the standards are said to be difficult to read, they contain a wealth of important information about what the W3C is doing and which standards it will update or release in the near future. Use the following addresses to find your way around the W3C's vast Web site:

Home page:
http://www.w3c.org

The latest copy of the XML specification:
http://www.w3.org/TR/REC-xml

The latest copy of the XSL specification:
http://www.w3.org/TR/xslt

The latest copy of the XPath specification:
http://www.w3.org/TR/xslt

Organization for the Advancement of Structured Information Standards publishes standards for XML vocabularies like DocBook, and publishes conformance tests for XML and XSLT:
http://www.oasis-open.org

O'Reilly XML.com is useful for new and experienced XML users:
http://www.xml.com

Also, you can download the sample code for this book, get up-to-date information about standards the book discusses, and get a free copy of Excelon Stylus Studio at the author's site:
http://www.designs2solutions.com/LXIAW

GLOSSARY

Absolute units A unit that represents a discrete, or specific, value. Examples of absolute units include meters, miles, and degrees.

ADO An acronym for Microsoft's ActiveX Data Objects, ADO is a unified approach to accessing data from a variety of sources, including databases, text files, and XML documents.

ASCII An acronym for American Standard Code for Information Interchange, ASCII is a relatively old system of character encoding that has widespread industry adoption. However, it has depreciated in favor of Unicode. ASCII encodes characters by associating a number with each character. The problem with ASCII is that it can encode only 255 characters and assumes that only English can be encoded. Whereas Unicode is an internationally standardized encoding method that's capable of encoding characters and symbols from the world's major current and historical languages.

ASP An acronym for Microsoft's Active Server Pages, ASP is a set of technologies that Web developers use to create interactive Web pages using Microsoft's Internet Information Server (a Web server product). ASP is capable of combining static (unchanging) HTML content with scripting language commands that are carried out by the Web server to deliver dynamic content to end users.

Attribute Part of an XML element that adds information through annotation. Attributes are less structured than XML elements, so they require special consideration when you're processing an XML document. Attributes are usually used to annotate an element, as opposed to introducing new information. However, the industry has not established any broad guidelines for using attributes in XML documents.

Axis A relative reference in an XPath expression. XPath supports thirteen axes, including relative references to self, siblings, parents, children, and ancestor nodes.

Breakpoint An arbitrary location defined using a debugger. When a debugger encounters a breakpoint, it halts processing and essentially freezes the state of the system, allowing you to inspect it and locate problems in your code.

Browser A generic term for a specialized application used to view Web pages on the Internet, such as Microsoft's Internet Explorer.

Character code Represents the numeric value of a text character. For example, the ASCII character code for the letter A is 65.

Character data A special block of data in an XML document that the XML parser ignores, which lets you include characters that the XML parser does not otherwise allow.

Character encoding A method of numerically representing textual information. A computer stores all information numerically. This includes images, documents, and XML documents. The computer converts (encodes) all characters into numbers and stores the numeric representation. These numbers, and the method the computer uses to encode characters, are referred to as character encoding.

Character sequence A specific sequence of characters that are significant to XML and XML parsers. For example, the character sequence `<![CDATA[` appears at the beginning of a character data section, and the character sequence `]]>` appears at the end.

Character set A set of characters supported by a particular character encoding. For example, ASCII supports the US-English character set.

Child A general term for nodes that are enclosed within an XML node (element).

Client-side A general term for the processing that occurs on an end-user's computer. This term originates from the processing model that's pervasive throughout the Internet in which processing is divided between a server, specifically a Web server, and a client that uses a Web browser to access that server. Web servers often send special instructions that are carried out by the browser, which then returns the results to the Web server. This effectively divides processing between the Web server and client.

Complex type An XSD type that allows you to define your own data types.

Component A general term for software that resides on a computer but plays a supporting role, as opposed to an active role. A component can usually be used by active software, like a word processor, to provide certain services. For example, a spell-checker component can be used by a word processor and an e-mail program to check your spelling.

Compositor Refers to a means of defining a complex XML element through XSD, the XML Schema Definition. There are three types of compositors: sequence, choice, and all. You use a compositor to describe the essential characteristics of a complex XML element, and you use other facets and XSD elements to define the remaining characteristics.

Constraint Defines and enforces limitations on information to ensure that it's entered correctly or conforms to a specific format.

Content Management System Abbreviated CMS, this term describes special software that manages the content on a Web site. A CMS produces a Web site by combining information from a variety of sources, including databases, XML documents, and even information from other Web sites. Some simple CMSs merely help you manage the files that make up a Web site, while more complex CMSs are capable of a variety of tasks, including managing advertising campaigns, generating e-mail newsletters, and tracking Web site use.

Content model Describes what an XML element can contain in terms of any subelements and data. There are four basic types of content models: empty, element-only, mixed, and any.

Convention An informal practice that's not standardized by a single entity but is commonly used throughout an industry. For example, you use the xsl prefix to refer to the XSL namespace when creating an XSL document. That's a convention.

Country code A standardized notation for referring to the name of a country without using the country's common name. For example, the United States country codes are US, USA, and 840, and Canada's country codes are CA, CAN, and 124. Country codes are usually used in the value of the xml:lang attribute, in conjunction with ISO-639 language codes, to indicate what language an element's content is in.

CSS An acronym for Cascading Style Sheet, CSS is a standardized means of applying formatting to HTML and XML documents.

Data model Information that describes the structure of a document or other structured data.

Debugging The process of finding a problem, informally referred to as a *bug*, in code that you're writing. Debugging sometimes involves the use of a specialized application called a *debugger*.

Depreciated When something is depreciated, it's still supported for older applications but that support will cease at some point in the foreseeable future. It still exists and is usable in older applications, but it's not recommended for newer applications.

Document Type Declaration Part of an XML document that describes certain aspects of the document. Confusingly enough, the document type declaration often contains a reference to a DTD, or Document Type Definition.

DOM An acronym for Document Object Model, a DOM is a logical representation of a document that allows developers to programmatically (using program code) manipulate it using a cohesive object model. There are various types of DOMs available, including XML DOM and HTML DOM, which developers can use to manipulate XML and HTML documents.

Drag and drop A visual approach to editing a document, using the mouse instead of the keyboard. Drag and drop involves selecting an element on the screen using the mouse pointer, dragging the selected element to another location, and dropping it at the new location.

DTD An acronym for Document Type Definition, it's a type of XML schema that's part of the XML specification.

Element A well-formed set of tags that represents an essential part of the XML syntax. XML elements usually have a start tag, content, and an end tag. Some elements can stand alone with a single tag, using a special notation for an empty element.

Element only element An element that contains only other elements.

Entity reference A specialized notation that represents special characters or parts of documents (if the entity resides in a DTD).

Facet A common term for a *constraining facet*, which is used in XSD to limit the possible values of data contained in an element.

Font A specific typesetting or style of typesetting. Fonts change the way information is rendered in print and onscreen, without changing the information itself.

Formatting objects An aspect of XSL that makes it possible to transform an XML document into binary formats like PDF.

Hexadecimal An alternate system to conveniently represent numbers in a form that's easily interpreted by both computers and users.

HTML An acronym for the Hypertext Markup Language, the publishing language of the Internet. Web pages contain HTML to format information in your browser.

Identity An aspect of an element that uniquely identifies it from all other elements in the same document. Identities are usually referred to as *identity constraints* and are applied to a specific attribute in a group of related elements.

IEEE An acronym for the Institute of Electrical and Electronics Engineers. The IEEE is a global professional society serving the interests of the public and members of the electrical, electronics, computer, and information technology fields. The IEEE plays a role in developing standards that are used in computing. Contact the IEEE at http://ieee.org.

Instance document A formal term describing an XML document that refers to a schema. The schema is said to validate the XML document; therefore, the XML document is considered to be an instance of the schema (the document that the schema describes).

ISO The International Organization for Standardization, a worldwide federation of national standards bodies from more than 100 countries. ("ISO" is not an acronym.) ISO creates and maintains a number of important standards in various industries. However, its relevance to XML is based on character sets, country codes, language codes, and other important codes. Find out more about the ISO at http://www.iso.ch.

Key value A value that represents an identity. Key values have identity constraints to ensure that an element can be uniquely identified within an XML document.

Markup language A general term for data that combines with existing data to add new information, structure, or annotations, without changing that existing data.

Mixed element A type of content model in which an element contains both elements and text data.

Name collision This is when elements or namespaces from two different XML documents have identical names, but with different meanings. Name collisions can be avoided by using namespaces, and you can guarantee their uniqueness by using a UUID.

Namespace A logical grouping of related elements and attributes, a namespace represents a logical boundary that allows documents that use identical element and attribute names to be combined without name collisions.

Name-value pair A simple data format that combines an arbitrary symbolic name with an arbitrary value. An example of a name-value pair is any XML attribute.

Nesting Nesting occurs when elements enclose each other. This can occur to any level, as long as the nested elements are well-formed.

Node Refers to an element in an XML document in the context of the document's structure. XML documents are conceptually modeled using a tree structure made up of nodes. XPath expressions are based on the conceptual tree structure view of an XML document; as a result, XPath expressions refer to nodes.

Parent Describes the relationship between a contained element and its containing element. The containing element is referred to as the parent.

Parsed character data Also referred to as PCDATA, an XML parser reviews parsed character data and processes it along with the rest of an XML document. All data in an XML document is PCDATA by default, unless you put it into a character data (CDATA) section.

PDF A popular format for representing documents in a platform-independent manner. Adobe Systems, a large U.S.-based software firm, developed the format and supporting software that has become a *de facto* standard.

Predicate Part of an XPath expression that's capable of further qualifying nodes in a node-set.

Prefix A expression that appears before the name of an element or attribute. Prefixes are usually associated with namespace names and make it easier to use namespaces.

Processing instruction An XML directive that is not part of an XML document's structure, a processing instruction often provides information to an XML parser or XML editor.

Prolog The first few lines of an XML document. The first line of the prolog is the most important because it contains the XML declaration. Most current XML documents do not include the rest of the prolog.

Pseudo-element Part of a CSS statement that represents parts of a document that are otherwise inaccessible to CSS. An example of a pseudo-element is first-letter, which allows CSS to manipulate an element's first letter.

Regular expression This uses a special syntax and a set of symbols to define a template to perform string manipulations and filtering.

Relative units A unit that represents an inexact value in place of an absolute value. The actual value is derived from combining the relative value with other factors through a calculation. Examples of relative units include percent, em, and ex.

Render The process of representing something on an output device. For example, a browser interprets HTML tags to render a Web page on the screen.

Restriction A limitation on the possible values that elements may contain.

RGB An acronym for Red, Green, Blue, the three primary colors a computer uses to render all colors.

Schema A representation of the structure of an XML document, a schema validates the document. As a result, an XML document is said to be an instance of its schema.

Scope The effective range or applicability of an element. In the context of an XML schema, scope refers to the applicability of an element's declaration. If a schema includes a global element declaration, it can refer to the element from anywhere in the rest of the schema. If the schema uses a local element declaration, that declaration is applicable within the element where it was declared.

Script A general term for programming languages like JScript, JavaScript, and VBScript. All of theses languages are designed to be easy to use and can perform complex tasks in applications like Microsoft's Internet Explorer. The term *scripting* derives from other programming languages on other platforms that are commonly used to perform simple tasks that make systems administration easier.

Server-side A general term for processing that occurs on a Web server. This term originates from the processing model that's pervasive throughout the Internet. Processing is divided between a server, specifically a Web server, and a client that uses a Web browser to access the Web server. For example, Web servers can access a database to look up the status of an order and return the result to a user's browser. This process encompasses the database lookup, rendering the Web page, and delivering the completed page to the end user's browser, all on the server-side.

Simple type A simple type is analogous to a text-only element, an element that does not have any attributes and contains only text (no other elements).

Software Instructions, written by developers, that are executed on a computer to provide some service or benefit.

Standard A practice or definition that's widely employed or recognized, the definition of which is controlled by a standards body such as the ISO or IEEE.

Syntax The grammar or structure of strings in a given language. Syntax defines basic usage patterns for a language, whereas the language defines the elements of the language itself.

Tag Part of an element. XML elements have start and end tags, and there is a very small syntactical difference between the two. Sometimes complete XML elements are incorrectly referred to as tags, which is probably a carry-over from HTML.

Template A model for matching elements in XSL. XSL uses templates to locate elements in a source XML document, and then renders the resulting document based on directives contained in the template.

Text-only element A element's content model, where an element can contain only text and no sub-elements.

Transform The process of converting something from one form or format into another. XSL transforms XML documents into other formats.

Unicode A method of encoding characters and symbols from all current and significant historical languages. Unicode enjoys broad industry support from a range of software and systems vendors. Find out more about Unicode, and access the specification, at http://www.unicode.org.

URI An acronym for Uniform Resource Indicator, a URI is the name of a resource. A person's URI is their name, and a book's URI is its title or ISBN. URIs are usually used in XML namespaces, which are often prefixed with the characters `uri:`.

URL An acronym for Uniform Resource Locator, the *de facto* standard for addressing Web sites and documents on the Internet.

UUID An acronym for Unique Universal Identifier, a special number that's guaranteed to be unique for all time. (No two UUIDs will ever match.) UUIDs are generated using a combination of hardware addresses, time stamps, and random numbers. They're used in XML to define a namespace name that's guaranteed to be unique and are useful in the absence of a controlled domain name. The supporting Web site for this book has a UUID generator you can use for your namespace names. See the Preface for details.

Valid An XML document is said to be valid when it conforms to the restrictions placed on it by a schema.

Visual editing A conceptual approach to editing or creating documents, as opposed to a text-based approach made up commands or directives. Visual editors often provide direct representations of abstract concepts, making them easier to understand. XML tools like XML Spy and Stylus Studio provide visual editors.

W3C An acronym for the World Wide Web Consortium, a standards body made up of a number of companies. The W3C manages standards for XML, XSL, CSS, and other important Web standards.

Web server A computer that delivers Web pages to users. When you type an address into your browser's address bar, you're actually accessing a Web server and requesting information from it in the form of a Web page.

Well-formed A document is said to be well-formed when all elements have start and end tags. All XML documents must be well-formed; as a result, XML parsers only work with well-formed XML documents. It's possible for a document to be well-formed but also invalid.

XDR An acronym for XML Data Reduced, an XML schema invented by Microsoft before XSD became a standard. XDR is supported in some Microsoft products; however, since XSD is a standard, XDR may become depreciated.

XHTML A variation of HTML that uses the same syntactical rules as XML.

XML parser Software that's capable of interpreting XML. An XML parser is usually a system-level component that provides essential services for reading and creating XML documents. For example, you can create an XML DOM in memory to allow programmatic access to an XML document's content and structure.

XML vocabulary A set of XML elements that are useful in a certain capacity. XSL is an XML vocabulary because it uses the same syntax as XML and is accessible through an XML processor. There are hundreds of XML vocabularies available.

XPath An acronym for the XML Path Language, a syntax for addressing parts of an XML document.

XSD An acronym for the XML Schema Definition, a schema dialect that addresses issues with other schema dialects.

INDEX

S

saving
documents, 88
XSLT Designer, work on, 289
SAX (Simple API for XML), 335
scenarios in Stylus Studio, 306
SCORM (Shareable Courseware Object Reference Model Initiative), 18
script element, 325
select attribute in XSL, 234
selection elements in DTDs, 124
selectors
in CSS, 244–245
XSD element, 188–189
selectSingleNode method, 57
self axis in XPath expression, 356
sequence compositor in XSD, 165–166
sequence diagrams, 40–41
serif fonts, 225–226
SGML (Standard Generalized Markup Language), 6–7
shared DTDs. *See* DTDs (Document Type Declarations)
sharing documents, 109
simple types. *See* XSD
slash (/), 3
SMBXML (Small and Medium Sized Business XML), 18
SMDL (Standard Music Description Language), 18
SML (Smart Card Markup Language), 18
SML (Steel Markup Language), 18
SOAP (Simple Object Access Protocol), 31–32
software, XML vocabulary for, 18
sort element in XSL, 238

source code control system integration, 208
Spanish characters, 92
standalone attribute, 115
standards, 6
start tags, 3, 12
character sequence for, 77
in HTML anchor element, 69
as XML element, 70
statements
CSS statements, 222
in RDF, 32–33
string attributes, 129–130
string data types in XSD, 147
string functions, 353
style files. *See* CSS (Cascading Style Sheet)
Stylus Studio, 201–202, 213–215
collapsed view of documents, 304
completing mapping with, 309–313
compositors for repurposing document, 302
debugging with, 210–211, 213–215, 298, 307–309
instance documents, editing, 206
item element in, 302
manual editing in, 311–313
new schema, creating, 300–303
repurposing documents with, 300
repurposing XML documents with, 298
root elements in, 304
scenarios for mapping, 306
system to item mapping, 309–310
tree view mode, 205
Visual Source Safe, integration with, 208–209
XML parser with, 216
XML-to-XML Mapping Stylesheet, 300, 303–309